CASTING BACK

CASTING BACK

Sixty Years of Fishing and Writing

Peter McMullan

RMB

RMB | Rocky Mountain Books Ltd.
rmbooks.com
@rmbooks
facebook.com/rmbooks

Cataloguing data available from Library and Archives Canada
ISBN 978-1-77160-174-0 (paperback)
ISBN 978-1-77160-175-7 (electronic)

Edited by Rhonda Bailey
Cover photo: Craig Somerville, Castabroad

Printed and bound in Canada by Friesens

Distributed in Canada by Heritage Group Distribution and in the U.S. by Publishers Group West

For information on purchasing bulk quantities of this book, or to obtain media excerpts or invite the author to speak at an event, please visit rmbooks.com and select the "Contact Us" tab.

RMB | Rocky Mountain Books is dedicated to the environment and committed to reducing the destruction of old-growth forests. Our books are produced with respect for the future and consideration for the past.

We acknowledge the financial support of the Government of Canada through the Canada Book Fund and the Canada Council for the Arts, and of the province of British Columbia through the British Columbia Arts Council and the Book Publishing Tax Credit.

DEDICATION

This book has to be for Daphne, my wife and patient partner for more than 50 years, the one person who has supported my love of fishing almost from its beginnings, who has willingly shared in our adventures from Haida Gwaii to New Zealand, from Northern Ireland to the Cook Islands, from the Bahamas to Bamfield. From brown trout at Lake Taupo to the rainbow trout of Babine's Rainbow Alley, from chinook at Langara Island to Atlantic salmon on the River Mourne, she has accepted with good grace dawn starts, inclement weather and the often fruitless hours we anglers tend to take for granted. Simply said, there is no way I can ever thank her enough for all she has done for me, as both a fisherman and as someone who finds writing about fishing to be almost but not quite as rewarding.

CONTENTS

FOREWORD
In His Blood

Peter McMullan says he was just a boy who was born to fish. Luckily for us, he was born to write too, and now both passions are brought together in one place.

In these collected works he ranges from the relatively genteel salmon rivers of Ireland, where he's never far from a pub, to wild steelhead rivers in British Columbia, where he's never far from bears. He navigates both with charm and humility.

Unfortunately I never got to spend any time with Peter on those Irish waters he writes about with such love, but I have been lucky enough to wade with him on several occasions on the Pitt River, a rush of glacial water that comes down out of the Coast Range near Vancouver, pouring into a deep tidal lake, whose rugged mountainous sides block any roads into the valley.

When I started the fly-fishing web magazine www.ariverneversleeps.com, it was with a small collective of writers, artists and photographers who were looking for a vehicle to connect with fellow anglers. It wasn't then, and it isn't now, about publishing for profit. Without ads, except for a handful auto-posted by Google that provide just enough to cover Internet costs, we were free to write about whatever we wanted without any concern for advertisers' interests.

But we were also without any income to pay writers. And how many people do you think are happy to write for free in this mercenary world we live in? Not many good ones, I can tell you, but those who are belong to a special group.

Peter said yes the moment he was asked to contribute and has for over a decade been one of the magazine's most steadfast supporters.

When the magazine co-publisher, photographer Nick Didlick, took on duties as head guide at Pitt River Lodge, we saw a chance to reward Peter, and invited him for a weekend of fishing after the main season was over and the last of the clients had left.

I'd known Peter for several years by then, first encountering him when I was a journalist working in Vancouver and he was the head public relations official for BC Hydro. He was an old-style flak, a kind now mostly gone, who felt telling the truth and answering hard questions from reporters was his duty. In other words, he served the public, not the executive staff of the day.

He brings that same honesty to his storytelling. If he says he caught seven salmon between 6 and 14 pounds, you can bet there weren't any 5- or 15-pounders in there. And he did get seven.

Unlike many, Peter doesn't count pulls, hits, or lost salmon as part of his daily tally. Oh yes, he remembers each one and will gladly share the stories with you, blow by blow, but he won't say he got ten fish, when he means he got three and seven got away.

I know this having fished with him – and having edited his stories.

One day on the Pitt I learned just how good he is with a fly rod, a skill he has never boasted about. As we fished up the river, my younger legs, and my eagerness to explore around the next bend, carried me ahead of him. But as I moved up, every time I looked back I saw Peter's rod was bent and he'd fallen into that fish-fighting stance he has with his feet spread to balance his weight. I imagine that's how he fought on rugby pitches too, alert and calm, and ready to knock you down.

"Fish on," he'd shout. Then later, as you could see him kneeling to release another salmon: "A beauty!"

That day I'd say Peter probably took two fish to every one I got. He never gloated or compared numbers. He did recite with absolute delight how this one had fought and that one had taken with a jarring strike. How one went down the rapids into the pool below. And how another threw his fly back at him. All of them, even the lost fish, delighted him equally. And he was just as thrilled to hear about my fish as talk about his own.

On another day we fished hard, didn't do nearly so well, but better than anyone could hope for, all of us taking nice bull trout. We got back to the lodge before dark, and as others gathered for cocktails by the airtight stove Peter suggested we go out to fish a slick run just below the lodge. He felt sure it held one more big fish. As the light faded I pulled out and headed back to the warmth of the lodge, calling out to him that I'd see him soon. I fully expected him to come back with a story of a big fish, taken just at last light. But he got far more than that.

About an hour later he came in out of the blackness, shed his coat and came quietly to stand by the fire. This wasn't like Peter. And he was pale.

"You look like you've seen a ghost," someone joked.

"Not that," said Peter. "A black bear stalked me."

He had been fishing in the promising run when he felt a chill and turned to find a big black bear watching him from near the water's edge. Then it moved closer, wading chest deep until it was only a rod's length away. Peter was as deep as he could go into the river's strong current. He faced the bear, and here is, I think, where many anglers would have gone wrong and panicked. Peter may have felt like trying to swim to the far bank, but knew in waders that would be fatal.

So he had a standoff with the bear. Experts on bears tell you to talk to them in a low steady voice. But they also say you should be instinctive. You fight if you think you have to, or, in Peter's case, you belt out as loud as you can every foul curse word you've ever learned. Then he shook his wading staff at it. The bear froze, I can only imagine that its eyebrows arched in shock, and it turned and lumbered away, stopping once or twice to look back as if to say, "Did that really just happen?"

It's impossible to know what the bear had in mind when it stalked him, or why it turned away at the last moment, but I expect the bear either knew not to mess with a tough old rugby player from Belfast, or it somehow understood he was just another old fisherman, out looking for a salmon like he was.

Somehow you know when you meet other anglers on a river whether they are skilled, or full of idle talk, just as you quickly know with a writer if the words are true. Peter knows his fishing. And his storytelling, as you'll see in this collection of a lifetime of his works, is honest. Even the bears know that.

–Mark Hume,
author of *River of the Angry Moon* and other books.
Vancouver, 2016

PREFACE
Tucked away but not forgotten

There can be no better place for a fisherman to make his home than the province of British Columbia, where fly-fishing opportunities remain an outstanding feature through the 12 months of the year.

By January the runs of winter steelhead are starting to build on Vancouver Island. As winter gives way to spring, it's time to think about rainbow trout in the multitude of lakes in the Interior of a huge and beautiful province. Or perhaps an encounter with an early spring steelhead in one of the northern BC rivers of the sprawling Skeena region.

The summer months are an invitation for ocean salmon fishing around the coastal waters of Vancouver Island, and further north too. These same fish, chinook, coho, sockeye, chum and pink salmon, start to enter their birth rivers in late summer and early autumn, providing countless freshwater fishing opportunities.

At the same time, Vancouver Island fly fishermen keep a close watch for pink and coho salmon appearing off the beaches that lie between Nanaimo and Campbell River, 153 kilometres to the north. Campbell River is notable as the home of the late Roderick Haig-Brown, perhaps the most famous fishing writer of them all and a longtime hero of mine. This same fall beach fishery continues much further up-Island as well.

The fall months also draw fishermen from across the globe to the great steelhead rivers of the Skeena Region, among them the Skeena itself, the Babine, the Bulkley, the Morice, the Kispiox, the Copper and the Sustut and many more.

As I look beyond my 80th birthday, angling challenges and adventures are never far from my mind. Retirement has allowed me to continue to combine my love of fishing and writing and to undertake the compilation of material for *Casting Back*.

These are my stories, from Ireland, Canada and New Zealand, some of them tucked away but not forgotten for more than 60 years.

CASTING BACK I ...
to how and where it all began

←———|

Early 1950s fishing diary extracts

1953

DEC. 29, spinning, Hudson Bay cherry bobber and spoon, ½-oz. lead, mild, medium dirty water. From bank, 1:10 p.m. Mike Rose, Bill Ballantyne and self. River Cowichan, Sahtlam. Steelhead trout, 8¼ pounds.

1954

JAN. 4, R. Cowichan. Fished all day with Bill and Mike. Neither hooked nor saw any.

JAN. 23, spinning, H.Bay cherry bobber, ½-oz. lead. Very cold, 3′ snow on ground, no wind, light snow falling, sunny. From bank, Bill, Mike Rose, Mike Rippingale, Lyle Wilkinson. R. Cowichan, Sahtlam. Steelhead trout, 8 pounds.

At the time the Victoria *Daily Colonist* fishing columnist – it could have been Jim Tang – wrote: "Sextette of young Victorians tried for steelhead Sunday in Cowichan River below Sahtlam. They caught two but hooked into a total of 10. Party was composed of Mike Rippingale, Bill Ballantyne, Michael Rose, Lyle Wilkinson, Jim Clements and Pete McMullan. The last two caught the fish. 'River is low and clear,' reported Rippingale."

JAN. 31, R. Cowichan. Saw nowt. Bill saw one and had one strike. Lovely day. River low and snow on ground. Fished Sahtlam and Pools.

MAR. 7, Bill and I went to Cowichan. Bill got a nice clean 9½ pound steelhead and I, once again, got nowt.

APR. 3, Fished Cowichan at Sahtlam. Water rising and dirty. Saw none.

My diary for 1954 also notes "an annual BC Resident Anglers Licence for 1954 costs $2." Today the same licence costs $36 plus $25 for a steelhead conservation stamp.

Hooked on fishing: A lifelong passion evolves

JUNE 1976, SPEAKING NOTES, ROTARY CLUB OF NANAIMO

Looking around, I can see any number of experienced fishermen and I just hope you came this afternoon for the food and the fellowship rather than expecting to hear how to take your limit every time you go fishing. If catching was all there was to it the majority of us would have given up long ago.

My own preoccupation with the sport dates back just about as far as I can remember. I am coming up to 41 and can say with absolute certainty that I have been fishing on a more or less regular basis since I was eight or nine. Certainly my interest in all forms of aquatic life goes back even further for I know we used to collect minnows and tadpoles and sticklebacks from a Cleaver Park pond near our home, in Belfast, when I was only four or five. Incidentally that pond has long since given way to an up-market housing development. That's progress.

Being an Ulsterman by birth, that is, a person from Northern Ireland rather than from Eire, also known as the Republic, most of my early memories are of fishing in Ireland, both north and south of the border. All this was long before the current tragic troubles, for religion never entered our lives in those days as it has over the last six or seven years.

Indeed, when it comes to fishing there is no religious divide in Ireland's 32 counties. Protestant and Catholic meet as equals on river and lake, and on the ocean too, and I will never forget a weekend spent in Belmullet, a small Co. Mayo village, in August of 1969.

At that time I was writing a weekly fishing column for the *Belfast Telegraph*, and I had travelled some 200 miles across the country to Ireland's west coast to research a feature on a popular international sea angling festival.

My wife, Daphne, and my son, Richard, then only four, kept me company on the long drive – no motorways in those days – and it just happened that we had left Belfast in the grip of a particularly dreadful outbreak of rioting and burning. Families were being driven from the homes, many of which were then set on fire, and by the Saturday night, the deadly shooting had started.

All this was brought home to us in a pub in Belmullet that same night, and in living colour thanks to the miracle of television. The entire population of the small village was stunned, but the big competition went ahead as planned the next day. That evening, when we had planned to drive back to Belfast, the local angling club secretary made it very clear that he simply would not permit us to go in the circumstances.

"It's much too dangerous," he told us, "so I have arranged for you to stay on in my house until things settle down." Remember, he was a Catholic and I a Protestant, meeting for the first time only 24 hours previously as complete strangers. That's fishing in Ireland.

I have jumped ahead a few years in this particular story. Going back to my boyhood, my time spent at a Co. Armagh preparatory school, between the ages of eight and thirteen, had afforded few worthwhile fishing opportunities outside the holidays. That all changed with the onset of the teens and five years as a boarder at Stowe School, what the English know as a "public school." The fact that the extensive grounds featured two well-stocked fishing lakes made a whole world of difference to my life, then and now.

Fishing in England was a new experience. This was coarse fishing as opposed to game fishing for salmon and trout. The Welsh and the Scots and the Irish still have access to some excellent salmon and trout waters at a modest cost; in England the sheer numbers of fishermen mean that such opportunities are often beyond the means of the ordinary working man.

So they turn to coarse fishing, to such freshwater species as roach and rudd, perch and pike, carp, bream and tench. Certainly there is lots of pressure, especially near the big cities, but nearly all the fish caught are returned to the water unharmed.

It was during this time of my life that I grew to love and cherish the early morning hours. The close season for all coarse fishing in England runs from March 15 to June 15 so that gave us six weeks before the end of term to slip away from our sleeping dormitories to fish for tench in the hours before breakfast.

From school in England, in the summer of 1953, I came to Victoria to stay with relatives and to attend Victoria College. Here I developed a taste for British Columbia, and it was this 18-month detour in my life that finally led just five years ago to my return to Canada with a young family, this time to Nanaimo and its venerable daily newspaper, the *Nanaimo Daily Free Press*.

Ever since, I have had ample fishing opportunities in our local rivers and on the ocean. The steelhead in the Nanaimo and Stamp rivers have been good to me as have the coho and the chinook salmon in the ocean, a fishery unheard of anywhere in the British Isles, where the coveted Atlantic salmon are only caught in freshwater locations.

Not so many weeks ago, while out fishing in the *Blueback*, a little eight-foot-long plywood dinghy, I had a memorable encounter with a killer whale. Unseen in the grey, first light of day, the whale approached one of my favourite fishing locations, not far from Clark Rock, and revealed its presence only when it exhaled. The sound of its breathing carried far in the still morning air.

The orca, surely a far better name for such an amazing creature, went on its way, leaving me to reflect on another magical fishing moment. By now you will have guessed I am something of a fishing fanatic. Yes, I'm hooked, always have been, always will be.

⟵⟶

1950s Stowe School: Fishing for memories

2014 *Stowe Corinthian*, THE ANNUAL MAGAZINE OF STOWE SCHOOL

The elegant Vancouver restaurant with its spectacular harbour and mountain views was the perfect recent setting for a reunion dinner. The Belfast-born, Old Stoic author and Daphne, his wife, have lived in Canada since 1971 with their two sons, Richard and Conor, now in their early fifties and late forties with families of their own. The other two men at the table, a second Old Stoic, also named Peter, and his friend John, were on their way home to England after a successful week's fishing for steelhead on the Skeena River in northern British Columbia.

Fishing, and in the beginning Stowe School, in the heart of England's rural Buckinghamshire, had brought the two Peters together again for the first time since they went their separate ways almost 60 years before. Their Stowe, in the early 1950s, was a very different place to the Stowe of today.

Sweets, bought at the school shop beside the tennis courts, were still rationed with wartime era coupons required; the inspiring, 550-acre, sprawling estate, with its many ornate temples, scenic drives and monuments, had yet to attract National Trust recognition and with it the ongoing restoration of both buildings and grounds. And there certainly were no girls and only eight boarding houses, not to mention the absence of so many other taken-for-granted aspects of life today.

Back then, with the aftermath of the Second World War still very real, the two Peters, McMullan and Houghton-Brown, were assigned to Temple House. McMullan started in 1949, the start of the final year of the era of J.F. Roxburgh, who had been the founding headmaster in 1923. Houghton-Brown, his good friend-to-be, followed in the autumn of 1950.

More than half a century has elapsed since then, and they both still love to fish. They moved on from the pike, roach, perch and tench that continue to populate Stowe's Octagon and Eleven-Acre lakes to fishing in the United Kingdom and Western Canada, for Atlantic and Pacific salmon, brown and rainbow trout and steelhead. When the urge to travel grew too strong, they also fished much further afield – Iceland, Russia, New Zealand and Alaska.

As boys in their teens Peter Houghton-Brown, an Oxfordshire farmer to this day, and the writer, now a retired editor and communications manager, fished together at Stowe whenever the opportunity presented itself. In the winter months pike were the principal quarry; in summer their attention turned to the handsome tench found where the Eleven-Acre Lake empties into the now restored Copper Bottom Lake. In their time, this was nothing more than a swampy marsh with an evocative name as a reminder of its previous grand history when Stowe House, then the ancestral home of the Dukes of Buckingham and Chandos, was one of England's greatest eighteenth-century mansions.

The tench demanded a dawn start, but no one ever seemed to notice that, in June and July, we were departing our dormitory beds to go fishing shortly after 4:00 a.m. On the way to the lake, Peter H-B recalls searching the dew-heavy grass on the South Front cricket pitch for lobworms. Along with bread paste, lobworms were the best possible bait for the tench, tenacious fighters weighing four pounds and more.

My first Stowe fishing rod was a whippy, khaki-coloured metal affair that possibly started life as an aerial on a British army tank, while the wooden Nottingham-style reel, which I still have, was bought second-hand for a few shillings from the tackle shop in Buckingham.

The other Peter adds: "Memories fade over 60 years but I do remember my best great aunt taking me to the Army and Navy Stores, of all places, to buy me a rod. A very helpful gentleman produced an Apollo spinning rod made of steel. They are not made any more but it was my pride and joy for many a year."

As we approach our eighties we both reflect on our Stowe days with considerable pleasure. I was no great academic but relished the traditions, the sports and inter-house competition, the friendships, the fishing, the incomparable setting and the day-to-day activities associated with an always quite remarkable educational establishment.

I know the fishing experiences most definitely helped to shape my life, as did the influence of history tutor, army officer (Military Cross, Normandy) and author Bill McElwee, who lived with his remarkable wife Patience at Vancouver Lodge, in those days Dadford village's unconventional cultural retreat and a welcoming oasis for visiting History Side pupils.

On one memorable occasion, Patience actually stuffed and baked a five-pound pike for us. Sadly it was not great eating despite a rich sauce, many spices and all her best culinary efforts: far too many bones. By comparison, her deep pie made from the breasts of young rooks, shot by his pupils under Bill's supervision, was quite superb.

In common with a number of other Stoics of that era, we shared a love of the countryside and traditional rural English pursuits. Fishing was just one of our hobbies. Meat, like sweets, was still rationed so there was a ready market among the masters – 2s/6d was the going price I recall – for the rabbits we snared in the neighboring estates or netted in their warrens as they tried to escape the ferrets we kept caged in a malodorous wooden shed beside the gymnasium.

Measured against today's norms, life at Stowe in the early 1950s was on the free and easy side, but we learned to be responsible and polite, to respect others and to enjoy our stunning surroundings, to make new friends and, of course, to follow the inevitable boarding school routines.

So many of our fishing memories from those days live on for me in the carefully detailed pages of "The Angler's Pocket Record," a cherished Christmas gift from my parents filled with neatly written notes of those long-ago fishing experiences. The Stowe part begins on January 21, 1951 – two small pike taken spinning and on dead bait from the Octagon Lake – and concludes on March 15, 1953, "very cold, stormy," when Peter H-B and I landed six Eleven-Acre pike on perch live bait, none especially large but a fine way to close out the 1952–53 coarse fishing season.

By then we were often fishing from a handsome canvas-over-wood punt that we, together with Peter Steveney, also from Temple House, had built as an ambitious school woodworking project. It served us well and, for a time, was to be found moored in the old boathouse on the Octagon Lake. I still recall my father's astonished reaction when he saw the end-of-term bill for "woodworking materials."

All you have just read is a reflection of a bygone time but very much a defining aspect of my life. We can only hope the present generation of Stoics and Old Stoics feel as good about the school when, in 2074, their turn comes to look back 60 years. Perhaps they too will be fishermen.

←———————

Sixty years and counting

MARCH 2005, *www.ariverneversleeps.com*, VANCOUVER

As we get older, our reflections on past fishing adventures become ever more selective. The disappointing days, for the most part, slip off the memory shelf never to be recalled. The good days grow in stature, the clarity of the images forever shining bright along with the hope that there is still time to add to the collection.

Admittedly, I have to be one of the lucky ones, for I have been fishing seriously for close on sixty years, first in England as a boarding school boy and then in my native Northern Ireland and, since 1971, in British Columbia, Canada. For the most obvious of reasons, it's good to be able to report no significant decline in effort or enthusiasm.

An early riser, both by nature and habit, I can still wake well before dawn, ahead of the alarm clock's raucous call, grab a quick breakfast and then drive dark roads swept with wind and rain, and sometimes even snow, before making my way down to the river in hope of a chance at an elusive winter-run steelhead.

Or, as spring gives way to summer, I can have my 14-foot aluminum boat in the water and the rods rigged and fishing for feisty chinook salmon long before 6:30 a.m. That's when the first ferry pulls away from Departure Bay terminal on its 95-minute trip from my hometown of Nanaimo on Vancouver Island across the Strait of Georgia to Horseshoe Bay and mainland British Columbia.

Only weeks back, such an effort, timed to meet a low slack tide, was rewarded with a chinook of just over 18 pounds, one of those prime, early season fish, fattened through the winter on a diet of mature herring. The chinook flesh was neither red nor white but rather varying subtle tones of pink. Grilled with butter it made for superb eating.

One more for the book of memories so many of us keep, some mentally, some in diary form, others through carefully recorded notes, perhaps now computer-based, supported by lots of photos of people and places, of fish and fishermen.

In my case there are also the treasured clippings from a long-ago career with the *Belfast Telegraph*, where I was encouraged by then managing editor Jack Sayers and sports editor Malcolm Brodie –

two giants of the newspaper business – to learn to write about an already-maturing passion for fish and fishing.

Naturally, not all that early work has survived, but numerous fading examples remain to this day at the bottom of a desk drawer, precious reminders of a time when I fished at every opportunity for brown trout and for the salmon that come back each year to Northern Irish rivers like the Mourne and the Strule, the Lower Bann, the Glenarm, the Maine, the Moyola and the Ballinderry.

My very first day as a cub reporter, not yet 20, was on January 1, or perhaps January 2, 1955. For the second half of the 1950s, I was an aspiring young journalist finding my way in a strange and exciting new world. Personal budgetary restraints meant most of my fishing was on unrestricted, public waters, free from the constraints, and expense, of private beats and angling club membership fees.

Those doors opened later and the quality of my fishing improved accordingly. However, it was still the River Moyola – one of the Lough Neagh tributaries and public water –that provided me with my very first Atlantic salmon, a bright fish of some 10 pounds that holds a very special place in my heart to this day. It would be nice to be able to recount how it was taken on a home-tied fly, fished on a venerable, handed-down split cane rod, but the truth is altogether more prosaic.

No one in my family had the slightest interest in fishing or fish, beyond what ended up on the table, usually from the local fishmonger. There was no heirloom tackle to be cherished, no tradition of fly fishing to be passed on from father to son. Happily, my own consuming love of the sport now lives on in our two sons, with more recently arrived grandsons Finn and Jack sure recruits for the future.

Eldest son Richard caught his first trout off Lower Lough Erne's Eagle Point at a very young age, nearer three than four, so it should not be too long before Finn and Jack, sons of Conor, Richard's younger brother, are being encouraged to follow in the footsteps of their grandfather, uncle and father. That should help to keep us all young at heart.

Now turn back the clock an exact half century to the Moyola, the river falling and clearing after a mid-week spate. It was a Sunday, late in June 1955, and my 350 cc Royal Enfield motorcycle had made quick work of the dawn run on all-but-deserted roads from Belfast through Antrim, Randalstown and Toomebridge to the pool at the new bridge.

I was just weeks away from my 20th birthday, and salmon fishing was still a challenge for the future. This was a day for brown trout, nothing more, and I had yet to invest in my first fly rod.

Small blue and silver Devon minnows, an older Mitchell spinning reel loaded with five-pound breaking strain nylon, and a fibreglass rod seemed more than adequate, and inevitably, there was no landing net, no sharp-pointed gaff.

The pool below the bridge proved unproductive so I clambered back up the sloping rock sill, the flow threatening to top my thigh boots, and began to cast upstream and into the deeper water close to the far bank.

That was where I hooked, played and eventually manage to secure – the word "land" hardly works in the circumstances – my very first Atlantic salmon as it made a final, tiring dash for the lower pool.

At the time I wrote in a feature for the *Belfast Telegraph*: "As I floundered after it, the fish caught behind a projecting rock halfway down the slope and I was able to dive on it before getting my fingers through its gills.

"Not pretty by any means and certainly not enough to impress the lone bystander, leaning over the parapet of the bridge, who remarked, in the broadest of Ulster accents and to no one in particular: 'Man, there was someone watching over him the day.'"

Salmon fishing became a defining priority from then on, and as the 1960s went their way, I had the good fortune to learn to fish with a fly for salmon and to enjoy access to some of the best of the local waters. Among them were the River Mourne and the River Finn, the latter just across the border in Co. Donegal, and Lough Melvin, in Co. Fermanagh, where we would troll for and occasionally catch spring salmon in March and April while fishing along the Garrison shore.

Then there was the early season fishing for brown trout on the Six Mile Water, a river dear to my heart to this day since it was on the stretch above Templepatrick Bridge that I began to fish seriously with a dry fly, often accompanied by close friends and Antrim Angling Club members Jim Telford and Moore Anketell. The dark olives began to hatch around midday in March and April and there were times when a few hours snatched from journalistic duties would be rewarded with three or four handsomely spotted fish.

Other days we came home empty-handed, convinced the trout we could see rising steadily in the straight stretch above the bridge were just too well educated, had already ignored the efforts of too many fishermen. No doubt that identical strain of brownies, generations removed of course, are still leaving dainty rise forms in the very same spot.

Truly that particular decade, the 1960s, was good to me in so many other ways, both professionally and in meeting and marrying Daphne Love, then a young teacher and a partner who has always understood my deep-seated love for fishing and who supported me in our eventual family move to British Columbia in 1971.

Long before then, spinning tackle had given way to two split cane trout fly rods, both by R.C. Moore of Belfast, and a 14-foot, three piece Hardy Wye split cane salmon fly rod. Heavy by today's graphite and carbon fibre-based standards, the Hardy Wye was still a beautifully finished rod that helped me to cover the more distant lies on larger rivers like the Finn and the Mourne.

Moore's fishing tackle shop, on Belfast's Royal Avenue, was most conveniently located immediately opposite the *Belfast Telegraph* offices. It was the rare day when I did not find an excuse to call in to talk to Bob Moore and Ken Rankin, two respected experts in their time, and their apprentice Roy Graham, from Lough Erne's Boa Island, where his father, Jack, was a noted boatman, fisherman and a great character.

The Erne days were another highlight, with big brown trout to be caught on trolled lures in the spring before the annual mayfly hatch brought old friends together to stay and fish from Brendan and Mamie Faughnan's lough-side home. Schoolteacher Brendan could sing like a lark and was wonderful company on the water as we worked the drifts with wet flies and dapped naturals, always watching, hoping for the sudden, splashing rise of a fish.

Later in the day the spent flies, easily seen dancing in the trees and above the shoreline bushes, would drop back on to the surface of the lough to offer quite superb sport to the carefully cast imitation Spent Gnat dry fly.

Anketell and Telford, from Antrim, one the postmaster, the other a policeman, were regular visitors in those distant days along with Ballymena's George McCartney, Omagh's Bertie Anderson and Mike Murray, a cheerful Scot who really cherished his fishing opportunities. Time moves on, and while so many of them are no longer with us, they will ever remain a part of my fishing life, fine companions on the water and also later in the evening when the time came for another toast, another song, another story.

Even earlier there was the boyhood lure of Joseph Braddell and Son (founded 1811) and the shop in Belfast's Arthur Square where the Clarke brothers, Harry, Bobby and Jim, not forgetting "young" Jim, sold and repaired fishing tackle and shooting equipment under the watchful eye of their father. While the father's Christian name escapes me, the essential, old-fashioned image remains of a small, elderly man in a dark jacket and a shirt with a high wing collar. Subsequent research tells me his name was William James Clarke, and he had joined the firm as a junior salesman in 1890.

The polished wood shop fittings were from a much earlier age, and this was in the late 1940s and early 1950s. I vaguely remember a central display case that featured stuffed game birds, rows of new rods hanging in their cloth bags, and gleaming shotguns. Also drawer after partitioned drawer of trout and salmon flies and a steady stream of familiar faces, all regular customers willing to answer the questions of the boy who lived to fish.

For the most part their names are long forgotten but a few still come to mind: Finaghy mechanic Davy Moore, who sold me my first motorcycle, Lex McVeigh, Billy Murphy, the only one of my own generation, Billy Armour, Wilbur Little and George Lough, a stalwart member of the Pickwick Angling Club "instituted 1911."

My sense today is that this was an era when sinking fly lines were pretty much the norm for salmon fishing and, by then, my bookshelf included a copy of the classic *Greased Line Fishing for Salmon* by "Jock Scott," pen name of A.H.E.Wood.

This 1930s title encouraged me to try sink tips and floating fly lines in what was, in the main, a summer and early autumn salmon fishery. Later, much later, the same approach and flies continue to serve me well for steelhead on Vancouver Island and on the rivers of northwestern British Columbia's Skeena Region, notably the Babine, the Morice and the Bulkley.

Some great Irish days followed and I have the handwritten notes to remind me of one in late June, 1970 when I hooked eight Mourne grilse, landing four weighing up to six pounds, all on Shrimp flies tied by Newtownstewart's John McAleer (see "Fish worth toasting," page 66). Then there was the 12-pound Lower Bann salmon caught on a No. 12 – small indeed – Claret and Hare's Ear fly at Movanagher on June 18, 1969.

That was most certainly another one for the memory book in that I was fishing for brown trout, for which this private beat is best known, and using the better of my two split cane trout rods. Today that rod hangs in virtual retirement on the wall of the room where I write, the set in the tip joint a reminder of a notable catch.

To this day it's easy to recall the lasting sense of a Lower Bann salmon that, for a while, was totally beyond my control as it charged downriver from The Flat, below the Movanagher weir, through The King's Hill, a heavy, boulder-filled stream, eventually to be netted in the deeper waters of The Neck – what excitement.

Then there was the autumn grilse from the River Strule, downstream from Omagh, that was eaten by a pig, at least all but the tail, which was still visible in the corner of the animal's mouth when I came to collect it. What happened? Salmon grilse are dainty little fish, This one weighed no more than five pounds and the noosed length of cord, securing it to a convenient tree branch, had slipped free of the slender wrist above the tail. And we all know, pigs take no prisoners when it comes to an opportunistic meal.

To my way of thinking, that is still what my fishing is all about. Not so much the catching but rather the whole essence of the sport, the anticipation, the day-to-day experiences and adventures, the friendships and the trips, the many and varied locations, the tackle, the traditions and always the golden memories of those very special days, some long ago, others yet to be enjoyed.

In British Columbia we have long been supportive of a catch-and-release ethic. In our freshwater trout fisheries we use only single, barbless hooks. Again, it's the law. This conservation-driven approach means there should still be plenty of salmon and trout for grandsons Finn and Jack when they and their friends come of fishing age.

May their lines be tight, their fish bright and strong and their days on the water every bit as rewarding as mine have been.

CASTING BACK II ...
in print for the first time

← ═══

Angling interest high in Northern Ireland
MAY 1955, *Belfast Telegraph*

Ten years ago, for most people angling was just another hobby. Now it's a major sport complete with international matches.

In Northern Ireland, every season shows an increase in the sale of licences. Last year there were 4,695 salmon and trout licences sold in the Coleraine district, an increase of 252 on 1952.

In the Ballycastle district, there was an even greater rise, from 461 to 782. Sales so far this season indicate Ulster anglers will be out in greater numbers than ever before. They are fortunate, for with only a ten-shilling licence, they can fish for brown trout and Lough Neagh dollaghan trout in practically any river in the province. For an extra pound they can turn their attention to salmon.

Their counterparts across the Irish Sea have a very different story to tell. It's a sad one, for overfishing, pollution and preserved waters make it almost impossible for the working man to enjoy a day's fishing on a salmon or trout river.

Many Ulster anglers are inclined to be a little snobbish. With so many miles of salmon and trout fishing on their doorstep, they are contemptuous of such humble coarse fish as the pike and the perch. Co. Down, for instance, is teeming with lakes that the English angler would rave about, but as they only hold coarse fish, they are ignored. Lough Neagh, too, is home to thousands of these neglected fish.

At Toomebridge, where the Lower Bann River leaves the lough, there are times when it is possible to catch perch by the dozen. In Ulster the brown trout takes over as the most sought-after fish, and there is hardly a river that is not well stocked. The Upper Bann is one of the best rivers near Belfast, and it has some excellent wet and dry fly stretches. Good fishing spots are around Corbet, Katesbridge and Ballyroney, all easily accessible by bus from Belfast.

Lake and reservoir fishing for trout is very popular but the majority of the best waters are preserved by clubs and associations. Lough Erne is famous for its large trout and the mayfly hatch, around late May and early June, is an irresistible attraction.

Salmon and sea trout start their annual spawning runs sometimes as early as the middle of May, although this is unusual. The main runs commence in July and continue through until October. Among the most popular salmon rivers are the ones that flow into Lough Neagh, with the Maine, Moyola, Ballinderry and Blackwater the largest of these tributaries.

Salmon are caught both on flies and by spinning with small spoons and Devon minnows. There is a fairly even balance maintained between the devotees of each particular method. The Lough Neagh rivers are not the only ones that have runs of salmon. The fact is they appear in nearly every Northern Ireland river with access to the sea.

Running at the same time as the salmon in the Lough Neagh rivers are a species of fish peculiar to Northern Ireland, the dollaghan. These are large trout that live only in the lough (see "Taking trout the commercial way," page 52 and "Lough Neagh trout can be caught," page 63) and which, each year, come into its feeder rivers to spawn.

In size they can range from two to fifteen pounds with the average nearer five or six pounds. Like the salmon, they do need fairly high water flows to draw them into the rivers.

And what of the prospects for this year? So far the fishing has not been spectacular, but to the fisherman, "hope springs eternal."

A red-letter day on a Glens of Antrim river

DECEMBER 1956, *Belfast Telegraph*

The 1956 angling season in Northern Ireland will be remembered not for the number of fish caught but for the ever-changing weather conditions that marred its later months.

The weather never really settled into any fixed pattern. One week, rivers would be in full spate and the next, in many cases, they would be just a trickle.

For some reason or another the northwest of the province had more early summer rain than the rest of the country, and in consequence, the rivers in this area benefited considerably. Those in the Foyle System, including the Finn, the Mourne and the Derg, all enjoyed excellent runs of both salmon and sea trout.

The picture was not so bright for the fishermen who rely mainly on the Lough Neagh feeder rivers for their sport. These did not have a really decent flood until early in August, and then there was often too much rain, leaving them unfishable for two or three days at a time. The Ballinderry made up for this in the final four or five days in September, just before it closed, for then the dollaghan started to take well and some big catches were made.

Lough Melvin fished better than it has for a very long time and, when closing day finally arrived, it had given up more than 200 salmon and many more good trout.

In 1955 I caught my first salmon of the year while fishing on the River Moyola in the last week of June. This year I had to wait another month before the big moment arrived. I was in Co. Donegal, on the River Owenea (see "Only in Ireland: The one that got away," page 55), one of the most attractive rivers I know and one that usually fishes best in July.

This year was no exception and, with Ireland's west coast getting more rain than the east, there was a good run of fish in the river when I arrived. It's a river that rises and falls very fast after rain and I counted myself fortunate to kill a couple of salmon and half a dozen sea trout in the few days that I was able to spend on its banks.

From the Owenea I went to the upper reaches of the Finn (see "The River Finn: A Co. Donegal delight," page 69), where I had three perfect days' fishing. Although the actual catch was not great in numbers, the fishing itself and the scenery made up for this and a great deal more.

Every year provides at least one true "red-letter day" and 1956 was no exception. Mine came on October 2 when I was fishing one of the small spate rivers that run down through the Glens of Antrim.

The water was low and clear, and for the first part of the day, I had fished flies but without success. Then I changed over to my spinning tackle and a one-inch blue and silver Devon minnow on line with a breaking strain of only four pounds.

In conditions such as this I think a heavier line becomes too obvious, and as the pools I was fishing were slow moving and unobstructed, I had no great fears of the line being broken in the event that I hooked a fish. In any case, I had taken salmon on the same river on identical tackle on previous visits so saw no reason to change my tactics.

My third cast sent the little minnow up and across the head of a run that opened into a deep pool, one bounded along one side by a steep rock face. Three turns of the reel's handle and I was able to watch the minnow racing through the water just below the surface.

Suddenly, out of the white mass of foam and bubbles at the near edge of the run, came a grey shape. As it seized the lure and came tearing out of the water I saw that it was a salmon of five or six pounds. It fought well, spending more time out of the water than in it, and was finally beached at the tail of the pool.

After replacing my trace, just in case it had been frayed, I started to spin again, this time directly upstream. On the first cast I had a sea trout follow the minnow right to my feet; on the second came a hard strike, almost before I had started to reel in.

It was another salmon and a good one. It jumped only once, showing a deep flank, and when finally landed, after a fight lasting a good 15 minutes, it weighed a little over eight pounds.

Both this one and the first fish I caught had fresh scars on their tails, and I wondered if an otter had held them for an instant between sharp, pointed teeth before they broke free ... only to fall victim to the treble hook of a minnow lure a fraction of their size.

After wrapping both fish in damp ferns and placing them high up in the fork of a tree, well out of the reach of a river rat or other vermin, I moved on upstream, fishing as I went.

In one pool I saw three salmon splashing but they were not interested in my offerings and it was not until the light was fading that I hooked and landed my third salmon of the day, one of about six pounds.

Earlier in the season, in mid-August, I was on the Whitewater, a pleasant little stream near Kilkeel. It's very much a spate river, and on this particular day it was running in what was nearly a full flood. The water was far too dirty for flies or even small spinning lures, so I decided to try a "garden olive," or common worm.

It did not take long to bait up, and after the worm had drifted down along the bottom of the pool three or four times, I felt the line tighten and then start to move upstream against the current. When eventually netted over a pebbly bar, one that in normal conditions would have been high and dry, what I thought was a small salmon proved to be a sea trout of almost three pounds, my largest ever.

On riverbank with rod and line

JANUARY 1957, *Belfast Telegraph*

Ever since I started being interested in the hobby of the immortal Izaak Walton, my friends have been asking me, "Why do you go fishing?" and "What pleasure can you possibly get from angling?"

This is the first time I have either tried to answer their questions or, for that matter, attempted to define for myself the fascination of fishing.

It all started when I was quite a small boy in short pants. The seaside resort of Bangor was, to me at least, an immense number of miles away from my home in Belfast; to go there by train for a day's fishing from the pier was quite an adventure. My tackle was simple but my enthusiasm was unbounded, and a catch of a couple of plump, shining mackerel or even a few codling or a flat fish made my life a sort of heaven for many hours.

Later, when I was 13, I went to a boarding school in England. In the grounds, and within easy walking distance, were two good-sized lakes that were home to various species of coarse fish, notably pike, perch, tench and roach. For the next five years, I hoarded pocket money to buy line, weights and hooks and spent valuable studying time quietly out of sight in a sheltered bay with a crimson-tipped float the focus of my attention.

By the time I left school at 18 I had gained the reputation of being a hard worker – at my fishing – and my keenness, far from being dulled, was sharper than ever.

In the few years since then I have been across the Atlantic to British Columbia, Canada, where, among other things, I earned a living outside college hours in the commercial fishing industry, unloading fishboats and then stacking the salmon by the hundred in a freezer facility. Now I am back in Northern Ireland and I am still fishing.

I do not think it necessary to be landing fish to have a successful day. It is enough to be out of doors, surrounded only by the sound of moving water and the life it supports.

My own preference is to fish alone, and I fail to understand the people who clutter up the banks of a river in little groups of three and four. By all means have a companion, but let him go his way and you yours and arrange to meet later in the day at an appointed time to swap stories and enjoy refreshments. The lone angler who is reasonably quiet sees so much more and is also far less visible to his quarry.

Had I had a companion by my side one evening last summer, I probably would not have been able to watch a big otter moving sedately down the middle of a river in Co. Down. Nor, I imagine, would I have been able to pass an absorbing 10 minutes spying on a kingfisher, gleaming like some rare jewel, as it fished for minnows in the River Lagan a few miles above Lisburn.

Certainly it would be a lot cheaper for me to buy the fish that I catch from the whiteness of a fishmonger's slab. I have never worked it out, but the few salmon, as an example, probably cost me at least four pounds for each pound of fish.

Why then do I go fishing? The reasons are most certainly neither gastronomical nor pecuniary. To me it is a form of escapism, and when I can't be on the riverbank, I like to dream about "the one that got away" or about some of the events that have enriched a day's fishing.

One such moment came when I was fishing on a remote lake on Vancouver Island, off Canada's West Coast. The lake is a vast sheet of water bounded on one shore by high mountains, the slopes of which run straight down into its icy blue depths. I was on the opposite shore when I heard a strange sound, one not unlike the far-off complaint of a rusty hinge.

I looked all around me but could see nothing. Then, lifting my eyes to the mountain peaks, white with snow for 12 months of the year, I saw the reason for my puzzlement. Almost level with the peaks were a host of small, black shapes strung out in an untidy V-formation. It was a huge skein of geese going I know not where. Maybe their destination was some remote island on the barren northern coast of British Columbia or perhaps somewhere warmer in the south.

This sight alone made the two-day trek into the lake and the accompanying non-stop war with mosquitoes and "no-see-ums," minute, mean-biting insects, worth all the effort.

So it is with all fishing. The lure is in what the future holds, the next day, the next pool or the next bend in the river.

Northern Ireland anglers with choices to make

MARCH 1957, *Belfast Telegraph*

There are those who regard angling as one of the dullest of all pastimes. Their idea of a fisherman is of someone seated on a little stool beside a placid lake while watching a rod and float and dozing in the sun. Nothing could be further from reality, for fishing is a most active sport, one that provides any amount of variety.

Every time the fisherman assembles his tackle, by lake or riverside, the conditions will be different. Unlike the tennis or rugby enthusiast, who plays on a court or pitch of identical geometrical proportions, the angler's beat is always changing, from day to day, season to season and even at times from hour to hour.

In summer a river may be low and clear today yet in high, brown flood tomorrow. Or there can be a full gale blowing down a mountain lough while the fisherman covers a rising trout in a calm, sheltered bay.

There is variety, too, in the angler's equipment, sometimes too much variety. One has only to walk into a fishing tackle shop to see what I mean. Glass cases full of shiny new rods of varying lengths and weights immediately catch the eye, as do cabinets full of countless boxes of lures and flies, skilful creations of fur and feather with no two patterns quite alike. Adding to this expensive array are orderly rows of artificial lures, coloured like jewels.

All this equipment is stocked for the convenience of the angling fraternity, one that can be divided into two classes: fly fishermen and others. The first are interested only in catching salmon and trout on artificial flies. The others will use imitation minnows, spoons and even garden worms to achieve the same ends.

Between the two lies a gulf as wide as Lough Neagh and one that is just about as likely to be filled. The reasonable argument of the devotees of the fly is that the angler casting spinners and artificial lures into a river or lake is both scaring the fish and lessening the chances of others fishing in the same water.

With the ever-growing popularity of the fixed spool reel, which enables even a beginner to cast 30 or 40 yards with less than an hour's practice, they have good cause to complain. They know that in a day's fishing even an expert fly fisherman could not cover a fraction of the water available to the man with spinning tackle.

There is also no disputing the fact that the angler who is spinning will prick but will not hook a large number of fish that are thus less likely to take again. I believe that the fish are there to be caught, and I am prepared to vary my tactics according to the conditions. Fly fishing remains the traditional way to catch trout and salmon, and it's the one from which I derive the most pleasure.

However, there are times when weather or river conditions do not favour the use of the fly, and it is then that I am quite happy to spin or even to fish with a bunch of worms, incidentally one of the best ways of deceiving a salmon when a river is in flood.

The ideal solution to the problem is to have certain waters preserved for fly fishing only, but as this is really not practical, my way seems as good a solution as any.

February in Northern Ireland is always a poor fishing month, and of the rivers that are legally open, only the Lagan is worth a visit. I have already spent two enjoyable days on its banks for a total bag of one 12-ounce trout. Now we are into March, and with every river in the province again open, I have high hopes for the days to come.

←——————

Hopeful thoughts of an angler

APRIL 1957, *Belfast Telegraph*

A new rod, like the thought of a fresh fishing season, is something that fills me with pleasure. Into its comfortably shaped cork handle, into its finely tapered tip, has gone the skill of the craftsman backed by the experience of years. All that remains is for the angler to prove its worth.

It's a long time now since I last allowed myself the luxury of such an expensive item of tackle. In the shop it seemed out of place, an object that was for sale, a reason for one man to give money to another.

On the riverbank all that is changed. The rod is the most important part of the angler's equipment. Without it he would be helpless, for how else can he cast to within reach of the fish that he hopes are waiting out there, innocent of man's deceit and his fly or lure?

My new split cane rod received its baptism a few weeks ago on the River Blackwater, in Co. Tyrone. It was not a spectacular christening but it would be churlish to complain of a brace of brown trout, each weighing nearly three-quarters of a pound. They both fell for a Greenwell's Glory fly and both had their home in a fast moving run beneath a tall tree, then leafless, now showing a green mist on its branches that will soon become lush foliage.

Spring is a pleasant time of year in the country whether, like myself, you are there to take a trout or, like others, just walking for pleasure.

At the beginning of March, winter is still fresh in our memories and there is always frost and sometimes even snow to come. But, as the weeks go by and April arrives, summer seems suddenly much nearer. The winds become gentler and the buds, so long in forming, start to open.

The trout, too, appreciate the coming of spring, for now the olives begin to hatch and they are able to build up the strength that has been sapped by the efforts of spawning and then the fight to stay alive through the long, dark months when most anglers remain close to home.

As far as actually catching fish is concerned, I have not yet enjoyed any really memorable days but there has always been something to hold my interest.

Last week, on the River Lagan, I watched what must have been the father of all water rats feeding from the carcass of a drowned hen. He was as large as a kitten and so close to me that I could see his nose twitching as he pulled with sharp teeth at the pieces of flesh he gripped between his paws.

Lough Melvin, in Co. Fermanagh, is one place to which I always like to return. It holds as good a stock of trout as any lake in Ireland and has a fine run of salmon each year. From now on they will be starting to come to the fly, but in the early part of the season, they are taken trolling a lure, sometimes natural, sometimes artificial, behind a slowly moving boat.

This has to be one of the most peaceful forms of fishing. Nothing disturbs the angler's thoughts save the splash of the waves against the side of the boat and the sounds of the oars as they move through the water. Above the fisherman there is often the strange, liquid cry of the curlew drifting away toward the Co. Leitrim hills.

Suddenly all is changed. A salmon has struck the lure and the peace is broken by the excitingly strident sound of an emptying reel. It's the moment every fisherman waits for. Perhaps it will be my turn soon.

Angling Trust may provide tourist bait

JANUARY 1959, *Belfast Telegraph*

Another angling season opens in two days' time. When it closes nine months will have passed and the province's total count of licensed fishermen will have climbed to a new peak. In all some 10,000 individuals are expected to have paid fees varying from ten shillings to two pounds for the privilege of fishing in the rivers and lakes of Northern Ireland.

These facts in themselves are not surprising, for since the end of the war there has been a marked and steady interest in the ranks of the angling fraternity throughout the United Kingdom.

What is surprising is that this growth is continuing in Northern Ireland, an area where the level of sport now available is of a far lower standard than it was five years ago, let alone at the time when peace was declared in 1945. Not only are the fish fewer in number, they are also smaller in size.

I use the word *fish* loosely to cover both the native brown trout and the migratory salmon and sea trout. Of course, there are other fish to be caught in Ulster waters, coarse fish like pike and perch, bream and rudd.

This decline in our angling standards has been an admitted fact for some considerable time. Until recently there has been much talk but little action toward remedying the matter. Now, at last, definite plans are in hand, plans that should, given the necessary support and enthusiasm, do much toward putting our piscatorial house in order.

I refer to the proposed Northern Ireland Fisheries Trust, whose articles of association, I am told, will be very similar to those of the like-named body that has been operating in Eire since 1952.

The trust, which must have official government backing to succeed, would be a limited company with a permanent, paid staff.

Its duties would centre around the development of angling – both coarse and game – in rivers and lakes throughout the province.

A few anglers of the old school have cherished the thought of founding just such a trust for a number of years. Now they have banded together, at the original invitation of the Armagh Angling Club, as a group whose main purpose is to maintain and then to better the present angling standard in the Six Counties.

Members of the group are drawn from all over the province and from all walks of life. They are, at present, 10 in number and have as their secretary Mr. Roy Gallagher, an Armagh bank official.

The creation of such a venture is obviously placing a considerable responsibility on the shoulders of these 10 men, but this is tempered by the knowledge that they have the personal support of Lord Brookeborough, Prime Minister of Northern Ireland. Both he and his wife are keen anglers, and it is at his request that he will be receiving the first official draft of the trust's plans within the next three weeks.

When I met with Mr. Gallagher earlier this week I asked him the obvious question: "Where will your waters come from?"

To this his reply was: "There are a number of sources. There are some free waters that we hope eventually to take over and improve. In other cases we will negotiate for the fishing or trespass rights on various stretches of river, through the riparian owners, and we are also hoping to benefit through direct gifts."

Mr. Gallagher emphasized that the trust would not make any approaches toward rivers or lakes at present controlled by angling clubs unless specifically requested by the bodies concerned.

This does not mean the trust does not anticipate support from the clubs. On the contrary, it already has the active backing of a considerable number of them and expects this to swell once their enterprise becomes a working concern.

Finance will obviously be a problem and, for this reason, the trust must have government backing. At the start they are hoping for a grant of 6,500 pounds. This would probably have to come through the Tourist Board and is roughly equivalent to the sum paid out each year by Ulster anglers in rod taxes and licence fees.

At present this money goes to the local boards of conservators, who are responsible for the maintenance of our rivers and lakes, but the general feeling is that the angling community, as opposed to the commercial fishermen, are not getting fair value for their money.

Added to this sum will be the membership fees paid by those anglers who join the trust. This will give them the right to fish in any of the trust's waters.

In the Republic of Ireland (Eire) this fee is seven shillings and sixpence and brings in a yearly income of almost 2000 pounds, to which is added State grants amounting to 11,700 pounds in 1957. I imagine that, to start with anyway, the Northern Ireland fee may be slightly in excess of that paid by anglers in Eire.

Of course, south of the border, angling is big business and this point was stressed to me by Mr. Erskine Childers, Eire's Minister for Lands and Fisheries, when I met with him in Dublin. "Last year," he told me, "more than 100,000 visitors came here for the fishing spending on average between 20 and 30 pounds each."

As if to emphasize his point, the pipe-smoking minister continued: "In the next five years our government expects to spend 60,000 pounds to improve the salmon fishing. Seven rivers, now closed to these fish by obstructions such as weirs and falls, will be opened. The first of these will be the Inagh, in Co. Clare. Our salmon exports are worth 600,000 pounds a year so you can see that the development of this type of fishing will aid both the commercial and the tourist trade."

This year the Eire Government's income from angling will rise from 66,000 pounds to 80,000 pounds through increased rod licence fees and the export levy of two pence per pound that applies to all salmon sent out of the country before June 1. After this date the figure drops to one penny per pound. Much of this revenue will go toward improved water protection and the mechanization of bailiffs with both cars and motorcycles.

No wonder Mr. Childers sounded satisfied as he told me how the development of Eire's inland fisheries in 1958 had shown the most striking progress of any aspect of their economic expansion program. "We feel," he said, "that we have given the program a great lead by the number of visitors we have attracted through angling.

Although he is not an angler himself, Mr. Childers is a far-sighted man. He knows that the development of angling is important, but so too are the visiting anglers' creature comforts.

It would probably be true to say that Eire has a greater angling potential than Northern Ireland, for it is a bigger country with a greater area of river and lake surface. However, the majority of anglers who come to Eire in a visiting capacity are seeking not game species like salmon and trout but coarse fish like pike and bream.

Ulster is especially rich in coarse fishing opportunities. There are lakes that never see an angler from one year's end to another. It will be the exploitation of such places by the new trust that will bring English anglers north of the border. For them coarse fishing is not only a sport; it is the attraction around which their whole way of life revolves.

Listen again to Mr. Childers: "I would like to see some form of angling trust that would cover the whole of Ireland. If this is not possible then I would like to think that your new trust and ours will work together as closely as possible."

CASTING BACK III ...
to trout and Atlantic salmon

←———|

Lean times for salmon fishers

OCTOBER 1955, *Belfast Telegraph*

After a dismal succession of damp, sunless summers, 1955 will stand out for a long time in Ulster fishermen's memories.

For the majority of people, recollections of summer 1955 will be happy ones of clear blue skies and long dry spells. But for the anglers and the commercial men, who depend on salmon for their sport and their living, the memories will be anything but happy. In fact, 1955 has been one of the worst years.

The total value of the Northern Ireland salmon catch is usually about 250,000 pounds. The Foyle Fisheries, by far the largest, landed 79,000 salmon worth 46,000 pounds in 1954. The Bann Fisheries last year had a total catch of between 12,000 and 14,000 fish, worth 60,000 pounds.

This year's returns have not yet been made public, but it is expected that in nearly every case they will be considerably below those of last season.

The primary reason for the decline was the abnormally dry weather that delighted the holidaymakers. The total rainfall for July and August, when the majority of the fish usually run, was only 2.9 inches when the average is more than 6 inches.

The drought meant that the rivers were in a very low state, and the salmon remained in the estuaries. When the rain came it was too late as the close season had started on nearly all the rivers.

The Bann Fisheries have had a poor season. When the fish were running early in July the floodgates, at Toomebridge, were opened fairly wide and the fish traps, at Coleraine, caught no fish at all. Mr. William Duff, Fishery Inspector for the Coleraine Board of Conservators, estimates that the loss over this one period was about 3500 pounds.

The loss of the Coleraine fishermen was to the gain of the men who set their nets in Lough Neagh, above Toomebridge. Some of them were able to show returns that were 300 per cent up on last year.

The control of the floodgates at Toomebridge, which is in the hands of the Ministry of Finance, has been a talking point for years. The ministry has a treaty with the Farmers' Union to maintain the height of the lough at 52 feet above sea level. If it is allowed to rise above this mark, flooding of valuable town and farmland immediately follows.

If the level drops below 52 feet then sand contractors and the Royal Air Force are not able to use their boat moorings on the lough and the water intakes of various authorities and industrial concerns are made useless. It is a situation full of problems.

Of the Co. Antrim coastal fisheries, only two report a reasonably good season. At Portbradden, owned and fished by Mr. Archie McKay and his three sons, a dry summer is appreciated, for it means the salmon stay longer in coastal waters. "It follows that the longer the fish are in the sea the better chance we have of catching them," says Mr. Bertie McKay.

How much damage has all this done to future fish stocks? Very little, according to Mr. Dan Cochrane of the Ballycastle Board of Conservators. He says it been a good spawning year for salmon on the River Bush.

A day for dapping on Lough Corrib

July 1957, *Belfast Telegraph*

Dapping for brown trout may not be an especially advanced form of fishing but it's one that has a special appeal on some of the great Irish loughs during the months of May and June.

A live mayfly is impaled upon a hook and, with the aid of a favourable wind, allowed to float on the surface of the water before a drifting boat. The rods are long, sometimes more than 16 feet from butt to tip, and they are not always as light as they might be. The ample length is essential if the fisherman is to benefit from even the lightest of airs.

Sitting with his back to the wind, he holds his rod at an angle of some 45 degrees and allows the unfortunate insect, attached to a silk line by a nylon cast, to be carried out to land on the water a little more than a rod's length away.

This year the first reports on our arrival on the shores of Lough Corrib, in Co. Mayo, were far from encouraging. It was too hot – even in the west of Ireland where rain and clouds are common fare – and the emerging mayflies were drying off and taking flight before the trout had a chance to snatch them up. Also, the hatch was some two weeks early this year and had never produced flies in any great numbers.

Corrib is a lough of great charm and beauty, its surface broken by countless islands, some densely wooded with firs and others clothed only with coarse grass dived into fields by neat dry-stone walls.

Our first day was spent under a sun of almost tropical ferocity, but the newness of the experience for me did much to compensate for a fishless day.

One of our problems had been a shortage of natural flies, but by the start of the next day, we had gathered a good five dozen from the bushes on the sheltered side of one of the islands.

We were afloat again shortly after breakfast and, by lunchtime, had three trout, of around a pound and a half each, in the boat. None, however, had fallen to my rod. Happily my luck was about to change, for to return fishless for a second day would have been too much to endure.

We were drifting slowly over a shallow shelf when my fly vanished in an oily swirl. This was the testing time; a too hasty strike and the fish would be away, leaving behind a bare hook and perhaps the sense of a hearty tug on the line by which to remember it.

My fears proved groundless. The trout was well hooked and soon the reel was singing the harsh song that only an angler can appreciate. The pressure told and now the fish was close to the boat and just a few feet below the surface.

In the net and quickly dispatched, my trout was one to be admired, perfect in form, small in the head with deep spotted flanks and a body that was firm and, I knew, with flesh that was pink and perfect for eating. It weighed just over two pounds, not large by Corrib standards but more than satisfying mine.

As we rowed back to shore, the setting sun was leaving a track of silver-topped waves behind us. My shoulders were aching and I was both tired and not a little sunburnt. But I was absolutely content, for I had gone dapping and caught my trout.

←⊣

Taking trout the commercial way

MAY 1958, *Belfast Telegraph*

A cuckoo called derisively from wooded Ram's Island, a mile off Lough Neagh's Co. Antrim shore. The two fishermen, their boat anchored in the shallow water, looked at their empty net and shrugged their shoulders. "That's the way it goes," said the younger of the two. "You can't be catching them all the time," said his partner.

Northern Ireland's Lough Neagh, at 151 square miles the largest lake in the British Isles, is world famous for its eels but it is also home to countless numbers of trout, known locally as dollaghan, and also pollan in addition to pike, perch and bream. The last three have only a small commercial worth at present and it is to the trout and pollan that the local fishermen look for a living when the eels are out of season.

I spent a day with two of these men, Felix and Sean McGarry, both professional fishermen with homes on the shores of Sandy Bay, at the mouth of which lies Ram's Island.

Although they are not related, as their names might suggest, they have been fishing together for a number of years and have developed an understanding of each other and of the lough itself that can only come of long experience.

Felix is the older of the two and has been fishing for 26 of his 38 years, following in the footsteps of his father and his grandfather. To him go two-thirds of the profits, for he is also the owner, and indeed the builder, of the sturdy 20-foot, wood-planked boat on which their living depends.

Sean (26), is recently married and the father of a two-month-old baby. His wife's side of the family have always been connected with fishing but his have not, and only recently he spent a year and a half working as a lorry driver in England. Family reasons brought him home shortly after Christmas, and he is now back fishing with the man who, he says, "taught me everything I know."

Theirs is not an easy living for it has no regular hours, no union contract benefits and no steady rates of pay. And all the time they are dependent on the mood of the weather and the wiles of the trout.

One week they may make 12 or 15 pounds; the next they could just as easily be storm-bound and take home only a couple of pounds. Despite the uncertainty is seems to be a case of "once a fisherman, always a fisherman." They are their own masters, doing something that requires considerable skill and from which they derive great satisfaction.

We left the anchorage at Sandy Bay shortly after breakfast, and until we reached the shelter provided by Ram's Island, our open boat, powered by a 24-horsepower lorry engine, had to force its way into the strong westerly wind that was sweeping across from the Co. Tyrone side of the lough, bringing with it biting squalls of sleet and rain.

Soon we had started to fish. The anchor was dropped and the 600-foot draft net, lengthened at both ends by another 100 feet of rope, was payed out in a huge circle. Then began the actual hauling of the net, a long and tedious task as its heavy folds were drawn slowly through the water.

Felix and Sean made it look easy, leaning against the weight of the net and bringing it in steadily, yard-by-yard, hand over hand. But it's not as simple as it looked; a few minutes' trial showed me that.

In theory any fish that are caught within the compass of the stone-weighted net are slowly but surely driven into its long, cone-shaped tail from which they have little hope of escaping.

As the two men hauled, I had time to look around. To our left were the Mountains of Mourne, their profile blunted by the distance; on our right, the pencil-slim silhouette of the television transmitting mast on Divis Mountain. And to our backs was the protective shelter of the island with a slow-winged heron passing by at treetop level.

Now the drawing of the net is nearly complete. The tempo of the men's movements quickens as the tail of the net is brought aboard ... but it's empty. This time the trout have had the last laugh. And so it is again on the next haul, for there is only one small trout within its meshes.

Then a hail shower came whipping across the lough, numbing our hands and lashing the surface of the water into an angry, hissing foam. When it had passed and the sun returned, the contrast of its warmth both welcome and startling, Felix decided to move to another fishing ground, a shallow shelf in the middle of the bay. His judgment proved sound for our next two hauls produced some 28 fish, all trout ranging in weight from one-and-a-half to five pounds.

The two men had been working now non-stop for some five hours and decided to call a halt for some food and to light a fire of driftwood on the shore. Fresh, pink-fleshed trout baked whole over the glowing sticks, eaten from the fingers and washed down with strong, sweet tea, made for a meal to remember.

Before we finally headed for home that evening they had set and hauled their nets four more times, taking another two dozen trout and one pollan, a small, silvery fish that looks very much like a herring. In all, their day's catch would have weighed in the region of 80 pounds and would sell at a wholesale price of about three shillings a pound.

As I left Sandy Bay, night was approaching fast. To the north, storm clouds, black and threatening, were piling up one upon another. My day's work was over, but the McGarrys had still to set their nets to dry and then to free the meshes from a covering of slimy, green weed. Perhaps the coming storm would stop them from going fishing in the morning, but they couldn't take the chance. They had to be prepared.

←————

Only in Ireland: The one that got away

FEBRUARY 1959, *Ireland's Saturday Night*, BELFAST

Anglers are noted storytellers and sometimes prone to exaggeration. Occasionally the tales of "the one that got away" have a basis of fact.

The one I have in mind most certainly has. The fish, a salmon, made good its escape not in the water but on dry land and after it had been dispatched with the time-honoured knock on the head from the wooden priest.

The whole affair has a slightly Irish ring about it and, not surprisingly, took place on the banks of a river in Co. Donegal, the Owenea. This is a lovely stream running through lush Irish countryside where fairies and leprechauns actually seem possible. Along its course the angler comes upon pools with names like Poul-a-Tuarn, The Gubbin and Wee Crambam.

It was the last day of the holidays and Fred Beckett, my companion, and I had struggled out of our beds before dawn. For a number of days we had been fishing the Owenea with modest success, and we hoped to finish on a high note.

A short drive down a bumpy bog road, running between high mounds of sweet-smelling turf, brought us to the river.

For a time our efforts were in vain. Then Fred called from a pool below where I was fishing. A salmon had taken his fly, and when I arrived, his rod was arched in a most satisfactory fashion. It was not a big one, perhaps weighing five or six pounds, but it was a fish. That was what counted, for it meant we would have something to show for our efforts on our return to Belfast.

Perhaps salmon, like humans, are not at their best in the early morning, for this one did not put up a great fight and was soon landed. It was then that we made our fatal mistake.

Not wanting to leave it concealed on the bank lest it provide a free meal for a hungry rodent, we decided to carry it with us, although neither of us had a suitable fishing bag or creel.

I found an old piece of string in my pocket and soon the salmon was hanging, head down, from the handle of Fred's landing net. Then, since it was not yet breakfast time, we set off to catch another one.

Half an hour later we had lost our salmon. Fred had gone on ahead, and as I caught up to him, I saw not a shining fish but a damp and sorry-looking piece of cord hanging forlornly from the handle of his net.

Obviously the quality of the string was not all that it might have been and the weight of the salmon, modest though it was, had proved too much of a strain. The string had snapped.

For the next hour we hunted high and low for that fish. We searched under rocks, in bank-side holes and hollows, in the river itself. Our efforts were in vain. It wouldn't have been so bad if we had been able to catch another one. But, of course, we didn't.

Later our friends looked at us in doubtful fashion when we told them about "the one that got away."

I don't think they believed us.

←⟶

Strong man's fishing season

FEBRUARY 1963, *The Observer*, LONDON

It was a Scot, with long experience of spring fishing for salmon on the mighty River Tay, who once spoke of a wind so cold "that there was no place to put my face." It is not hard to imagine his discomfort or to realize that Irishmen up and down the country will be subjecting themselves to equally unpleasant conditions within the next few weeks.

Indeed some of them are at it already, for the River Liffey, flowing icily beneath Dublin's stately bridges, has already given up a number of fish, and to the expert they are always fish and not salmon, among them one particularly fine 26-pounder. The River Bundrowes, in Co Donegal, also opened on January 1 and has already repaid a few of those who have braved the long journey to Ireland's far northwest.

Fishing at this time of year is no pastime for the weak in heart. Old men and ladies can go out and kill their share of salmon in June, July and August, but it is the strong men of the sport who make their mark in January and February, at a time when friends and relations are sitting snugly at home cursing the weather.

The men who do well are the ones who will stay out all day in an open boat on Lough Melvin or Lough Fern, in Co. Fermanagh and Co. Donegal respectively, patiently trolling natural sprats and artificial minnows, men who do not complain if a day's fishing with a heavy rod and long-numbed fingers brings no reward. Rivers everywhere run high in winter, and it takes strength of character and a steady hand to check a hooked fish that could easily tip the scales at 20 pounds.

It is, perhaps, the potential physical bulk of the catch that provides one of the greatest of all the attractions associated with Irish salmon fishing in the opening months of the season. Michael Wall landed one weighing 37 pounds on the River Suir on the 18th of February last year. Later in the month the River Boyne produced a fish of just over 30 pounds.

Spring fishing is, in fact, the specialized realm of expert fishermen with unlimited patience coupled with an ability to withstand the worst possible conditions for as long as may be necessary.

The financial rewards can be considerable, but it can be an expensive hobby and the fish don't exactly give themselves up when, and if, they are hooked. "First catch your salmon" could be the specialist's slogan, and it is the brave man who would deny him the right to cook or sell as the fancy moves him.

←——————|

Disaster at Glendun

JUNE 1964, *Creel Magazine*, ENGLAND
(PUBLISHED 1963-67)

The salmon, and there must have been a dozen or more in the space of a few yards, lay dead on the blackened beach, occasionally covered by the inky tide. The waters of the bay were stained far out to sea. The sand was fouled and strewn with debris. The river ran thick and brown.

Such was the aftermath of disaster, a reminder of the night that destruction came sweeping down the River Glendun , a sparkling little salmon stream that tumbles gaily through one of the larger watersheds that comprise Northern Ireland's famous Glens of Antrim. It is not one of the country's best-known salmon waters but it has a scenic charm all of its own.

Now its future hangs in the balance, for its salmon parr, its smolts and a high percentage of its spawning stock have been destroyed. Some, like the ones on the beach, were washed, choking, downstream to their deaths, while others lie buried deep beneath the mass of primeval filth that came surging down the wooded glen.

Natural disasters seldom affect the angler in Britain, but the men who look to the Glendun for their sport have bitter cause of recall that Sunday night in early November, 1963. It had rained for much of the day and the river was rising, bringing in some late-run fish from the short estuary, allowing others to press further upstream.

It was almost dark when 25-year-old schoolteacher Margaret McCormack looked up at the steep sides of the glen beside her riverside home some five miles from the sea. Above her the brow of the hill suddenly collapsed as huge boulders began to plummet down the slope.

Screaming, she ran for her brother while the very ground heaved beneath her feet. The two halted in their flight and turned in time to see their home carried intact out into the glen to stand for a moment before being engulfed by the moving tide of near liquid matter.

The flood hurled itself across the valley and up the other side, leaving its mark more than 30 feet above the level of the river. Then, as the water backed up foot upon foot, it broke again, this time toward the sea, carrying all in its path, spilling out to block the road, tearing away trees and bushes.

In less than three hours the damage was done. Nothing was left alive. Many of the Glendun's upper pools had been leveled, the spawning beds had been denuded and the fish suffocated by what was an almost solid concentration of peat.

Somewhere high in the moorland hills above the glen the ground had reached saturation point. The marshy land, quaking and insecure, had broken free, initiating a train of events that were to cause almost unbelievable havoc. Gathering momentum, the moving mass of water, turf, earth and rock gouged a great, dark scar across the face of the high plateau before dropping over the lip of the glen. No lives were lost, but many sheep, pigs and cattle vanished that night,

In 1900 a similar "moss flood" swept down the Glendun, so the story goes, and it was a full five years before the salmon returned in any numbers. This time, the local angling association is hoping to initiate a massive restocking scheme.

Although it produces the occasional fish in April and May, the Glendun is generally recognized as a summer and autumn river, receiving a fair run of salmon, grilse and sea trout from July right on until the season ends on the last day of October. In the months ahead, the fishing should be as good as ever, for the water will have cleared and successive winter spates will have dispersed much of the excess silt.

After this will come the lean years, for no amount of restocking can compensate for the loss of the smolts that would have soon been making their way to the sea or for the death of the salmon parr that would have followed them in 1965. Of course, some salmon did survive, for they had already reached the river's headwaters, high up in the glen. There would have been many more of them in another month.

Nature was not prepared to suspend sentence on the Glendun and its people. I was there on the last October day of the 1963 fishing season and was enthralled at the playful antics of a weasel that had made its home in the dry stone wall just below where the McCormacks' home stood. Now nothing remains but bleak and barren earth.

When the fly bobs up

MAY 1965, *The Observer*, LONDON

Only a few days to go. Then the news will begin to spread. In a remote Irish village the local postman will be asked to hand on a cryptic telegram. In a lonely cottage with breathtaking views of lake and island, a swarthy, weather-beaten man will sit down to pen what could be his only letter of the year.

Delivered in a day or two to city office and suburban villa, letter and telegram will cause a sudden disruption in family life. Staid business partners will put aside their balance sheets. Students will forsake their books, tradesmen their tools, their daily rounds. One and all will know that the fly is up, that the biggest brown trout of all are on the move.

For the Irish angler the annual mayfly hatch is a highlight of the season, an opportunity not to be missed, a time when the wildest dreams can be realized. It is a golden hour too for the people who cater for the itinerant fisherman. Hotels and boarding houses, and private homes as well, are full to bursting; boatmen booked out weeks in advance, boats for hire virtually unobtainable.

There is nothing quite like it to stir the angler's heart. The famous Irish loughs, Erne and Sheelin, Mask and Arrow, Corrib and Derravaragh, and others as well, will attract a regular clientele, all hoping to catch the trout of a lifetime, all determined to make the most of the foolish fishes' picnic.

The dainty mayflies spend the greater part of their lives as larvae in the silt at the bottom of the lake or river. Then comes the time of hatching, varying from the second week of May and on into the first two weeks of June depending on locale. For each fly, and they can number in the hundreds and even thousands, the climax of life is short and often frustratingly sudden.

Small trout, of two and three pounds, can be caught right

through the season, but the real monsters, great brutes running to six and eight pounds, tend to keep themselves to themselves, feeding in the deep, dark depths and generally ignoring the fisherman's pretty lures and flies.

Each year at mayfly time, discretion is tempered by greed. It is then that the trout take to surface feeding, gulping down fly after fly with enthusiasm and presenting a tempting target for the fisherman who seeks a tenant for the glass-fronted showcase above his mantelpiece.

Mayfly fishing has always been associated with the traditional sport of dapping, hunched men in drifting boat, tall rods held out to catch the wind, eye glued, unblinking, on the hook-impaled flies moving urgently from wave to wave. Comes a rise and the expert will pause for a moment or two before setting the hook with a deft turn of the wrist.

Beginners find the self-control the hardest part of all and are given various catch phrases to repeat before striking. Of course, Irish politics must play a part in the routine. In Northern Ireland the boatman will suggest "God save the Queen"; south of the border, in Eire, it's always "Up the Republic." History does not relate relative successes, but the pause remains essential.

Tradition dies hard and dapping will always have its followers. It certainly accounts for big bags of trout, not to mention "dapper's hump," an angler's complaint that makes itself known when back muscles revolt in the most painful manner after being tensed hour after hour in the same crouched position.

Happily the trout can also be outwitted with artificial flies. Some are dressed to imitate the hatching nymph, others the mature dun, the Green Drake, and the dark spent fly, the Black Gnat, that falls back to the surface of the water to lie spread-eagled and exhausted on completion of the mating cycle.

As in all forms of fishing, the weather is a major factor. Clear skies and a burning sun are deplored. They allow the emerging insects to hatch, dry their wings and fly away before the trout can twitch a tail. Ideal conditions call for plenty of broken cloud and a soft, dancing breeze with the mayfly's maiden flight retarded by the weather.

The past winter was long and hard, the spring more than a little delayed, so there is a school of thought that believes the hatch will be late this year. The angler knows the wait will be worthwhile. So do the trout, the terns and the gulls that come inland to glut themselves on mayflies at every opportunity. Also waiting are the barelegged local boys who find a ready market for live flies at three shilling a dozen – and more in time of need.

<hr>

Lough Neagh trout can be caught

JUNE 1968, *Belfast Telegraph*

For as long as anyone can remember, the myth has been perpetuated that Lough Neagh trout cannot be caught using rod and line. It can now be said with absolute certainty that this is nonsense, pure and simple. Some six or seven years ago a few fish were taken by prospecting anglers prepared to question accepted facts and, more recently, far more convincing evidence has come to hand.

Two separate groups of anglers, from Antrim and Lurgan, have been thinking along similar lines for some time and their efforts have been amply rewarded. Lurgan brothers Pat and Jim Mc-Caffery, along with a couple of friends, reckon they have caught 25 trout, ranging in weight from two and a half pounds to six pounds, fishing on the occasional evening since the start of the season.

Then last week John Laughlin, from Antrim, brought off the noteworthy feat of killing trout of six pounds and four and a half pounds while fly fishing from the shore at a place called Cattlebottom, not far from the town. This catch in itself was sufficient to rekindle my interest in the potential offered by the largest area of fresh water in the British Isles.

Over the past month I have spent long and unprofitable hours fishing on such well-known Irish trout loughs as Erne and Sheelin. On Wednesday, along with Antrim anglers Jim Telford and Moore Anketell, I set out, determined to put an equal effort into an attempt to take a Lough Neagh trout using traditional wet fly tactics from a drifting boat.

The exposed waters of Lough Neagh can be as rough as any sea, but the wind was only of moderate force and there was ample shelter in vicinity of Ram's Island. By the end of the day we knew for certain that Lough Neagh trout can and will take an artificial fly.

Coming home with the sun long since set, we could reflect on the excitement of seven trout hooked and played, not to mention eight silvery pollan landed, the best weighing a little short of a pound. As so often happens, not all the trout stayed hooked, but fish of two and a half pounds, taken by Telford, and one and a half pounds, caught by Anketell, more than proved the point.

Of the seven, four were hooked between noon and 6:00 p.m. with the other three coming during a spectacular evening rise to the abundant chironomid midge. Dry flies having met with little success in the past, we concentrated on casting wet flies, relying largely on a variety of nymph patterns, with Anketell hooking five of the seven fish on a fly that had a body of peacock herl.

I had more success with pollan, often described as a "freshwater herring," than with trout but have starkly etched memories of my encounter with a trout that weighed between three and four pounds. Fishing with only a three-pounds breaking strain cast, I had little option but to give it its head as it sent off on a run that took all 30 yards of fly line and then many yards of backing in one great, sweeping run.

This had to be one of the most spectacular fighting fish I had ever hooked, for it jumped wildly six or seven times and never once gave any indication of being under control.

As always among fishing friends there was some lively banter when my line came back slack and, in the opinion of the other two,

I had been too gentle in my approach. Be that as it may, Anketell was soon to lose two successive fish, holding them hard each time before they regained their freedom.

The fight of the Lough Neagh trout, which are generally hooked near the surface, is beyond compare, and I have no doubt that the time has come for the more imaginative of Northern Ireland's ever-growing army of anglers to give the lough an exhaustive trial.

The McCaffery brothers enjoyed exceptional fishing in March and April but have found an algae bloom, which is already discolouring the water, makes for difficult fishing in June and July. It settles in August and September and sport picks up again, so I can see no reason why dapping with a daddy-long-legs or a grasshopper, or both, should not be worth a trial.

Unfortunately there are few if any suitable boats available for hire. A small craft poses a real risk on Lough Neagh, for a sudden squall could easily be a prelude to disaster. Still, if the demand is there, I am sure it won't be too long before adequate boats are made available.

How big do these Lough Neagh trout run? I'll let Pat McCaffery have the last word. "My brother Jim hooked a fish that was feeding about a yard from the shore. It smashed a ten-pound nylon cast as if it was only two pounds. We saw its tail and back and then it made one great dash and wrecked him.

"The next day one of the commercial fishermen on the lough handed him back the Invicta fly that he had been using and told him that the trout weighed 22 pounds. I am sure he was not exaggerating for we have seen plenty of fish of between six and ten pounds and some much larger than that."

On Wednesday we watched as a couple of massive trout fed steadily just out of casting distance. Then there was another big one that came steadily up a calm water slick picking off natural flies. They are not all takers by any means, and this one ignored our offerings on three or four occasions as it moved away into the dusk.

Fish worth toasting

JULY 1971, *The Observer*, LONDON

The pints of Guinness, freshly pulled and still settling, made moist little circles on the bar. I was standing there running with water like some great blue sponge. Jersey, jeans, socks, hat and all might just as well have been taken straight from the river that ran a stone's throw from the door.

In normal circumstances my condition would have excited some comment, even in a Northern Irish pub well used to the strange ways of anglers. But this was no ordinary day, and the regulars at the bar must have sensed my elation. They asked no questions, only offered their congratulations.

The fish lay at my feet on the floor, freshly caught and, from their appearance, freshly minted too. There is nothing I know to beat the sight of a salmon fresh from the sea, every scale intact and throwing back the light. When they come in fours it is a very special day indeed.

The dedicated salmon fisherman can wait for years for the combination of circumstances that transforms just another day's fishing – and they are all special – into one that must go down in the book.

So it was for me on that day late in June on the River Mourne, near Victoria Bridge in Co. Tyrone. Atlantic salmon can be taken with worms from the garden and on spoons, with prawns and shrimps and with an endless assortment of lures fashioned from wood, plastic and metal. But for absolute fulfillment they must always be deceived by an artificial fly.

John McAleer lives a few miles upstream from Victoria Bridge, in Newtownstewart, and ties both salmon and trout flies with a skill tried and tested by a lifetime's experience. Hammie Burke is a river watcher who spends endless summer hours beside the stone-built weir at Sion Mills, below Victoria Bridge, counting the individual salmon as they fight their way up the sloping white torrent.

Both men had contributed to this my day of days. It was Hammie who had confirmed with a phone call that the fish had been running earlier in the week and this despite falling water that would soon leave the weir high and dry with the river's flow again diverted down the mill race. And it was John who had tied the gold, silver and Wilkinson Shrimp flies that were to serve me so well on the day.

The fish we toasted in the bar that night were typical of their kind, dainty Atlantic salmon grilse weighing between five and six pounds, perfectly formed and still carrying the distinctive sea lice to emphasize their so recent arrival in fresh water.

The Mourne is not a long river, only 10 miles from Newtownstewart to Strabane, but it is a large one by Northern Irish standards, carrying with it the lyrically named tributary waters of the Owenkillew, and the Glenelly, the Camowen, Drumragh, Strule and Derg – all salmon rivers in their own right. Its pools are substantial in many places, and the angler needs chest-high waders and a rod that offers both length and power.

The news that there were fresh-run salmon in the pools, that the water was at an optimum level to fish the fly and that a cloudy day with occasional light showers was in the forecast, was incentive enough. Wiser men were still in their beds as I made my first cast on a pool called the Feddans, feeling my way carefully around the angled rocks and over the jagged underwater ledges.

Nothing happened, nothing showed. Perhaps the fish had not yet come that far, or perhaps they had run on through the night to rest in the pools further upstream?

The story was the same at first from the Pan, a choice pool in its own right lying in the shadow of the now abandoned Mulvin railway bridge, and terminating in a short rapids leading into a heavy stream called Burnfoot. It was there, in the heavy water, that the first salmon took solidly on the far side of the river at the end of a long cast.

So the day went on, from peak to peak, from success to despair with one more salmon killed and then four lost, one right at the landing net and two more after being played for an appreciable time.

Three hours passed, all the time fishing hard, before a pool called Stralag provided ample reward for perseverance. It was well on into the evening when the seventh fish of the day intercepted my fly at a point marking the dividing line between calm and broken water, a classic lie.

This one played especially well, defying side strain and the drag of an extended line to hold station far out in the rushing current. Ultimately the pressure told and it came quietly to the landing net. The spell was broken. A second time down the same pool the performance was repeated, providing me with a fourth fish as perfect as the rest.

Dry-shod and weary, I should have made my way gratefully toward the comforts offered by Noel Finlayson's bar at the bridge. Instead, Stralag seemed worth another try. Almost immediately I misjudged the angle of the deceptive ledge at the head of the stream and did an unexpected, unwilling vanishing act. Casting and concentrating one minute, shoulder deep and struggling for a foothold the next, before a hasty exit with waders filled and clothing soaked.

I have caught more salmon in a single day in the past, with seven from the Strule the absolute limit. They were taken in the autumn on spinning tackle and, to my mind, their currency was accordingly devalued. Four landed and four others hooked and lost, and all on the fly, that's fishing of a high order, enough and more to restore confidence in the future of salmon angling on the Mourne and the other rivers that make up the Foyle system.

The River Finn: A Co. Donegal delight

JUNE 2001, *Belfast Telegraph*

Business types collect business cards – and so do fishermen. Indexed properly, they can provide an invaluable reminder of places visited, contacts made and goals achieved.

The card I have in mind has to do with fly fishing for Atlantic salmon on a storied Irish river, one that tumbles down from high ground in Co. Donegal on its way to the tidal reaches of Lough Foyle and finally the Atlantic.

It was Glenmore Estate agent Thomas McCreery, over a welcoming cup of tea in his farmhouse kitchen, who suggested where we might find a bed for the night after our first evening on the River Finn.

The cream-coloured card with its green typeface and accompanying sketch of the two-storey, steep-roofed premises said it all: Harkin's Bar and Restaurant, Brockagh, Cloghan, Co. Donegal. Accommodation Available, Meals Served Daily, Music at Weekends. What more could we possibly want.

My old friend Dave Lane, the "sturgeon general" to those who recognize his pioneering sturgeon research and hatchery work at Vancouver Island's Malaspina College, was happy to concur. We had just driven due west 170 brisk miles from Dublin, noting the negligible traffic and sensing that many smaller streams and rivers were definitely on the high side after heavy rain earlier in the week.

The Finn is prime water for the salmon fly fisherman, especially its swift-flowing reaches above the town of Ballybofey. Sourced from Lough Finn, in the Blue Stack Mountains, and further enhanced by the contribution of its major tributary, the Reelan, the system supports a perhaps diminished run of prime spring fish in March and April. Then come the strong returns of sprightly smaller summer salmon, grilse to the locals, together with the sea trout, white trout to the Irish.

While most of the best water is in private hands or controlled by local angling clubs, there is good visitor access to be enjoyed at more than reasonable prices. The upper part of the Finn, where this tale is set, has more than 30 named pools with another 11 on the Reelan. As I recall we paid a daily rate of a little less than 10 pounds. And this at a time when the cost of game fishing in both Britain and Ireland is fast soaring beyond the reach of all but the very rich.

The Finn's two prime beats, Ivy Bridge, with eight pools, and Annich, with ten, each limited to three rods, cost between 25 pounds and 34 pounds a day for each rod, the lower rates applying in April, May, August and September.

Dave had heard my stories of earlier adventures on the river, back in the 1960s, and was anxious to be fishing sooner than later. Modest sums exchanged hands for that evening's fishing and for the next day as well, with the prospect of falling water levels to enhance our chances in the morning.

It was time to move on, across the Ivy Bridge, stopping briefly to admire that famous pool of the same name far below, and on up the hill to Brockagh, not so much a village as a tiny roadside hamlet that looks out and across the deep, river-worn valley of the Upper Finn, its borders a patchwork of neat fields and traditional dry-stone walls.

On our arrival, Mrs Harkin's greeting had all the warmth of a summer's day. Yes, she had beds available, a room apiece as she wasn't too busy, and yes, we could eat when we came back from the river. And when should we aim to return? "Don't you worry, the bar'll be open and we will get you something" was her promise.

Harkin's Bar and Restaurant has been a family-owned business for more than 50 years. Mrs. Harkins now has her daughter back to help after a nursing career in London, another small example of how increasing Irish prosperity is bringing its people home.

It would have been a wonderful climax to return at dark with a bright fish in hand, but it was not to be. We found the water was still coming up, typical of any Irish spate river, one that responds quickly to rain in the hills and yet can then steady and start to drop within hours. Earlier we might have fished the so-called "creep," seen the telltale signs of rising water as the first grasses and twigs float free, giving hope of a taking fish responding to the changing conditions.

Dinner that night was as memorable for its setting as for its quality. Our places were set at the long wooden bar, where we enjoyed fine steaks with chips and all the trimmings. A turf fire warmed our backs while the locals supped their pints. Later, very much later I recall, there was Irish whiskey and lots of fishing talk, for it's not every day that a pair of Canadian anglers find their way to Brockagh.

To his lasting credit, Dave stayed the course. I was in a deep sleep, in my own bed let it be said, before the bar finally called "last drinks" for the night. Dawn came all too soon, as it invariably does in such circumstances, but we were still on the river shortly after 6:00 a.m., fortified by early morning tea and biscuits.

We worked the upper pools first, Letterbrick, also called New Bridge for obvious reasons, the Corner Pool, where I had taken a couple of good fish so many years before, and finally Herns. Then it was time for breakfast, the full Irish version with fried eggs, sausages, bacon, tomatoes, slices of black pudding and potato bread – and more if we had had the appetite. And the bill for dinner, bed and breakfast, 21 pounds each, which was quite amazing value.

The rest of the day passed all too quickly. We headed for water familiar to me over the years, to a long beat that ran from the Chapel Steps through pool after quality pool, deep water and streamy water. The Sea Trout Pool, Martins and Pattons, each holding the promise of a fish to the very next cast. Had we had the energy, we could have worked our way right down to the Rock Pool, the last of the estate fishing below the now vacant Glenmore House.

Dave was using my ten-foot, seven-weight, Scottish-made Clan rod, nicely balanced and well able to deal with what was in the river at the time, early summer-run fish in the three to eight pound range with the chance of an occasional larger salmon.

I left him fishing his way carefully down the Chapel Steps, encouraged by the sight of a small grilse landed by a local angler just after he arrived, his fly swimming perfectly down and across a strong stream, one confined by a rock shelf reaching out from the far bank.

My objective, my hope for the day, lay half-a-mile downstream at Keys High Water Pool. I fished with a No. 8 double Gold Shrimp fly before changing to a Thunder and Lightning, working my way through a succession of deep pockets, where I felt the salmon must surely lie, if only briefly, as they push on upstream toward the Chapel Steps.

The take, when it came at last, well into the morning, was in Keys, just below and out from the massive midstream boulder that forces the current toward the right-hand bank.

The 13½-foot, double-handed Sage rod had made easy work of the moderate casting distance, and the fish pulled strongly at the Shrimp fly, boiled once just below the surface and was gone.

My sink tip line had only just tightened to the hand, but it was most certainly an offer, albeit a fleeting one. One chance, only one chance, as it is so often with Atlantic salmon. Of course there were no regrets, only vivid recollections of the potential of a classic river in a totally beautiful and ever so Irish setting. When, if ever, will I return? A lifetime is too short for all the fishing that we hope still lies ahead of us.

That was that for my day, an expedition to a most favoured place, an opportunity to share past experiences with an old and valued friend, one whose reaction to the whole affair was summed up over a recent New Year's dinner when he said: "You know, we'll have to find a way to get back to Mrs. Harkin's one of these days."

Dave's day on the Finn was a mirror image of my own, a single fish played almost to the bank well down the Chapel Steps before the hook pulled out. An experienced fly fisherman and a skilful fly tier, he took the disappointment well, for this was his first crack at Atlantic salmon. He could have been disconsolate, but that's simply not in the character of this always-cheerful companion.

My hope all along was that Dave would have had a first fish on the bank before the start of our long drive back across the country, almost from coast to coast. It was not to be, but we still brought home with us our memories of the day, and that surely·is so much an integral part of fishing the world over. As we get older we can only hope these treasured images from the near and distant past remain in focus as we look forward to the next time.

Cowichan River invitation

NOVEMBER 2001, *www.ariverneversleeps.com*, VANCOUVER

The big Cowichan River boulder stands well to the left of the summer-weight stream, its feet now in water only inches deep, its shoulders bleached by sun and wind.

Back in March the same rock was close to mid-river, just upstream of an all but submerged outcrop islet. First impressions were of a potential holding place for a worthwhile fish, a robust resident brown trout or perhaps a late-run steelhead.

By July the picture is much changed and yet the location, its water level diminished by a good few feet, remains full of promise. The stream, strong enough in spring to make for a challenging, deep-wading crossing to the edge of the outcrop and then to the relatively calm water behind the big stone, still runs strongly as it curls back toward the fallen remains of a substantial tree.

The aquatic shelter this windfall provides close to the bank stirs the imagination. The pool below is wide and deep, offering perfect cover for fish of all sizes. As the square cast traverses the flow we anticipate the take.

Concentration is at a high pitch, the senses never more attuned to the moment. No brown trout this time, instead a 15-inch rainbow comes to a nymph pattern in bright sunshine to prove its vulnerability to the right fly. Then it plays strongly, twisting and turning in the clear water.

Cowichan River fishing is seldom easy, but the surroundings are visually superb. Densely treed along its fly only upper reaches, it offers a shaded, forested walk beside a series of lovely pools and runs upstream from the long since abandoned 70.2 mile railway trestle.

From its source at Lake Cowichan, the river hurries along an often-rugged course of some 27 miles (43 km) to its tidal estuary in Cowichan Bay with 98 named pools to invite the fisherman along the way.

The visitor can expect brown and rainbow trout over the 12 months of the year. Chinook, coho and then chum salmon arrive in late summer and early fall, and the steelhead run from December through April.

Water levels are the key for the fly fisherman. The lake and the weir at its outlet provide a controlled flow, but after heavy rain in the hills there will be days when levels are too high for effective fly presentation. High water limits wading opportunities too.

Walking from pool to pool has to be an essential part of the whole Cowichan experience with so much to see, so much to enjoy. In season there are otters and hummingbirds, eagles and mink, mergansers and woodpeckers and all the other smaller songbirds.

March, April and May bring the best of the dry fly opportunities, and the river is good again in the fall and early winter when an abundance of salmon eggs catches the attention of the resident browns and lures the rainbow trout down from the lake. During high summer, when water temperatures rise, the river falls to a more easily waded level, but fishing pressures ease as anglers avoid imposing undue stress on the resident brown trout.

The Pitt River and promise of a big fish running

JANUARY 2005, *www.ariverneversleeps.com*, VANCOUVER

Remote yet still accessible, the Pitt River and Danny and Lee Gerak's lodge of the same name bring a sense of unique opportunity to the sport fishing scene in British Columbia. There are lodges, rivers and lakes aplenty in this huge province of ours but the large majority, or at least those offering fishing that counts as out-of-the-ordinary in terms of the quality of the experience, are invariably located some distance removed from the main population centres.

That, of course, is an essential part of their charm, for there is nothing worse than the pressure that comes with overfishing. Resident stocks suffer in terms of numbers and average size, and anyway, who really wants to fish shoulder to shoulder with – or even within hailing distance of – complete strangers. Overfishing is a fact of life in so many places, and for the most part, we accept it as such with good grace as part of the compromises we must make if we are to continue to fish at all.

To come to the Pitt River Lodge – as I did in late October with Mark Hume, Nick Didlick, Glenn Baglo and Mike Smyth, respected journalists, writers, photographers, friends and colleagues from the fishing website www.ariverneversleeps.com – was to take a step back in time.

One minute we were snarled in Sunday afternoon highway traffic in Vancouver as incessant rain drenched the coast; an hour later we were well on our way by boat up Pitt Lake, eager in the anticipation of a return to an era when all rivers in this part of the world were in their prime, full of fish and located in places where the hand of man had still to leave its mark.

True, the rich forest resource of the Upper Pitt River valley has been exploited in the past, and, to a degree, still is being exploited. But the logging operation that once supported the long-since-dismantled township of Alvin and its pioneering population of some 250 hardy souls is being scaled back and should be shut down altogether within a couple of years. Later we learn from our co-host Lee at Pitt River Lodge that Alvin was named after a Nova Scotian farmer and logger, Alvin Patterson, the first settler in the valley in 1901.

As it happens, the very nature of the wild and often braided watershed is such that the visual impact of the logging can be largely ignored. At the same time the network of gravel logging roads provides access from the estuary, where the river meets the lake, upstream for some 26 kilometres, almost to the very edge of Garibaldi Park. There, for some reason, all fishing ceases.

Here in British Columbia we have every reason to take great pride in our superb provincial parks, and one wonders why such a total closure is deemed necessary. Surely a catch and release, fly only experience would help to attract discerning fishermen to an area of extraordinary natural beauty? As our resource industries, forestry, mining and fishing, continue in decline, so tourism becomes an increasingly important source of revenue and jobs. Fly fishing is as good a way as any to attract visitors from south of our border with the USA and further afield as well.

Danny Gerak knows full well the challenges faced by a commercial fisherman, but now his boat, the 32-foot Fraser River gillnetter *River Wind*, is an integral part of a Pitt River Lodge transportation system that includes a fine old, yellow school bus and a rugged, red four-by-four crew cab truck. The boat provides the key linkage between the lodge and the pickup point at Grant Narrows, less than an hour's drive from downtown Vancouver, where the tidal Pitt Lake runs into the Lower Pitt River on its way to meet the mighty Fraser River.

In calm conditions, and it can be really rough at times, the run up or down the lake takes about an hour and a quarter. Had the rain eased, we would have been able to enjoy our first sight of this wilderness on the very edge of civilization. There are some holiday and weekend homes at the lake's edge, but they are dwarfed as steep, forested slopes climb into the clouds. On a fine summer's day the boat ride would be an experience in itself; for our crew the warmth of the cabin's oil stove was good reason to stay inside.

Just as the *River Wind* carries guests, equipment and supplies on the first leg of the journey, so the yellow school bus is used between the dock and the lodge, where over the years, our hosts, Lee and Danny, have created a remarkable home away from home. Here guests are immediately welcomed as family, and visitors are encouraged to make the most of a still maturing enterprise, one that owes everything to the relaxed and informal way the owners go about their business.

First came the cabins in the early 1990s, two of them relocated from elsewhere in the valley. Then the lodge itself, completed just a year ago, built from locally cut cedar and fir and notable for the noble proportions of its massive, open plan main floor area.

The lodge provides every comfort, with full board and lodging for up to eight guests in four double rooms. The four cabins – Bugtussel, Rocky's Longhouse, Loft Cabin and Boise Bunkhouse – stand close at hand. Each accommodates between four and seven guests who look after themselves while enjoying evening access to the main building.

The silent, dripping forest is all around us, ancient, moss-hung trees with stories to tell, the green-roofed, two-storey lodge standing proudly in the middle of a substantial clearing. For those with an urge to wet an immediate line, a one-minute walk will bring you to the river.

Not that we were in any great rush to go fishing. After all, four full days lay ahead, dinner was cooking and we knew we would have the river to ourselves for most of the time. Expectations were high, the bar was open and there were flies to be tied by those with prior experience of the Upper Pitt. In particular, a fresh quota of Kelsey's Hopes spun effortlessly off Didlick's nimble fingers.

A night of continuing rain did nothing to disturb the sleep of the big city quintet. Danny's pre-breakfast check confirmed the river was still on the rise, not surprising in view of the volume of water still pouring down from on high. Nevertheless, there was a spirit of optimism in the air, inevitable when dedicated fly fishermen get set to go about their business.

In passing, Danny mentioned he was having problems with the heater in the crew cab truck he uses to bring visiting fishermen to the river. Soon we knew what it was to travel rough logging roads in a mobile sauna, a condition exaggerated on the way back with six sodden, wader-clad bodies generating a level of interior moisture that would have been of fully tropical proportions had the day been any warmer.

Liberal use of a wad of paper towel just about kept the windscreen clear for the undaunted driver, while his passengers remained confident that he at least could see where he was going.

So the time passed. On the river for most of the daylight hours, eat and drink, talk fishing, play pool, glance at the latest satellite war news from Afghanistan, incongruous as it seemed in the circumstances, and then to a dreamless sleep. Two wood stoves make for comfortable, cozy living in the lodge with the mounted, antlered deer heads perfect for hanging the chest waders, hats and jackets that were always bone dry again come morning.

With no other guests in residence, Lee had lots of help in the kitchen. The dinner duties were evenly shared between those with culinary talents, mostly Baglo, who had also provisioned the expedition in some style, and those of us who accepted our lot as humble dishwashers, with not one breakage to mar the effort.

And how was the fishing? The answer has to be "met all expectations," and this despite an unexpected dearth of coho salmon at that particular time. There were certainly coho in and just above the canyon pools but not too many takers to the fly. Didlick's fish was an exception to the rule but, perhaps responding to undue pressure, it promptly turned a fine, three-piece fly rod into a five-piece version in less time than it takes to tell the tale.

Over the four days, we all caught and released our share, the majority of them delicately pink-spotted bull trout, some close to five pounds, in greater or lesser numbers depending on a variety of factors, prime among them being location and effort. There would be abundance of fish in one stretch of water and few or none in another, but the sense of expectation, of something good about to happen, was ever present.

With radiophones to hand, we were quick to hear who was doing well and who was struggling – a useful innovation with obvious safety implications when a group is spread out over three or four kilometres of wilderness river. Keeping count with suitable recognition and retribution for the "top rod" at the conclusion of each day enhanced the occasion, as did the recounting of the various mishaps that befell the group.

My encounter with a curious black bear (see "Three bulls and a bear," page 273) was an early talking point, while Danny made his mark not once but twice with headlong plunges into the chilled water – unusual behaviour for an esteemed guide, one who has known and cherished the Upper Pitt since boyhood. But for a leak in the casing, Didlick's underwater camera would surely have been called into service to capture the moment.

I had my first experience of bull trout, resident fish according to Danny and not to be confused with the sea-run Dolly Varden that appear at certain times of the year, big char that frequently weigh into double figures. The bulls were just that, bullish, strong and eager takers of a wet fly cast square on a sink tip.

Often the best of the fishing came at the very tail of the run, just where the water breaks, with the larger fish eager to turn and make for the rapids as backing followed fly line in quick order. One such was my best fish of the trip, in prime condition and a full 25 inches in length despite the loss of an eye at some earlier stage of its life. "Ah," said the wag on the radio, "that has to be one-eyed Oscar, we know him well."

By mid-week, as the water level dropped and clearing skies

revealed fresh snow on high ground all around, talk turned to dry flies and rainbows. And this, remember, was in the third week of October.

The others had their first contact with surface-feeding rainbows on the Wednesday, but they were working a stretch of the river well above me and, for whatever reason, met up with rising fish while I saw no surface activity. On the final day it was a very different story. It was mid-afternoon when Baglo and I found ourselves on opposite sides of a perfect, broad stream, an even flow of super clear water carrying with it at least two species of mayfly, one large and one small, riding the current in significant numbers.

Just before the hatch came on in earnest the rainbows started to snatch at the sunk fly. Soon they switched to taking duns on the surface with a series of eager, splashy rises close to both banks, in midstream and toward the tail-out as well. The fishing was totally absorbing. My trout came eagerly to a No. 10 Gray Wulff, five out of five hooked and played, with all but one brought to hand for a quick release.

If ever an artist is looking for the picture-perfect river rainbow, then he or she should spend time on the Upper Pitt, for these were classic examples of the species, hard-bodied, beautifully marked and in superb condition. Life can never be easy in a river as wild and boisterous as the Upper Pitt. Its resident fish, whether they be bulls or rainbows, have to be of the best possible stock if they are to survive and prosper.

Mine were all in the 13- to 16-inch class, while Baglo finally lost one he estimated to be around 18 inches. Further upstream, where the hatch was on a good hour before our fish began to move, Hume, Didlick, Smyth and Gerak met up with even larger rainbows, to emphasize, if any emphasis is needed, just how good the dry fly fishing can be on this wonderful river.

For some years catch and release has been the accepted order for all Upper Pitt River species, and so it should be. The river's many boulder-heavy runs and shaded back channels, some constant, come changing from season to season, and even from one big flood to the next, offer the active fisherman a marvellous variety of waters, deep glides, runs and streams, pockets of all sizes and always the prospect of a big fish on the move.

Fly fishermen and those who use spinning gear as well appreciate the rare quality of the overall fishery and treat it with respect, even reverence. That approach makes for the survival of a healthy and stable stock.

The majestic valley setting, with its surrounding mountains, rushing tributaries and abundant wildlife, is an absolute visual feast. Bear, deer, cougar, bobcat, eagle, hawk and osprey all have their place in the Pitt River ecosystem along with the fish – the trout (rainbows, bulls and cutthroat), the Dolly Varden, the steelhead and the five species of Pacific salmon. We visit, admire, enjoy and take our leave.

On behalf of your October guests and friends, thanks so much, Danny and Lee. It could not have been any better. And, on a more personal note, Lee, your special "tatie farts" at breakfast provide strong competition for the potato bread so dear to the hearts of we folk with Northern Irish roots.

←————

The Cowichan: A special river

AUGUST 2013, *Chasing Silver Magazine*, FINLAND

There's not another river like it, anywhere. Not on Vancouver Island, not in British Columbia and certainly not in any of the other nine Canadian provinces and three territories barred from access to the Pacific Ocean by the mass of the Rocky Mountains.

With viable stocks of the three Cs of the Pacific salmon family, chinook, chum and coho, along with steelhead and the closely related rainbow trout, as well as cutthroat trout and brown trout, the Cowichan has always been a very special river. And for many it's the resident brown trout, along with its proximity to two major cities, which distinguishes it from all the other BC rivers.

On the historical side, the Fisheries Research Board of Canada (1946) wrote: "The brown trout was introduced into British Columbia in 1932, 1933 and 1934 from Wisconsin and Montana as eggs purchased by the Dominion Department of Fisheries. The eggs were placed in hatcheries at Cowichan Lake and Qualicum Beach and later the young were liberated as fry, fingerlings and yearlings into the Cowichan and Little Qualicum Rivers on Vancouver Island in an attempt to provide a fish for summer angling."

Earlier, back in 1935; A. Bryan Williams wrote in *Fish and Game in British Columbia* (Sun Directories Ltd., Vancouver) that 308,000 brown trout eggs were received in 1932. "The distribution that year totaled as follows: Little Qualicum River 50,000, Cowichan River 176,000." In the following two years the Cowichan received 13,543 and 2,817 eggs and the Little Qualicum 74,868 and 14,511 respectively. The so-precise egg count speaks to an amazing attention to detail more than 80 years ago. Williams served as BC's first Provincial Game and Forest Warden from 1905 until he retired in 1934.

The Cowichan browns have since become a well-established stock, but brown trout are only very occasionally encountered in the Little Qualicum River, although very large specimens can still be found in Cameron Lake, that river's source. There are also some browns in one other Vancouver Island river, the Adam, to the north of the town of Campbell River.

The Canadian real estate industry, always anxious to boost house sales, preaches the doctrine of location ... location ... location, and the Cowichan River meets that test most convincingly. Nanaimo, my hometown with a population closing on 90,000, is a comfortable hour's drive to the north while Victoria, the provincial capital (345,000), is a similar distance to the south. That makes for an easy day trip in either direction, so the river can be busy at weekends but seldom if ever during the week, which suits my retired generation.

Along the way, linked by a much-improved highway that extends almost 500 kilometres, or some 300 miles, north from Victoria to Port Hardy, lie the smaller communities of Ladysmith and Duncan. The river itself is equally friendly when it comes to access. Well-established forest trails and, in places, an abandoned pioneer logging industry rail track, lead to mile after mile of most attractive pools and runs. There can be few more pleasant places to be on an early summer day with the trout rising to a hatch of March Browns, mayflies or perhaps even tempting black ants.

A new river can be a daunting challenge for the first time visitor. The Cowichan has long been an exception to the rule, with lots of good information to be gleaned from books, the Internet and from the excellent river map produced by the Victoria-based Haig-Brown Fly Fishing Association, www.haigbrown.ca. The map costs C$12.75 and can be ordered from the association; it is also available at sporting goods stores in Victoria, Langford, Duncan, Cowichan Lake and Bowser. Proceeds from map sales are directed to the association's conservation fund.

Books profiling the Cowichan in some detail include *Game Fishing in the West*, by Mike Cramond (1964), *Outdoors with Alec Merriman* (1967), *Fly Fishing British Columbia*, edited by Karl Bruhn (1999), *Famous British Columbia Fly-Fishing Waters*, by Art Lingren (2002) and *Ultimate Trout Fishing in the Pacific Northwest*, by Larry E. Stefanyk and other contributors (2011).

My own experience of this cherished river dates back to the early 1950s, my teenage college student days, when snow, ice and treacherous roads a long, long way from today's modern highway standards did not inhibit weekend steelhead expeditions from Victoria. One of my cherished old diaries shows fish landed on December 29, 1953 and January 23, 1954, both around eight pounds and taken on spinning gear with upwards of three feet of snow on the ground in the New Year.

Vancouver Island winters now are generally a lot kinder, or at least it seems that way to me in these later years, and the fixed spool Mitchell spinning reel and my clumsy-looking Hudson Bay cherry bobber lure have long since given way to a double-handed fly rod, Intruder-style fly patterns and fast sink tips. Of far more importance, the steelhead continue to return to the Cowichan each winter, seemingly in improved numbers over the past few years.

My most recent direct contact came on February 13 of this year, 60 years on from that memorable, first ever steelhead for the long-ago teenage fisherman. The diary extract reads as follows:

"A Wednesday with Gordon Shead as my companion for his first look at the river. Fished the fly only stretch from 8:30 a.m. until 3:00 p.m. and then went to check out other convenient down-stream access points, Stoltz Picnic Grounds, Bible Camp and Sandy Pool. Hooked and later lost a decent fish in the Cabin Run using an unweighted Pink Intruder on a 560 grain, integrated sinking tip line. Fish hit hard and played strongly, two jumps and then off when almost ready to beach. Saw one other smaller fish show twice at tail of the pool. Thought this was my earliest steel-head ever on the fly but wrong – same date in 2002 hooked and lost one on a Muddler in the Spring Pool. Encountered only one other fisherman. River running at 51 cubic metres/second, a nice enough flow for fishing the fly."

A well-used trail through the forest to the Spring Pool pro-vides a convenient starting point to enjoy the year-round fly only stretch, one that extends upstream to the Greendale Road Trestle, near the village of Lake Cowichan, and downstream to the aban-doned 70.2 mile wooden trestle, an essential element of the for-mer logging railway. To walk and fish, for either steelhead or trout, all catch and release, from Spring Pool to the 70.2 mile bridge can fill the better part of a day and can be wonderfully rewarding, both physically and spiritually, regardless of whether or not fish are encountered.

In recent years there has been a steep decline in the numbers of winter-run steelhead entering rivers on the east coast of Vancouver Island. The Cowichan does appear to be holding its own, although the runs most definitely do not match up to those recorded in earlier years. It's these steelhead, together with the trout, that sustain the continuing popularity of the river, both for the locals like myself and for anglers, fly and gear alike, from further afield who cherish the opportunity to experience one of the province's best known, and historically important, fisheries.

Provincial government "angling effort and catch" statistics, based on anglers' returns, show just over 10,000 Cowichan steelhead caught (9355 released) in 1988–89, an exceptional year. In only one of the next 10 years did the recorded total fall below 3500 with the annual average close to 4200. Since 2000 the annual catch has only twice exceeded the 3000 mark, in 2001–02 (3301) and 2011–12 (3061).

All this adds emphasis to the need to ensure the river receives the fullest possible measure of care and attention, from fishermen, from local and provincial government authorities and from a forest industry that has left an indelible and often damaging mark on the Cowichan Valley down through the years. Last year record dry weather conditions in the late summer and early fall brought river levels down to a crisis point, one which prevented an estimated 1000 chinook, from a run of only 5000 fish, from entering the river to spawn.

That quickly led on to the formation of a well-organized group, One Cowichan, to urge the provincial government to allow for a greater level of local control over the amount of water being retained during the summer in Lake Cowichan, an impressive 20-mile-long (32 km) body of water extending over 200 square miles (518 square km).

It's the old story of too great a demand being placed on a strained resource, with Crofton's coastal pulp mill, and thus precious jobs, long guaranteed a minimum daily flow from the lake, the level of which is controlled by a weir at the outflow. Decisions are expected sooner than later, and hopes are that the recently re-elected Liberal government, in Victoria, will respond to the concerns so strongly expressed by all the rightly concerned parties.

In the meantime, anglers will continue to enjoy the opportunities provided by Cowichan steelhead in December, January, February and March and then trout, both brown and rainbow, in April, May and early June, by which time rising water temperatures convince many rods to look elsewhere to avoid unduly stressing any fish that may be hooked.

In their stead the river becomes a favourite haunt for swimmers, campers and picnickers, for tubers and canoeists, prompting one fisherman to ask: "Who wants to hook a babe in a bikini as she floats past in her tube?" Who indeed?

Where the browns, a most handsome fish, are concerned, there is apparently a school of thought – presumably a minority viewpoint –that would prefer to see all Cowichan River brown trout eliminated as an invasive or non-native species. It's hard, if not impossible, to imagine such a program being approved, let alone instigated. Yet ironically, this seems to be an opinion supported by the late Roderick Haig-Brown, the world-renowned author from Campbell River.

Writing in *The Western Angler* (1968, Wm. Collins Sons & Co., Toronto), he says brown trout should not be planted "in waters where he will be competing with fish that are already providing satisfactory sport. The risk is too great."

Haig-Brown continues: "Unfortunately, the boards of trade and the individuals who persuaded the authorities to plant brown trout in British Columbia chose Vancouver Island for the experiment. These waters are already used by cutthroat, steelhead and the five Pacific salmon. That the feed in them is insufficient to support a heavy fish population is clearly shown by the migratory habits of the cutthroat trout. So it was, or should have been sufficiently obvious that, if the brown trout were able to establish itself, it could only be at the expense of some native species. The only question was, which species?"

Much of the lower river, which extends to close on 30 miles (48 km) from lake to ocean, is closed to all fishing between August 1 and November 15, to protect incoming salmon runs. Later in the year, coho and chum in particular are a big attraction, with all intending visitors advised to check carefully regulations that can vary from year to year, and even from month to month, according to circumstances.

In 2003 the Cowichan became the third river in British Columbia to be accorded Canadian Heritage River status, and the seven-page online brochure, published by the Canadian Heritage Rivers system, is an excellent information source.

Describing the river it says: "The Cowichan River supports an impressive balance of natural, human heritage and recreational values. The river also supports hundreds of species of fish, mammals, birds, insects and amphibians in a lush oasis just minutes from urban areas. Not only is it a pillar of economic stability in the region but it also allows for a myriad of recreational activities, from swift water kayaking to peaceful nature walks, all taking place around a river flowing through a glaciated valley in a stunning landscape."

Trout fishing on the Cowichan is at its very best in April and May. This year, with friend and next-door-neighbor Wayne Davidson, I had a chance to spend two days on the river in a drift boat with Kenzie Cuthbert, veteran guide, proud lodge owner with his wife Kyt and expert, innovative fly tier. As we fished, landed and released brown trout of up to almost three pounds and enjoyed the passing scenery, the peaceful surroundings, the birds and the fresh riverbank and forest growth, we had a chance to discuss the river, its fish and its future prospects.

For Kenzie, in his 25th year of guiding on the river, the outlook is positive in the extreme, but at the same time, he acknowledges there are challenges ahead, in particular management of water levels and storage and maintaining adequate flows during periods of low water. Then there is the threat, one unfortunately not unique to the Cowichan, posed by seals and sea lions waiting to intercept incoming salmon at the mouth of the river. "There were 300 of them there, plus or minus, last fall and who knows how many fish they were taking each day," he says.

His view for the long-term future of the Cowichan is summed up in a single word "excellent." He elaborates, "The number of rainbows we are seeing is way up and they are larger than normal. The brown trout do not seem to be hurting at all. There were plenty of steelhead this past winter and the good fly fishermen were catching them, which is not always easy on this river. Of course they were helped by low water in February.

"There is definitely a concern with the chinook run, but the chum and coho numbers were away up and the fry count just now (early May) is very high. Just today I must have rescued up to 150 from one little puddle that was about to dry up," he says.

On the overall state of the fishery, Kenzie had this to say: "Fish stocks and the fishing itself are among the best ever. The 2012 chum run was around 400,000, and we have had large runs of coho for the past three years. We are also averaging daily high numbers of brown trout, and I would estimate there are some 3000 of them in the upper river at the moment. We know they can be hard to find when fisheries staff undertake a swim count as they are quick to hide among the sticks, bushes and log jams."

He adds that a really large (and now very rare) Cowichan River brown trout would weigh about 14 pounds. "The largest caught by any of our lodge guests is around 10 or 11 pounds, while our biggest steelhead this year would have gone 20 pounds and was 39 inches in length." All this comes from a man who caught his first steelhead as an 11-year-old with his tutor Herman Mayse, one of the original guides in the area.

The changing nature of steelhead fishing on Vancouver Island is evident by the fact that up to 90 per cent of Kenzie's guided clients are now fly fishermen using double-handed rods. "That has been especially noticeable over the last two years and particularly so in the season just past, when the collapse of the Stamp River winter steelhead run meant many more rods on the Cowichan," he says.

In addition to running his guiding business and, with Kyt, operating their beautiful, two-storey, four-bedroom riverside lodge, Kenzie has also made his name over some 20 years as an award-winning fly tier and designer.

He has developed a patent pending, eco-friendly, lead-free eyes-n-tubes system. "I make and package them right here at the lodge," he explains, "and then send them to a distributor in Vancouver. They are also available for purchase through the Internet and come in a number of variations, with sizes from no weight at all up to 5.4 grains per eye if you want the fly to go deep.

"The eyes work really well with nymphs and muddler patterns, and we can manipulate the fly with them so that it always fishes hook up. I have always tried to have my flies work this way as it stops fish from being caught deep in the mouth or in the gills and means less messing about removing the fly. We can even make a fly that, if dropped into four inches of water, will still flip over before it hits the bottom."

With the lodge, open since September 2002, now well established and with interest in the river and its fish continuing at a high level, it's no wonder he and Kyt are so optimistic about the future.

"I come from a local family dairy farm, a 24/7 business that makes you look at almost any other job you can do to get away. My office now is a much nicer place to be." We all should know by now that being a professional fishing guide can be hard work, but it's easy to appreciate his point of view.

CASTING BACK IV ...
to Pacific salmon

←———|

Salmon from the sea

JANUARY 1956, *Angling*, UK (PUBLISHED 1936–56)

The majority of anglers in the British Isles are prepared to believe the stories told by other anglers. But when I returned from Canada in December 1954 after living in Victoria, British Columbia, for 18 months, I told my friends about catching salmon in the sea and they just laughed at me. "Salmon in the sea!" they exclaimed, "Why, that's impossible and anyway it wouldn't be sporting." I am still trying to convince them that it's both possible and practical. And sporting.

There are five distinct species of salmon living in the Pacific, but only the spring or chinook and the coho or silver salmon are of any interest to the angler. The pink, chum and sockeye salmon seldom take a lure and are usually caught in the nets of the commercial fishermen.

These salmon are only vague relations of the Atlantic salmon that we know. In shape they are similar, although the spring is usually shorter and deeper than the coho. In size the coho is the smaller of the two, averaging between six and ten pounds. The springs run much larger, and it has been known for specimens of more than ninety pounds to be taken in the nets. The average weight varies from place to place. At Campbell River or Port Alberni, two of the Meccas of spring salmon fishermen, a forty-pounder would cause no special comment.

Their life cycle, too, is very different. Instead of running up the rivers to spawn after three or four years and then returning to the sea as spent fish or kelts, the Pacific salmon all, without exception, die after spawning. The spawning runs commence in late August and continue into December. When the rivers are low it is possible to stand on the bank and watch the salmon going up in the thousands. Indeed, the annual chum run in the Goldstream River, near Victoria, is quite a tourist attraction.

After they have spawned, the fish die slowly, and many wild animals take advantage of this free meal on their doorstep. In the shallows of one of the remoter rivers, it is not uncommon to see three or four black bears scooping up the dying salmon and throwing them on to the bank to be eaten later.

Once the salmon enter fresh water, they tend to lose interest in the angler's lures. Consequently, nearly all the sport fishing for them takes place in the sea, most often by trolling from boats.

Methods, like the average size of the fish, are many and varied. My favourite spot was Saanich Inlet, near Victoria, where, owing to the very deep water, we used wire lines of about 30 pounds breaking strain and trip weights of up to two pounds. These were attached to the line in such a way that they would drop off (trip) when a fish struck.

While wire lines were a necessity if one wished to catch really large springs, they could be dispensed with when one was fishing for coho and smaller springs. For them, a nylon or cuttyhunk line of 10 to 12 pounds breaking strain and three or four ounces of weight were quite sufficient.

As for lures, every fisherman has his own particular fancy. Some use spoons, others plugs. Yet another may swear by a bucktail or streamer fly trolled fast not far off the back of the boat. I have tried them all and, with one exception, have found that one was as good as another. Of course, it varies from day to day according to conditions. When the salmon are feeding on the large shoals of herring that come into the inlet in late August and September, a blue and white bucktail is particularly effective.

The exception mentioned earlier was herring strip, a bait that served me very well at all times. Cut from the side of a medium-sized herring and then trimmed of all its surplus flesh, it was fitted in to a plastic holder called a Strip Teaser and secured with a toothpick. The teaser prevents the bait from disintegrating after a short time in the water and also gives it the necessary action. When fishing perfectly, the lure, with a single hook, should be revolving slowly.

Although it is by no means an essential, many fishermen like to attach their lures to a flasher. This is a piece of highly polished or chrome-plated metal about ten inches long and three inches wide. It is curved in opposite directions at each end and, when drawn through the water, darts from side to side, towing the lure behind it, the whole impression being that of a small, wounded herring making frantic efforts to escape.

The technique used in this type of fishing is fairly simple. On reaching the fishing grounds the boat is slowed down to trolling speed, and the lures, with at least two rods being used, are let out to the required distance, which can vary from 30 to 300 feet depending on depth and conditions. Then the angler settles back and concentrates on steering the boat. I know it sounds dull, but wait until a fish strikes on both rods simultaneously. It's happened to me twice and something akin to bedlam has followed.

As to the cost of all this, I found it to be very reasonable. In British Columbia it is necessary to have a licence only to fish in fresh water. This means all the salmon fishing in the ocean is free, with the angler's only overheads the cost of his tackle and, if he does not own a boat, boat rentals. And a big advantage of fishing in the sea is that it cuts down on the loss of lures by nearly 100 per cent.

The price of fishing tackle is also very reasonable. A good trolling rod costs about four pounds ten shillings, with a five-inch trolling reel from the Victoria shop of famous local maker Peetz priced at three pounds ten shillings. Add another two pounds for lures and line and the whole outfit will cost an even "tenner," cheap compared to the price of salmon fishing on this side of the Atlantic.

Boat rentals vary in price with the popularity of the location. I used to frequent Peard's Boathouse, in Brentwood Bay, where a rowboat cost me two shillings an hour while one with a small inboard engine would be three shillings and sixpence an hour.

There are very few places where a guide is considered an essential, and a complete stranger can reasonably expect to catch a salmon first time out. To maintain the very high standards of sport fishing in British Columbia waters, the federal government recently instituted a bag limit of five salmon per day per person with heavy fines imposed on anyone caught taking over their limit.

In conclusion, a few notes on the culinary qualities of the Pacific salmon for those anglers who like to cook what they catch. Generally I found the flesh to be considerably redder and oilier than that of the Atlantic salmon. I believe the coho to be the best eating of them all, followed by the spring. The sockeye is the most valuable commercially and provides the largest proportion of primary grade Canadian canned salmon.

←———|

A chinook for sharing with family and friends

JULY 1985, *Belfast Telegraph*

The dinner party with an old friend from the Canadian Broadcasting Corporation, Canada's admirable equivalent to the BBC, had moved to its logical, liquid conclusion. John Lysaght, originally from Co. Cork, is a part-time Fraser Valley sheep farmer and he and his wife, Ann, had feasted us on home-bred lamb, the equal of anything I can recall from the Mournes of Northern Ireland, or from Wales or New Zealand for that matter.

Inevitably, they had complemented the lamb roast and the freshly picked strawberries with Canadian wines of a quality appropriate to an imminent journey overseas. After all, were we not looking ahead just a matter of days to our first return as a family to our Northern Ireland roots? Thirteen years had elapsed since our decision to move to Canada's West Coast from Belfast, and now the small boys of the early 1970s were young men in their mid and late teens.

The fisherman's return would have to be marked in the only possible way, by the capture of a Pacific salmon large enough to share among the friends and relatives we planned to visit in England, Wales and Northern Ireland. Time was running short, and the next morning's expedition, planned all week with due attention to marine forecasts and local fishing reports, was truly a make-or-break undertaking. Failure was inconceivable. A reputation was on the line.

Dawn came early that Sunday, just a few short days ago, but then in our approaching middle age, three short hours' sleep is scarcely sufficient to recharge even the most willing batteries. It seems, in retrospect, that it has nearly always been that way, the conflict between what are so knowingly called "the pleasures of the flesh" and that ever-present, all-consuming urge to simply go fishing.

When I was a 16-year-old boarding school student in the early 1950s, high expectations accompanied those illicit first light awakenings. I can still recall the cautious progress through a silent, sleeping dormitory and the long walk down through dew-laden fields to the serenity of an 11-acre lake and the challenge of the resident tench. The tench were totally without merit on the table, or so we were told, but marvellously strong and stubborn fighters in those weeded depths.

On those far off summer days, carefully cultivated lobworms or yesterday's bread kneaded into a thick, moist paste were the baits. A scarlet tipped quill float was the visible link between hand and eye and the fish that sent up rings of tiny bubbles as they fed in the clearing beyond the lily pads at the outflow to that particular lake.

Later came the dancing days and the growing realization that an undue emphasis on matters piscatorial could be viewed by some members of the fairer sex as a definite social handicap.

Again the conflict, again the early morning inspiration after too few hours in bed, the pleasure of driving on all but deserted Northern Ireland roads and finally the opportunity to be the first man down a favourite pool or run in late June or early July. That's when the grilse and summer salmon were appearing, true to their ageless calendar, drawn in from the sea to their natal rivers and streams by an instinct that we still do not fully understand.

Then there were those early season Irish outings on the Co. Donegal rivers Bundrowes and Finn, on Co. Fermanagh's Lough Melvin and Co. Donegal's Lough Fem, days cold enough to line the rings of the rod with a coating of ice, days when hands and feet lost all sense of feel, days when a spring salmon on the bank or in the boat was as much a tribute to physical endurance as it was to fishing skills or simply sheer good luck.

No one who has had the good fortune to fish for Atlantic salmon over a period of years would ever condone, let alone voice, a critical thought against the species. *Salmo salar* remains the ultimate challenge, the fish of all our dreams, the pinnacle on almost every angler's scale of ambition.

Tradition and mystique have played their part in placing the Atlantic salmon on something of a pedestal, contributing in no small measure to so many of the extreme pressures facing the species today in all parts of the British Isles, in Norway and in the rivers on the eastern seaboard of both Canada and the USA. We can only hope that the efforts, the campaigns, the negotiations being undertaken in so many different countries by so many different people will not prove to be a case of too little too late. Too much ground has been lost already, and it is in all our interests to encourage in every way possible the preservation and enhancement of the Atlantic salmon.

But I digress.... We were talking earlier of that early morning experience, of the magical moment when all of a sudden it is light enough to fish a fly down and across with certainty, to tie up a cast with a minimum of fumble-fingered ineptitude. There are certain days, special days, when it all comes together exactly as planned, when the pieces of the individual fisherman's jigsaw fall neatly into place, when that initial early morning momentum is translated into a day to remember, a day such as I was privileged to experience earlier this month. It was not, you must understand, a day notable, as some are, for the quality or the content of the conversation, for on this occasion I fished alone. Nor was it a day marked down by the sheer size or numbers of fish caught. And that can happen too, although not very often.

No, it was a day, or to be more precise, a stretch of five or six early morning hours, memorable for the absolute fulfillment of those pre-dawn expectations, for the sheer delight of the experience, for the simple fact or being able to go fishing in familiar waters and to catch a salmon of a size sufficient to emphasize yet again the quality of the sport available to so many people living within easy reach of the coastal waters of British Columbia.

Hard to believe as it may seem to those in the United Kingdom whose fishing activities focus on the freshwater pursuit of the Atlantic salmon, the large majority or Pacific salmon are taken in a saltwater setting. Every year, anglers in their thousands put their trust in a range of lures and baits limited only by their own imagination and by the ingenuity of a tackle-making trade that seems to have something new up its sleeve for almost every month of the year.

I come from a traditional background of Irish salmon and brown trout, caught in the main on artificial flies, and I suppose it was to be expected that my preferences on the Pacific coast would owe much to those earlier light tackle traditions. My split cane rods have given way to 11 feet of comfortably balanced tubular fibre-glass. The reel I use on most occasions could be mistaken for a fly reel but was made in Japan for saltwater usage. It holds more than 600 feet of 25-pound breaking strain nylon ending in a two-ounce banana-shaped lead and a seven-foot-long leader not that much heavier than the ones I used years ago when a neatly tied fly was the lure of the day.

The salmon we seek so enthusiastically in the Pacific are feeding fish in their saltwater prime, building up strength and bulk on a day-by-day basis in preparation for their final spawning run, a journey that invariably culminates in death. Unlike with the Atlantic salmon, there can be no recovery and return to the sea, no further growth as a prelude to a second spawning.

For all five species of salmon caught off the Pacific coast of British Columbia and north to Alaska, as well as further south off the coast of Washington, Oregon and Northern California, to spawn is to die. Then the limp and wasted bodies eventually break down to add fresh nutrients to the water, and the land as well, as their eggs ripen and hatch and the cycle starts anew.

When it comes to lures, we all have our preferences, regardless of where we fish. For many of the boats working the Strait of Georgia – the waters that lie between Vancouver Island and the mainland of British Columbia – the first choice at all times of the year is live herring, which is readily available at some marinas and priced at between £2.50 and £3 a dozen, not unreasonable when measured against the cost of fresh salmon steaks.

The day that led to this particular story was certainly one for mooching live herring, and the 90-minute, 27-kilometre boat run across the Strait of Georgia from Vancouver was broken only by occasional brief stops to change the water in the bait tank.

Without such consideration the shining five- and six-inch herring would quickly have lost their will to survive, and I would have found myself with a dozen or so corpses. These would have been great for ling cod and other bottom-feeding species but something less than completely attractive for my intended quarry, the predatory chinook salmon I hoped to locate in the deep channel that lies between Gabriola Island and nearby Entrance Island.

These are familiar waters indeed, a favourite stopping point over the last 13 years and a location where a concentration of tides tends to attract and hold the schools of immature herring upon which the salmon feed. There had been fish, and good fish, well into double figures, taken there during the preceding week.

That much I knew from an earlier phone call to a Vancouver Island contact who fishes the area on a regular basis. And the tides were favourable, with a low slack due around 8:00 a.m., a situation bettered only by a similar change at first light when the fish will at times feed with something approaching reckless abandon.

On this particular day there was no indication of the anticipated early morning bite. Two hours went by and there was still not a fish in the box. True, I had had one on briefly, but the take had been tentative and the hooks never made solid contact, leaving me with nothing more than a dying bait, its sides slashed deeply by the distinctive teeth marks of a chinook salmon.

At times such as this the alternatives become increasingly clear: hold on and hope that the fish have not moved away overnight and that, eventually, they will indeed start to bite, or pull out and try somewhere else. It's never an easy decision, one not to be taken lightly. This time I held my ground and was duly thankful.

I had rigged a fresh live bait and it was swimming freely, the point of the small treble hook through its nose, a slightly larger single hook located just behind the dorsal fin. With 50 feet of line out and some 75 feet of water showing on the depth sounder, the stage was set for what almost immediately presented itself as a strike. The subsequent contest between fish and fisherman left nothing to be desired.

The larger chinook will sometimes take a bait with all the savage presumption of the true ocean marauder. This was just such a fish. One moment the long rod was moving rhythmically in its holder, the slender tip mirroring the motion of the drifting boat in a gentle sea. The next minute it was suddenly bowed back as the lightly checked reel gave line at an alarming rate. No need to set the hook this time.

For 30 minutes or more the action was fast and furious. Start the motor and turn the boat into the wind to follow the still running fish, thankful for a well-filled reel. Steer with one hand and hold the rod high with the other. Call out to the shore casters to watch their lines as the big salmon dashes toward their rocky vantage point.

Slip the motor out of gear as the fish turns again and sounds straight down beneath the boat. Then retrieve suddenly slackening line as the salmon checks and makes for the surface. No time to think about aching wrists as it breaks water only feet from the stern in a welter of spray.

One great heart-stopping jump, high enough to catch the eye of the now attentive group on shore, then another long, surging run, this time just below the surface with the line cutting its own tiny, hissing wake through the water. As the pressure begins to tell, the fish's early strength gives way to an altogether more dour and dogged approach, short and deep runs, head almost straight down, broad, spotted tall sometimes thumping against the taut leader in a way that could so easily lead to a sudden break.

This is the most testing time of all. The prize is there for the taking, but there are no guarantees. A frayed cast, a weakened or poorly tied knot, a worn hook-hold – anything can go wrong, and sometimes does, leaving the fisherman with nothing more than a memory of what might have been.

Happily, there were to be no last-minute disasters, no reason for excuses, no cause for recriminations. The landing net was ample for the occasion, and soon I had the fish in the box and quickly dispatched. It was hooked deep inside its mouth, almost in the throat, in a manner that suggested it had literally charged at and engulfed the bait.

This particular chinook weighed just short of 23 pounds, not exceptional for the species – one of over 50 pounds was taken not far south that same day – but large enough to satisfy all my personal expectations as well as those of my soon-to-be-visited family and friends. My efforts from then on lacked something of their earlier concentration and determination. I had no further strikes, and soon I set the surviving herring free in anticipation of the return trip to Vancouver.

I understand it was Mark Twain who once wrote: "Nobody with a full stringer of fish goes home by way of the back alley." With more than 20 pounds of homecoming salmon safely on board, I was all set for the return run across the Strait of Georgia and, of course, for the long-awaited journey that will bring us back to Northern Ireland and, dare I hope, to a sampling of even a few of those rivers and lakes known and loved since childhood.

<hr />

Sunshine Coast coho comeback

MAY/JUNE 2002, *The Outdoor Edge*, VANCOUVER

They are an integral part of the lives of everyone living on Vancouver Island's east coast – the jagged mountains that appear, and as often disappear, across the Georgia Strait. Where we see those mountains meet the water, we have the Sunshine Coast and a fishery respected by those on the spot but of only passing interest to Island folk. That's a pity, for it seems they don't know what they're missing.

"The Sunshine Coast" is a wonderfully evocative description of a strikingly beautiful stretch of BC coastline that extends from Gibsons more than 60 nautical miles north to Sechelt and on to Powell River and Lund. The Alaska cruise liners pass that way almost daily in season as do power and sail boaters on their way up Georgia Strait to explore Jervis Inlet and other famous and more distant destinations.

We all know how the marketing men go to endless lengths to find just the right words to promote their products. And you thought that was something new. Far from it, as I discovered when I tried to pin down the origins of the generic title *Sunshine Coast*.

As it happens, Andrew Pinch, marketing director for Tourism Powell River, had already asked the question. He learned it came into vogue at the turn of the last century, the brainchild of an unnamed resident of Hopkins Landing, near Gibsons, who wanted to upstage his less fortunate friends on Vancouver Island and the Lower Mainland.

Some 100 years later, the Sunshine Coast retains its own character and identity, very much a part of small town BC, cherished by the locals and popular with tourists and big city people who can be envied for their summer homes and cabins along the coast, sundrenched retreats with spectacular ocean views across to Vancouver Island.

For the fishermen, both freshwater and saltwater, it's an area that definitely deserves a far higher level of recognition than it currently enjoys – that is, outside those in the know, the majority of them locals. The Georgia Strait salmon fishery, of which the Sunshine Coast is a major element, has had its ups and downs over the years, more down than up of late. Inside water coho stocks have been in the steepest of declines through the 1990s, a factor matched by a comparable fall-off in the overall sport fishing effort.

That is, until the summer of 2001, when there was good evidence from many sources, both from saltwater fishermen and from those who frequent a multitude of rivers, streams and creeks flowing into the strait, that there were significantly more coho around than there had been for a considerable time. Some areas enjoyed a limited retention fishery for marked hatchery coho while others had ongoing catch and release regulations and, as a consequence, continuing light pressure on the species.

It's too early to know what Fisheries and Oceans (DFO) may have in mind for 2002, but everyone is hoping for some easing of the restrictions with respect to where hatchery fish may be retained. Equally, there has to be recognition that coho stocks cannot possibly be rebuilt in a single year, that fishery managers must move with the greatest caution to ensure numbers continue to grow on a consistent basis. The secure future of all coho has to be the only concern.

Everything depends on ocean survival, on the numbers of fish returning from the outcome of each succeeding year's spawning cycle. I asked Terry Gjernes, the DFO's Nanaimo-based recreational fisheries advisor for the south coast, for his outlook for 2002. He came back with a response that has to be seen as something more than just encouraging.

"We now know there has been a substantial increase in ocean survival of the Strait of Georgia coho stock, and this could lead to increased retention of marked hatchery fish in 2002," he says.

We couldn't have asked for better news. And there is more. "We use Black Creek, between Comox and Campbell River, as an indicator stream for the strait, and in the fall of 2001 it had its highest ever return of coho, albeit from a strong brood year. We rate the overall situation on a scale of 1 to 4, and the Strait of Georgia coho outlook now stands between 2 and 3, or between 'below average to average' returns and 'normal to average' returns. That's a really dramatic improvement," says Gjernes.

It does not follow that every coho stock in every river and stream has come back to the same extent, but the crisis years of the 1990s might just be about to be consigned to history. The warning bells have sounded and there can be no relaxation in the emphasis on conservation, or on the maintenance and enhancement of spawning opportunities for the remaining precious wild stocks that many feared might be lost forever.

The renewed sense of optimism is heartening for all concerned, especially for people like Powell River's Sam Sansalone. Taking time off from planning his new tackle and outdoor sports business, due to open in March, he told me: "We have always had great saltwater fishing around Powell River but not too many know about it. Five minutes from the harbour and you are off the hulks in front of the mill, where there can be really good trolling for chinook, especially in May and June.

"Other local hot spots include what we call the sandbanks, on the southeast side of Harwood Island, and Kiddie Point, also called Coho Point, on Texada Island. There was outstanding fishing last summer around Grant Reefs, south of Savary Island. In August and September, we work closer to shore and around Grief, Myrtle, Albion and Kelly or Black Points on the mainland side of Malaspina Strait," Sam says.

Trolling depths vary according to the time of year, with the general downrigger range somewhere between 50 and 130 feet. Coyote spoons, in the Wonderbread and all silver prism versions, are proven and very effective favourites along with army truck, tiger prawn and black and white hoochies, fished on long leaders behind red and green plastic flashers. Anchovies also have a role to play for those who like to ring the changes between lures and baits.

Over the past couple of years, Sam, with a background in the tackle and marine equipment business, both on the road and behind the counter, says chinook numbers have increased along with the average size. "Generally they used to come in between eight and 16 pounds, but now we are seeing plenty of fish between 17 and 22 pounds and I know of at least four over 30 pounds that were caught last summer." As has been the case elsewhere in the strait, the local area coho stocks have picked up significantly, with returns to the Lang Creek hatchery, south of Powell River, responsible for an excellent beach fishery for coho, chinook and good-sized cutthroat trout. It's a similar story from the Sechelt beaches at Davis Bay and McLean Bay, superlative fly fishing for week after week in late summer and fall, mainly for coho but with the occasional chinook to set the heart racing.

While both sides of the strait benefit from the presence of all five Pacific salmon species heading for the Fraser River and its tributaries, and to other rivers to the south of the border, the productivity of the many local hatcheries plays an important role in providing enhanced opportunities for sport fishermen.

Bob Dixon, a longtime Sechelt baker who finds a 4:00 a.m. start to his working day gives him more time to fish, is perfectly placed to make the point. As a professional guide, fisheries consultant and writer with his own company, Davis Bay Sport Fishing, he spends much of his spare time on the water. When he is not fishing, he turns his considerable energies to his work with the Sunshine Coast Salmon Enhancement Society.

This is a major community undertaking, one with hatcheries at Chapman Creek, Soames Creek and Gibsons. There is also a smaller, satellite hatchery that recycles warm water from the Howe Sound Pulp and Paper Mill, at Port Mellon, for a chinook operation. In addition there is a close relationship with the McLean Bay hatchery, in Sechelt Inlet at Four Mile Point, run by the Sechelt Indian Band under contract to DFO.

This hatchery each year releases up to 150,000 chinook smolts, raised from Lang Creek stock, with the returning adults offering the best big fish opportunity on the coast in late July and into September.

Trolling across from Four Mile Point at between 80 and 100 feet with black and chrome Coyote spoons and black and white hoochies brings great rewards. In 2001 more than 70 fish were recorded in the official catch census. They averaged around 10 pounds with many at least twice that weight and a few over 30 pounds. And this fishery recurs every year.

The DFO contributes limited funding to the Sunshine Coast Society's hatchery program, but the bulk of an annual operating budget of well over $100,000 comes from community sources, so all aspects of continuous fund-raising are a high priority. "We get tremendous support from the local people and that makes all the difference," Bob says.

The society's hatcheries rear and release upwards of 70,000 coho smolts each year, along with 150,000 chinook, and in odd years, 250,000 pinks along with a few thousand each of steelhead and cutthroat. The coho brood stock, upwards of 100,000 fish, is seined each year in McLean Bay and held for stripping and rearing at the Chapman Creek facility. When the time comes to release the smolts, they are taken back to McLean Bay, ensuring strong and regular returns each year.

Tom Poulton, who runs Sechelt's Tips Up Charters, works from his 17-foot boat and recalls one recent summer day off Sangster Island when there were coho in abundance. "I was by myself and I hardly had time to sit down. Another day, we had a humpback whale follow us for a good half mile, between Sangster and Seal Reef. That was a unique experience and quite unexpected. Often it was only about 100 feet off the boat."

Like all good guides, and indeed so many of the people who look to the Sunshine Coast waters for both fishing and other recreational opportunities, Tom likes to bring some variety to his fishing. "When the salmon are off we will try dropping down to the bottom for cod or we will put down traps for crabs or prawns," he says. He confirms there are more coho around now than for years, adding: "You certainly can see them but I can't always get them on to the hook."

Both Bob and Tom look to the immediate future with confidence. "You could say I am walking around with a big grin on my face," says Bob. "We have come through the Georgia Strait coho disaster, caused by El Niño in the 1990s, and the outlook is very hopeful.

"In fact, last year, for the first time since 1990, I was able to take out nine charters and specifically target coho each time. That was a big change and we are very fortunate in that we have been marking our hatchery releases, which means fishermen have been allowed to retain two adipose-clipped fish a day in certain very specific local waters, along the Sechelt waterfront from Port Salashan to Snicket Park."

With some mature coho appearing as early as June, as a result of the regular release of smolts raised from the Capilano River brood stock, Sunshine Coast fishermen can anticipate a long and productive salmon season. Bob regards Easter weekend as changeover time, when the resident winter chinook fishery starts to give way to the first of the larger, migratory runs moving down the strait.

"Even though the level of fishing effort has dropped off because of what happened to the coho in recent years, I believe chinook stocks have stayed fairly solid, especially between Pender Harbour and Roberts Creek.

"In 2001 we experienced a major change in the feeding cycle when the fish started to encounter very small herring, less than an inch long. The one lure that worked consistently well for me was an ancient and tiny #2 chrome Tom Mack spoon. I actually found it in some old tackle left to me by my wife's grandfather," Bob recalls.

He places great emphasis on matching lure size with bait size, fishes leaders of at least six feet in length and feels that salmon along the Sunshine Coast were definitely flasher shy in 2001. He likes to troll a single rod with bait, herring, anchovy or strip, behind a flasher, on one side of the boat and then ring the changes with two lures on the other side.

"I work the single rod hard and watch it all the time. That's my go-to outfit and I rely on it to get at least the one fish that will make the day for the visitor. That's how a rolled anchovy caught my wife a 28-pound local ladies' derby winner off Cotton Point on Keats Island, in Howe Sound, last summer."

Explaining how he sets up his gear, Bob adds: "On the other side I will run a lure on the bottom line with no flasher behind a one-ounce banana lead. This helps to keep the lines apart since the flasher tends to lift a little. The lure with a flasher will be set 10 feet further up the line."

Contrary to the generally held opinion, Bob believes fish hooked on a flasher play harder if for a shorter time. "The visitor will always remember the blast that comes from a big chinook when it first runs 100 feet or more. That's a lot more exciting than having it thrashing around the boat," he notes.

As to favourite spots, he spends a good bit of his time in the

Davis Bay area, south of Sechelt, where a firm, sandy bottom will hold needlefish or lance fish, both very attractive to salmon. The outside of the Trail Islands, to the north of the town, is another reliable producer.

"There is plenty of heavy structure, reefs and rocks, and if you can pick your way through the alleyways and channels you will find the fish. If you are not careful it can be a bit of a nightmare for boats using downriggers but also very productive."

Bob, who runs a 16-foot boat, uses a trailer for maximum mobility and will range all the way from Gibsons north to Secret Cove in search of salmon, "There is a good bottom off the Thormanby Islands, just to the south of Secret Cove, and that's another place where I expect decent results," he adds.

A quick look at the chart for the central portion of the Strait of Georgia shows immediately why the Sunshine Coast is so popular with the saltwater fishing fraternity. There are a multitude of bays and inlets, some protected and some open to the weather, along with countless rocks, reefs, islets and islands, all offering the prospect of great fishing at the right time.

The residents know, in general terms, when and where to expect the salmon runs and plan accordingly; visitors can count on a warm welcome and good information for the asking wherever they go along this fish-rich coast.

Langara Island results a contrast to Georgia Strait

SEPTEMBER 2003, *The Herald*, GLASGOW

Home again to Nanaimo after an enthralling five days in pursuit of huge chinook salmon at the Langara Fishing Lodge in the Queen Charlotte Islands, now better known as Haida Gwaii. No really big fish to my rod this time and thus no challenge to my previous best of 37 pounds, one surpassed by two pounds last year by Richard, my eldest son. We live in hope for the next time.

Communications in various forms has been my lifetime career, as it was my father's before me. This, in turn, has opened the doors to countless angling opportunities here in Canada, in Ireland, England and Scotland as well as in such distant locations as the Bahamas, Norway, New Zealand, South Africa and the Cook Islands.

Fishing has been an integral part of my life for as long as I can remember and it was the seemingly unlimited quality of the sport here in British Columbia that brought me to Vancouver Island for the first time as an 18-year-old student back in the early 1950s.

Those were really extraordinary days in terms of abundance of fish and, compared with what is the norm today, paucity of sport fishing effort. Now we have many, many more fishermen and far fewer fish in all but the most remote areas of the province, among them the waters off Langara Island.

As I write, dusk is closing in across the Strait of Georgia, the inland sea that stands between Vancouver Island and the mainland of British Columbia. It has been a near perfect summer's day, and yet only a handful of sport fishing boats are in evidence from my Nanaimo vantage point.

Thirty years ago these were constantly hard-fished waters that provided a reliable early season return to a local fleet of commercial salmon trollers, boats that employed a variety of lures on heavily weighted wire lines, raised and lowered by mechanical winches known as gurdies.

Now the commercial boats are almost totally excluded from the strait while the stocks of the once numerous coho salmon have been depleted to such an extent that I have only caught one since May, a six-pound fish that I released in the hope that it would live to complete its spawning journey.

Virtually all Georgia Strait coho stocks, what is left of them, are subject to catch and release regulations. The runs of chinook salmon are in better health, but they too are subject to a range of regulations aimed at preserving the existing resource and eventually restoring it to its former strength.

The daily limit used to be four salmon of any species, day after day after day with no requirement for a licence to fish in salt water. Now there are licences for residents and visitors with a 65-centimetre minimum size limit for chinook – that's a salmon measuring just over two feet in length and weighing six to seven pounds.

Each fish kept must be entered on the licence, and no more than 15 may be retained from the strait in a year. And, of course, only barbless hooks may be used. Surprisingly, there is still no close season, and I can take my boat and go fishing at any time during the year.

The situation now being addressed with some urgency derives from a multitude of factors. These include climatic changes in the Pacific salmon's ocean environment and mounting commercial and sport fishing pressures along with the impacts of industry and population growth on spawning rivers large and small.

For all that, sport fishing for salmon in these parts remains very much a viable option and was still capable of providing me with a near 20-pound chinook within sight of my home a matter of weeks ago. There have been others as well in double figures to keep the interest up but nothing like the old days.

The season is just over for the Langara Fishing Lodge, where they finished on a sensational note with a Canadian television crew on hand to record the rod and line capture of a new lodge record halibut. It weighed all of 258 pounds and measured some seven feet from nose to tail.

It was caught off the west coast of Langara Island from a boat also named *Langara Island*. My second son, Conor, just happens to be the pilot, so he is on his way home with a fishing story to end all stories. That is, until the next big one.

Salmon on a different scale

SEPTEMBER 2003, *The Herald*, GLASGOW

There are fishing trips and fishing trips, but few if any worldwide to match what is to be experienced in the waters off the northernmost tip of the Queen Charlotte Islands, now more usually known as Haida Gwaii. We are 600 miles from Vancouver, within sight of Alaska on a clear day and accessible only by air or boat.

The floating Langara Fishing Lodge, on Langara Island, has been here for 16 years, tucked away in the sheltered Henslung Cove. This is home away from home for up to 60 dedicated fishermen (and women) who fly in for four- or five-day stays from May until mid-September.

The Langara people were pioneers, opening up new sport fishing frontiers to provide salmon fishing for the five distinct Pacific species, chinook, chum, coho, pink and sockeye – all prime fish taken in salt water by anglers using a fleet of boats with both guided and self-guided options available.

The mighty chinook pass through these waters on their way to rivers as far away as California. These amazing fish are the true backbone of the increasingly important British Columbia sport fishing business, one that operates in strength from here south to the border with the USA.

It's an enterprise that attracts both diehard fishermen and novices from all parts of the globe. None from Scotland on this trip as it happens, but memories are still fresh when it comes to the exploits of the Scottish Salmon Slayers, a group last here in 1996 under the inspired leadership of Scottish rugby's Iain and Kenny Milne, cricket's Dougie Barr and car rallying's Andrew Cowan.

They caught their share of fish, in keeping with their reputations as expert Atlantic salmon men, but nothing approaching the majesty of the 50-pound chinook boated by first-time visitor Dave King.

With guide Jeremy Wall – who would be a gillie or a boatman in the UK – handling the boat with expertise, the battle ran its course over a tense 80 minutes. "For a long time the fish was the boss and we nearly lost it in the kelp bed off Coho Point," a delighted Dave King said later.

With the big fish, by no means a record breaker, safely netted, they returned to the same spot and promptly hooked another one, this time a hard-running chinook of 32 pounds.

Both fish were taken in close proximity to a flotilla of anglers' boats, and it was easy to sense the heightened expectations as they drifted further offshore each time before rounding off a superb morning's adventure.

Since 1989, the Langara chinook record has stood at 78 pounds, truly an extraordinary fish, with this year's best so far just over 60 pounds. Not too far away, an American guest at another lodge last month boated a monster salmon weighing 82 pounds. His son caught one half that weight on the same day to underline the amazing potential of this area of the North Pacific. Every strike is a possible record breaker. That is what keeps so many fishermen coming back year after year.

Unlike Atlantic salmon, where a percentage returns to spawn again, all the Pacific species die at the completion of their cycle. And, unlike Atlantics, they can also be caught in the sea as well as in fresh water. Baits and lures are very much a matter of personal preference, and the range is infinite.

At Langara, few venture beyond the tried and tested cut plug herring mounted on two barbless hooks. This is fished slowly from 20 to 50 feet below the surface behind a banana-shaped lead weighing between six and eight ounces.

Barbless hooks have been mandatory in all British Columbia waters for the past three years, with no impact on the sport fishing success rate. According to Langara operations manager Mike

Neilson, "Very few fish are lost for this reason, and it makes for much easier catch and release."

⟵————|

Pacific salmon fall to sea lice

FEBRUARY 2009, *Chasing Silver Magazine*, FINLAND

Eric Hobson remembers cutting his angling teeth on chub minnows in Ottawa's Green's Creek at four years old. Today, he is an avid fisherman who travels extensively in pursuit of tarpon and taimen, steelhead and chinook salmon. More importantly, in terms of the survival of some of Canada's most important fisheries, he is challenging the commercial interests and the politicians who continue to turn a blind eye to a developing environmental disaster on the coast of British Columbia, Canada's most westerly province.

Hobson is a professional engineer from Calgary, Alberta, and a partner in Northridge Canada Inc., a private investment company. He is also an independent investor and a director of numerous private, public and charitable organizations. As an active philanthropist, he founded and leads the Save Our Salmon Initiative, or sos. This organization is dedicated to protecting British Columbia's wild salmon stocks and marine environment from negative impacts linked directly to the ocean farming of Atlantic salmon in open-net pens.

In the simplest of terms, open-net pen fish farms and their packed masses of thousands and thousands of caged Atlantics provide a perfect breeding ground for millions upon millions of sea lice, which in turn attach to and eventually kill untold numbers of immature wild salmon as they pass by and through the net pens during their annual migrations to the open ocean.

It's a situation all too familiar to anglers half a world away. They already have long-standing concerns over the effects of fish farms on past, present and future stocks of wild Atlantic salmon, as well as sea trout, in Scotland, Ireland, England and Norway and on the same species of salmon in some eastern Canadian rivers. But, until comparatively recently, sport and indeed commercial salmon fishermen on Canada's Pacific coast were, for the most part, unaware of the growing threat.

That's no longer the case. Now fish farming promises to have a greatly increased – and perhaps to some unwelcome – public profile as British Columbians prepare for a provincial election in May of this year. The present Liberal government led by Premier Gordon Campbell stands accused of downplaying the sea lice menace; the opposition New Democrat Party is expected to see this as another opportunity to put pressure on their political rivals. Public opinion, and with it votes, can be influenced because British Columbians, and indeed most Canadians, definitely care about environmental issues.

In a recent article in Canada's nationally circulated *Globe and Mail* newspaper, Mark Hume, a well-respected and knowledgeable commentator on fishery matters, wrote: "The salmon crisis will come to rest at Mr. Campbell's feet because of the way his government has embraced salmon farming, promoting an industry that scientific research is increasingly blaming for damaging wild salmon stocks by causing sea lice epidemics." The headline on the story read: "Campbell's doomed policies on fish farming will be tough sell to voters."

Eric Hobson was alerted to the problem four years ago while on a steelhead fly-fishing trip to the Babine River in north central British Columbia. "Pierce Clegg, who was my guide and who owns the camp, mentioned one night how plans were being made to licence salmon farms on the approaches to the Skeena River," he recalls.

Clegg was greatly concerned about what this would mean to the Skeena system's salmon and steelhead runs. He lent Hobson a copy of *A Stain Upon the Sea* (2004, Harbour Publishing, Madeira

Park, BC). This book about the West Coast salmon farming controversy features significant and highly critical contributions by six leading experts, including Alexandra Morton. Morton is the biologist and researcher who has done so much in recent years to highlight the threat posed by fish farms to British Columbia's wild salmon, in particular juvenile sockeye, pink and chum, and to other species as well.

In Hobson's own words: "Reading it made me very angry, and the more I read in my cabin, the angrier I became." From that campfire conversation and his late night study sessions sprang his determination to become involved. Now he is the director and prime mover behind Save Our Salmon, working to create a strategic approach to sustainable aquaculture in British Columbia. The Community Opportunity Foundation of Alberta, which Hobson co-founded in 1999, is overseeing the SOS initiative and has already provided $1.5 million for science, economic and legal research.

Hobson estimates SOS will spend another $400,000 this year to enable it to continue scientific fact-finding and to maintain its government and public education programs. And, while he identifies the ongoing sea lice problem as an environmental crisis, he also sees it as an opportunity for the British Columbia government to move beyond the present impasse to take a leadership role in finding and implementing lasting solutions.

"We have asked for a face to face meeting with Premier Campbell to offer to work with his government by sharing our knowledge and the strategies we have developed. We have established an influential Solutions Advisory Committee and want to see British Columbia assume a global leadership position in developing a sustainable salmon aquaculture industry, one that we believe will have to be based on closed containment technology rather than on open-net cages," he says.

To complicate matters, there is no one jurisdiction responsible for regulating all aspects of the industry, which is, in the main, foreign-owned (80 per cent Norwegian). The provincial Ministry of Agriculture and Lands issues the fish farm licences – and there are more than 80 of them strung along BC's 27,000-kilometre Pacific Ocean coastline – while the federal government's Department of Fisheries and Oceans is responsible for managing all wild salmon populations in their saltwater environment.

As more and more people become aware of the problems associated with farmed salmon, so the stakes become higher and the war of words becomes more intense. The Canadian province with the marketing slogan "Super, Natural British Columbia" takes special pride in its great natural beauty and in the wealth of its environmental resources, and the sea lice saga makes for depressing reading.

Alexandra Morton's original research was focused on the killer whales, also known as orcas, in the Broughton Archipelago. This isolated wilderness area of winding and protected sea inlets, forested islands, little-known rivers, soaring mountains and abundant wildlife is located between the northeastern coast of Vancouver Island and the mainland.

As the local runs of pink salmon, one of the five species of Pacific salmon, went into serious decline so grew an awareness of what was at stake – the very survival of a species critical to all aspects of the coastal life cycle. Subsequent research has shown that the problem extends beyond the Broughton to other areas of the coast where open-net pen salmon farms exist in high densities.

Without salmon, the First Nations people, who have been living in the Broughton area since long before the arrival of the white man more than 200 years ago, are denied an essential, historic food source. So too are the black bears and grizzly bears that depend on catching the salmon to build up strength and weight prior to winter hibernation, when their cubs are born.

Sport and commercial fishing interests are being affected, as is wilderness tourism, an annual $1.5 billion business built on providing opportunities and accommodation for visitors to come and observe bears, and especially the majestic grizzlies, in their natural habitat in an environmentally sensitive manner. Overall, tourism is an annual, multi-billion dollar contributor to the BC economy, one that could suffer a serious setback in the event of a widespread salmon run collapse.

In the past year, one marked by generally poor returns of all the Pacific salmon species to British Columbia's rivers, a decline has also been reported in the number and behaviour of the majestic orca whales that are a prime feature of the province's seascape. Chinook salmon are a staple of the orcas' diet, and even a temporary decrease in their numbers means trouble for the coastal whale population.

Without exception, all Pacific salmon die after spawning. In normal circumstances, the nutrients derived from the dead fish – and strong runs of the most abundant species can number in the hundreds of thousands and even millions – make for healthy rivers and riparian forests. These, in turn, support the next generation as they progress from egg to alevin, to fry, fingerling and finally to the smolt stage, when they migrate from fresh to salt water. That's when they become vulnerable to sea lice predation.

It's little wonder that Eric Hobson is so concerned or that his group is winning the support of a growing number of organizations and individuals. His hope is that the political leaders, both federal and provincial, will come to recognize the gravity of the situation sooner rather than later and will then take the necessary steps to address the problem.

A high priority would be an early decision, whether by direction or mutual agreement, to fallow or clear all farms located near river estuaries or close to routes used each spring by migrating juvenile salmon. Hobson is firm that no amount of habitat restoration and enhancement will help restore wild salmon if juvenile salmon do not have unobstructed access to the open ocean.

Each farm discharges its untreated waste directly into the ocean, as Hobson says, "like a plume from a big smokestack," in daily volumes on the scale of a town of 20,000 residents. The associated problems go beyond the presence of sea lice. For example: "We estimate there are 30 million Atlantic salmon in open-net pens in BC, and the industry relies on a chemical called SLICE to kill sea lice. It has a limited lifespan and we know that the lice can, in time, build up a resistance to it."

Other issues associated with fish farms include the considerable disparity between the volume of fish-based feed required to raise a much lesser weight of salmon; mortalities suffered by seals and sea lions when they become entangled in nets; the use of chemicals to maintain the health of the farmed salmon and even the actual culinary quality of the product on the consumer's table. And then there are the escapees – about 90,000 each year between 1987 and 2001 and another 19,000 in each of 2006 and 2007.

Seven years ago, when the sea lice infestation was first highlighted by Alexandra Morton, the focus was on the sudden decline of pink salmon runs in the Broughton Archipelago. In 2002 only 147,000 fish came back to spawn when 3.6 million had been expected. Late last year SOS, citing government counts, reported pink salmon returns to five key indicator streams in the Broughton area had fallen by up to 90% and constituted only about 2 per cent of the abundance in 2000.

"In Glendale Creek, a prime indicator stream, only 15,000 spawners were counted compared to 182,000 last year (2007)," the most recent SOS Update reports. Morton and colleagues co-authored a paper in *Science* magazine reporting that if sea lice damage continues, the Broughton pinks will be extinct in just six more years. This year's numbers are right on this trajectory to extinction.

Morton has expanded her research to show how sea lice are infecting sockeye salmon smolts on the Fraser River migration route as they pass through the Discovery Islands area, south of the Broughton. And she has confirmed sea lice can target young herring, a prime food source for salmon, and that the problem has spread to Clayoquot Sound, threatening juvenile chinook salmon in another fish farm location on the west coast of Vancouver Island. Previously abundant Fraser River sockeye runs have not met expectations in recent years. One wonders why.

At the same time, Morton has launched a series of initiatives designed to keep the issue very much in the public eye. These include an ongoing court challenge, an "Adopt a Fry" drive and a letter writing campaign asking supporters to flood Premier Campbell's mail with postcards cut out in the shape of a salmon to demand the removal of fish farms from wild salmon migration routes.

In a recent SOS presentation, Chief Bob Chamberlin of the Kwicksutaineuk/Ah-kwa-mish First Nation, from the Broughton, spoke movingly of the predicament facing his people. "What is happening to our pink and chum salmon is the key. We are an isolated community living in poverty. For the past two years there have been no food fish to catch in our area and that's unheard of." And he added: "Can you imagine not being able to teach your grandson to fish?"

Their concern made major news headlines when they announced they were going ahead with legal action against the Government of British Columbia. The class action lawsuit, launched in Vancouver on February 4, calls on the government to address the harmful impacts of open-net pen salmon farms on wild salmon in the traditional territories of the Kwicksutaineuk/Ah-Kwa-Mish First Nation.

At the same presentation, one of a series of four arranged for SOS sponsors and potential supporters, ecologist Dr. Craig Orr pointed out that Atlantic salmon are the farm fish of choice and described them as "the cows of the salmon world, very docile and ideal to raise in farms." With some farms holding upwards of 750,000 and more mature fish, he commented that this would represent a mass equivalent in size to 500 Asian bull elephants.

Orr, the Executive Director of the Watershed Watch Salmon Society, has written extensively on the subject, and it's worth quoting from a feature of his that appeared in the September 2007 issue of *The Osprey*, the newsletter of the Steelhead Committee of the Federation of Fly Fishers, under the heading "The politics of wild salmon: a brief update on the mess in British Columbia."

He writes: "We're talking adult mess with all the trimmings: science trumped by myopic ideology and communications spin; a calculated campaign to maintain the status quo using smothering uncertainty and massive fortification of denial; the failure to learn and apply lessons; personal attacks and dirty tricks; and change so stupefying glacial, it sets new standards for betrayal of public and ecological values.

"All this mess is firmly rooted in the recent and massive expansion of salmon aquaculture in the world's coastal waters – waters still harbouring a priceless-but-fragile legacy of wild salmon. Some 1,323,000 tonnes of farmed salmon (2005 figures) are now grown annually in the world, including a 'modest' 67,000 tonnes in the coastal waters of British Columbia."

According to the BC Salmon Farmers Association, total production in 2007 was 80,000 tonnes, with 85 per cent going to export for an annual value of $900 million. The industry, not surprisingly, vigorously disputes all claims that it bears responsibility for the sea lice problem and points to a worldwide decline in salmon runs, which it attributes to a variety of causes. These range from ocean warming and climate change to urbanization, logging, fishing and mining. All very convenient but hardly calculated to alleviate mounting concerns.

As Chief Chamberlin puts it: "What is happening is not consistent with good husbandry of the environment, yet the industry and the provincial government continue with what appears to me to be a policy of deny, delay and distract."

No one is more frustrated over the present situation, and its implications, than Eric Hobson. "Of course there are all sorts of moving parts involved, with climate change an example," he says, adding: "Why aren't we dealing with the problems that we can deal with quickly? We can turn this problem into an opportunity and it's totally under our control. That's the key. Everyone wins so why not do it?"

For British Columbians it's a most pertinent question and one likely to be asked more and more frequently leading up to the upcoming provincial election. Without doubt it's one the politicians will be expected to answer, both soon and with positive actions.

British Columbia is not the only Canadian province with concerns about fish farms. The government of Newfoundland and Labrador, on Canada's Atlantic coast, was been criticized in the 2008 General Report of its own Auditor General, John L. Noseworthy. Fish farm escapees rather than sea lice are the main issue.

The Auditor General's Report points to inadequate aquaculture facilities, insufficient inspections of aquaculture sites, problems with many aspects of cage emplacement, substandard fish handling standards, a decline in the number of site inspections, outdated industry codes of practices and an inadequate Cage System Audit Report with some cage nets failing a strength test.

In a joint backgrounder from the Atlantic Salmon Federation (ASF) and the Salmonid Council of Newfoundland and Labrador, the two organizations say the provincial government has failed to update and complete fish farm management plans and codes of practice.

Don Ivany, Regional Director of the ASF, comments: "We hope that the provincial government heeds a report by the Auditor General of Newfoundland and Labrador, outlining deficiencies in the present management of this industry, and takes steps to improve. This industry can have serious negative effects on the province's wild salmon populations.

"It is especially discouraging that the Code of Containment is deficient as lack of good containment leads to the breakup of cages and escapes of farmed salmon into the wild. This results in interactions with wild salmon in nearby salmon rivers and threatens the survival of these fish that are already in decline.

"We urge the province to provide adequate infrastructure to support current and future expansion of the industry. It must act quickly to finalize an aquaculture health management plan, and implement a comprehensive inspection system to discourage flaunting of the rules, which the Auditor General indicates presently lack the power of effective legislation," Ivany concludes.

Fish farm opponents take challenge to Oslo

MAY 2009, *Chasing Silver Magazine*, FINLAND

Opponents of open-net pen fish farming off the coast of British Columbia, Canada's most westerly province, will be attending two important company annual general meetings being staged in May in the Norwegian capital of Oslo. Opposition concerns are based on the linkage between fish farms, stocked with thousands of Atlantic salmon, sea lice and the deadly threat these parasites pose to wild Pacific salmon smolts migrating through areas where the many farms are located.

Norwegian companies, in particular Marine Harvest and Cermaq, which in turn owns Mainstream Canada, dominate the fish farm industry in British Columbia. Together they hold 108 licences. When added to the 17 licences of a third Norwegian company, Grieg Seafood, it means the Scandinavian country controls 92 per cent of the industry off Canada's west coast.

Canadian concerns, and they involve more than just sea lice, will be brought to the attention of stockholders of both Marine Harvest (75 licences) and Cermaq (33 licences), and the Oslo meetings can also expect to hear similar accounts from delegations from Ireland, Scotland and Chile.

Included in the Canadian group, travelling to Norway May 18–28, will be two high profile wild salmon advocates, marine biologist and researcher Alexandra Morton and Kwicksutaineuk/Ah-Kwa-Mish First Nations Chief Bob Chamberlin. Both these well-respected individuals have taken front and centre roles in confronting the fish farm industry and bringing the issues to the attention of the mainstream media and, through them, the general public.

Most recently Morton spearheaded an Internet-based postcard campaign that saw more than 13,000 individuals petition the government in Victoria with the message: "The science is in. Open pen salmon farming is driving Pacific salmon to extinction. Fraser and south Coast migration routes are now seriously affected by sea lice infestations. Take a stand now. Don't eat farmed salmon." All this under the headline: "Now dying of politics in rivers near you!"

The government, at time of writing, has chosen not to issue a public response, but with the May 12 provincial election only weeks away must sense that the fish farm controversy has the potential to become a major embarrassment in years ahead. Just as Newfoundland lost its once hugely abundant Atlantic cod fishery as stocks collapsed, so British Columbia faces the loss of its wild salmon.

Wild salmon have provided First Nations people with an important food source and a unique identity for thousands of years, and fish farms have been blamed by the Kwicksutaineuk for "the loss of cultural, ecological and spiritual integrity of the wild salmon habitat, including their ability to maintain cultural practices related to the wild salmon harvesting."

In other words, a way of life is under threat and, as a result, the provincial government is now being sued in the BC Supreme Court by the Kwicksutaineuk for allowing fish farms to be sited in the Broughton Archipelago in violation of their hereditary fishing rights.

The first quarter of 2009 has been highlighted by a number of significant developments in the ongoing controversy in British Columbia. First came a BC Supreme Court ruling that the Canadian government and not the province of British Columbia should be responsible for the regulation of fish farms. The judge has given the two jurisdictions 12 months in which to bring in new legislation.

Then came the news that Marine Harvest Canada, by far the largest of the Norwegian-owned companies, was going to appeal the earlier court decision. A company spokesperson stated: "Our concern is the failure of the court to recognize that the salmon we raise and harvest are the property of Marine Harvest. We have control over the entire life cycle of our salmon. We raise the eggs, hatch the eggs and then feed and care for them in captivity for about three years. We then harvest these fish directly from the pens they are raised in. The court's characterization of these fish as a 'fishery' is, in our view, incorrect."

While these interconnected threads have been developing in the public eye, the Save Our Salmon Initiative (SOS) has been continuing its work behind the scenes, meeting three times with senior federal and provincial officials for outcomes that are described as "cautiously optimistic."

SOS, noting that concrete actions are essential now, continues to press for reforms to the regulation of fish farms, for the introduction of closed containment rearing facilities in place of open-net pens, to prevent the transmission of pathogens and parasites between farm and the marine environment, and for the fallowing of fish farm sites at times when sea lice threaten migrating salmon smolts.

Fish farming and its negative impacts have to be of great significance to a province where the five species of wild Pacific salmon (six if you follow the biologists, who now include steelhead) have long been an economic driver. A once rich commercial fishing industry has been in decline for years. The sport fishery, especially in southern regions, is under pressure from climate change – and with it a decline in the ocean survival rates for the young fish – as well as logging, mining and the demands of population growth. All are blamed to a greater or lesser extent, and the salmon are suffering.

My own experiences over a span of 38 years more than confirm the transition of the east coast Vancouver Island saltwater sport fishery from dependable species abundance, especially for year round chinook and summer and fall coho, to one where the salmon are few and far between. And those that are hooked are more often than not quickly seized by one of an ever-increasing and voracious harbour seal population.

It's all very discouraging and definitely not a time for any further setbacks. I accept that the jobs provided by fish farms are important, especially in the present struggling economy, but not at a cost – any cost – to the environment. We must think to the future and a world that still has a place for wild Pacific salmon.

<hr>

Salute to Pacific salmon

NOVEMBER 2009, *Chasing Silver Magazine*, FINLAND

The white feather spirals down gently on the lightest of early August morning breezes. High on an ancient spruce tree on Graham Island's Guinea Point a bald eagle preens. Nearby, in a cluster of fishing lodges tucked away in a sheltered cove on Langara Island, a new day has started.

From its lofty vantage point the eagle has a view all the way to Alaska on a clear day. While watching the sport fishermen in their small boats, it can swoop down to snatch a quick seafood snack, competing with salmon, whales, sea lions, gulls, cormorants and other predators as large shoals of herring, under attack from both above and below, come boiling to the surface.

The setting is remote Haida Gwaii, until recently known as the Queen Charlotte Islands, or Islands of the People in the language of the Haida Indians who have lived there for thousands of years. This is a prime Canadian sport fishing destination, one of many such locations along the more than 27,000 kilometres that make up the spectacularly rugged Pacific Ocean coastline of British Columbia.

Salmon fishermen looking to Canada's east coast provinces, to the British Isles and Ireland, to Norway, Sweden and a few other select European countries, pursue a single species, the Atlantic salmon,

Salmo salar. By contrast the Pacific supports eight distinct salmon species, to be found from Alaska to California, with six of them of interest to anglers. The other two, the masu or yamame and the amago or biwamasu (*O. masou* and *O. rhodurus*) occur only on the Asian side of the ocean and fall outside the scope of this story.

All eight species belong to the genus *Oncorhynchus* and, in the accepted hierarchy of North American sporting precedence, are led by the chinook (*O. tshawytscha*), also variously known as king, spring, black mouth or, when over 30 pounds in weight, tyee salmon. Then we have the coho (*O. kisutch*) or silver salmon, and the pink (*O. gorbuscha*) or humpback (humpy), named after the distinguishing feature of the males as they approach spawning time.

Next come the chum (*O. kita*) or dog salmon, from the pre-spawning males' canine-looking teeth, and the sockeye (*O. nerka*), or red salmon, the most valuable of them all to the commercial fishery.

It's also worth noting that the scientific community has, since 1988, included steelhead trout in the genus *Oncorhynchus*, changing its Latin name from *Salmo gairdneri* to *O. mykiss*. While all Pacific salmon, without exception, die after spawning, this is not the case with steelhead. However, once it was determined that the steelhead is more closely related to the Pacific salmon than to the Atlantic version, that was that.

We fishermen living on the west coast of North America are fortunate to be able to pursue six of the eight Pacific salmon species. We can catch them with an infinite range of tackle and lures, from traditional and not so traditional flies to natural baits, from spoons to plugs and on to plastic lures in a rainbow of colours. Many of these lures imitate squid, which, along with herring, pilchard and anchovy, is a prime food source for salmon.

While the steelhead is a freshwater fish especially precious to generations of fly fishermen, we take the large majority of Pacific salmon in the open ocean, often many kilometres from shore. We also catch them while wading on the beach, in estuaries and in rivers and streams. Some of the larger river systems will bring the salmon hundreds of kilometres inland before they reach their spawning redds.

To the Atlantic salmon enthusiast with experience of fisheries in the United Kingdom and Europe, the North American version, focused on Pacific salmon, has all the makings of a fisherman's paradise. It offers unequalled opportunities and plenty of fish, some of considerable size, although it is not quite as simple and straightforward as it sounds.

Yes, the fishing can be exceptional in certain places at certain times of the year. And yes, in Alaska, British Columbia, Washington, Oregon and northern California there are, even today, many more salmon to be caught, in both salt and fresh water, than anywhere else in the world. But some Pacific salmon are in real trouble, not as a whole species but in specific Canadian and American locations.

A good example is British Columbia's Fraser River sockeye run that crashed this year (2009) from a forecast of 10.6 million fish to a mere 1.37 million, the smallest return in 50 years. Not surprisingly this collapse brought all commercial, sport and First Nations' fishing to a halt in an effort to preserve the survivors for spawning.

There are many theories as to the causes of this collapse, and it's hard to apportion responsibility. Some blame British Columbia's open-net pen Atlantic salmon farming industry and the associated sea lice that attach to and fatally weaken the immature sockeye smolts as they migrate north. Others suggest climate change and a yet-to-be-confirmed decline in ocean survival numbers.

In four years' time the Fraser River sockeye run might be in even greater trouble. Or it could just as easily bounce back with a strong return, proving yet again Nature's amazing resilience and capacity to survive against the odds. For the moment we wait anxiously for the 2010 run to see whether 2009 marks the start of a downward trend rather than a one-year blip.

In British Columbia, numbers permitting, the sockeye is a legitimate quarry for the sport fisherman in only a few places, including the mouth of the Fraser River, near the city of Vancouver, and in the long sea inlet leading to Port Alberni, on the west coast of Vancouver Island.

Trolling from boats with small lures and flies, and sometimes even bare hooks, will catch fish in these places. In fresh water it's a different story, with few hooked by what most anglers would consider legitimate means, that is, when the fish makes a deliberate decision to take fly or lure. Instead they fall to what is known as flossing tactics with the cast and then the lure drawn into the fish's mouth as the line swings across the current.

Over the years, and certainly dating back to the mid-1950s, there has been a steady decrease in the numbers of both chinook and coho returning to the rivers of the Georgia Strait, between mainland British Columbia and my Vancouver Island home.

What was a rich and dependable year-round sport fishery is now but a shadow of its former self. The once abundant coho have been especially hard hit. Blame the demands of a growing population and its appetite for more housing, improved and additional highways, expanded shopping malls, larger car parks and hydroelectric dams. Blame the long-term impact of logging and mining; blame the commercial fishery; blame climate change. All are contributing factors to the decline, and sadly there is no immediate solution in sight.

However, we did enjoy a much better run of chinook in May and June this year, while returning coho numbers were far above expectations in rivers such as the Stamp, on the west coast of Vancouver Island. The Stamp-Somass system also produced a sockeye run well in excess of the forecast, suggesting that poor ocean survival was not, after all, an issue. There was also a far better showing of pink salmon all along the coast and into the Fraser River, so the outlook is not entirely doom and gloom.

Also of note was the strength of the Vancouver Island offshore fishery for coho and chinook. Visitors to the west coast communities of Bamfield, Tofino and Ucluelet enjoyed the best sport in years. There were certainly plenty of fish around to encourage travel to the more distant offshore banks for the abundant salmon, many of them destined for rivers south of the Canada-USA border. Again, 2010 will confirm whether or not this bonanza marks a more productive era for salmon returns.

I noted earlier in this piece that the chinook stands proud at the top of the Pacific sport fisherman's wish list on account of its size, strength and sporting reputation. The world rod-caught record, from Alaska's Kenai River, was set in 1985 by a fish of 97 pounds four ounces. More recently the cast of a 126-pound fish, caught commercially some years ago, was offered for auction for a reported C$60,000.

My own personal best remains just ounces over 50 pounds, hooked on a trolled herring bait off Haida Gwaii's Lacey Island. It took all of 45 minutes to bring to the net and four times ran off more than 200 feet of line before spending long minutes holding directly beneath the boat, oblivious to the pressure being applied by my sturdy rod. Throughout the encounter, a puffin, as curious as it was colourful, swam close by. As the three-ounce lead broke the surface the bird moved in to investigate, anticipating a tasty meal.

The tension was electric until my fishing partner, Scot Iain Milne, had the monster in the net. Almost immediately we saw that the eye of the swivel between the lead and the running lie had opened up, leaving my improved clinch knot holding on by a mere fraction. One more good thrash, one missed pass with the net and this would have been nothing more than another tough luck Canadian fishing tale.

While much of the fishing for Pacific salmon species involves trolling from boats, often using downriggers and quick release devices to take the lure or bait down anywhere from 20 to 200 feet, there are still ample opportunities for the fly fisherman. Beach fishing, either by wading or from a pontoon or other small boat, has a strong following on Vancouver Island's east coast. Pink and coho salmon are the principal quarry with the occasional chum or chinook an unexpected bonus.

It's a classic late summer and fall fishery, one with its own special charm. The fish are still on the move, often in shallow water where they will reveal their presence by jumping or finning just beneath the surface. It can be a matter of watching and waiting, consulting tide tables and being in the right place at the right time. Then it's time for careful wading and precise casting using intermediate or slow sink tips with fly patterns tied to imitate a bait fish or a shrimp.

When the pinks are there in substantial numbers it's nothing to experience multiple hookups, always remembering the four-fish daily limit and the increasing importance of catch and release. The coho will also come strongly to cast flies, and this fishery is especially well established on the west coast of Vancouver Island, where Tofino is a popular centre.

Chinook and coho are also popular with the river fisherman who swings sunk flies as he would for Atlantic salmon. Often this will bring considerable success, especially when the fish are fresh run and not too far from the salt.

Chum also take both fly and lure well in fresh water and have a deserved reputation for teaching harsh lessons to less experienced anglers. Sometimes called purple tigers, in recognition of the vertical stripes they develop with maturity, they will battle with a frenzy and power all their own and easily smash a rod or tear off an entire fly line if undue pressure is applied too early in the contest.

While perhaps not the aristocrats of the salmon world – the crown most likely goes to the Atlantic salmon and the steelhead – there can be no questioning the Pacific salmon species' immense contribution to the North American sport fishing scene.

In particular, here's to the chinook and the coho, my favourites for so many reasons ... Beautiful to the eye, willing takers, strong fighters and wonderful table fare – long may they thrive.

Celebrating pinks

AUGUST 2010, *Chasing Silver Magazine*, FINLAND

Imagine, if you can, a wild salmon run where every fly fisherman has an opportunity to take home a four-fish limit each day, where it's nothing to hook, play and release a dozen, two dozen or even more in a matter of hours, all fresh and shining from the ocean. And this happens in locations where the fishing is available to all for the cost of a very reasonable licence fee.

This is not some exclusive Russian watershed, nor is it in far-away Alaska or to the distant south in windswept Patagonia. The Canadian rivers in this dream-come-true for any angler are easily reached by a paved highway. One Vancouver Island system is well within the boundaries of a medium-sized town; the other is further north at the end of a highway turnoff and another few kilometres of dusty gravel road, one where massively loaded logging trucks demand visiting drivers' absolute respect and attention.

Pretty well everyone knows about the biblical Adam and Eve, but how many beyond British Columbia's West Coast have ever heard of a pairing of rivers of the same names? Located on the east coast of Vancouver Island, some 400 kilometres north of the capital city of Victoria, the Adam and Eve systems come into sharp focus around midsummer and remain a popular if somewhat remote local destination well into the autumn.

As the season progresses, so the number of active fishermen on the two rivers, which merge within walking distance of the ocean, declines. Their runs of coho and chinook salmon can never match the amazing horde of pink salmon that swarms the lower reaches below the junction of the two rivers from mid-July and on into August before it's their time to spawn in September and October.

Look into a clear pool and marvel at the swaying black carpet of hundreds and hundreds of pink salmon as they hold in the current, one or more occasionally breaking the surface in a head and tail rise or leaping clear to fall back with a splash before vanishing into the crowd.

Or fish the flats as the tide presses forward from the sea and see the salmon showing and showing again as they thrust forward past the waiting anglers' flies and occasional lures, for this is a fishery where fly fishermen, both single- and double-handed, are definitely in the majority.

Although they don't come in their millions, as they can elsewhere, the pink salmon do arrive in their many thousands with this year's early Adam and Eve run estimated at between 20,000 and 30,000 as it built toward a final escapement that could approach last year's 392,000, a figure surpassed only once before, in 2000 when 430,000 returned.

In this system the pinks are the mainstay of a fishery that is available to all comers for the appropriate licence as issued by either the federal government, for the tidal stretch, a mile or so in length, or the provincial government, which has control over everything in fresh water.

Pinks, sometimes called humpies, reflecting the marked change in the body shape of the males as they approach spawning, are the most abundant of the Pacific salmon species. They outnumber chinook, coho, sockeye and chum and provide excellent sport for novice and expert fisherman alike, in the river, in the estuary as the tide builds and off the nearby beaches too.

For the European angler, whether he/she be fishing for Atlantic salmon in the Scandinavian countries or on the increasingly expensive and almost always strictly regulated rivers and streams of England, Ireland, Scotland and Wales, a really good day will be two or three fish hooked and perhaps one or two landed and often released to fulfill the spawning ritual.

When the pinks arrive off the east coast of Vancouver Island, and north along the mainland British Columbia coast all the way up to southern Alaska, so too do the fishermen, drawn by the prospect of almost certain double-figure days and by the fact of a generous four-fish daily limit. Unlike the other Pacific salmon species, pinks do not do well in the freezer but they can be canned, smoked and, best of all from my experience, eaten fresh from the sea on the day of their capture, perhaps cooked in camp on the barbecue or baked in the oven at home.

With a two-year life cycle and no overlap between odd year and even year runs, pink salmon were for years subject to heavy commercial fishing pressures. Then came a decline in their numbers before a subsequent reduction in effort on the part of the netsmen enabled them to rebuild.

Southern stocks are now described as healthy, as evidenced by returns to the Adam and Eve, all totally wild fish, and to the Campbell River and its tributary, the Quinsam, where a large hatchery, funded by the federal government's Fisheries and Oceans Canada, has been hugely successful. Further north, for reasons unexplained, recent pink returns have been far less encouraging, with a near collapse reported in some areas.

The 2009 run of pink salmon into the enhanced Campbell and Quinsam systems was not far short of one million fish, a modern-day record. This year's final count won't be of the same magnitude – perhaps in the order of some 500,000 – but still more than enough to meet all escapement needs, including those of the hatchery, and allow fishermen to start keeping up to four a day from July 15, a month earlier than usual.

With such abundance the local First Nations' A-Tlegai Fisheries Society was brought in to collect almost 16,000 salmon in a one-day Excess Salmon to Spawning Requirements (ESSR) operation in early August. These were taken right at the hatchery.

The heavily forested, and in places extensively logged, Adam and the Eve watersheds are in an area well away from any major population base, whereas the Campbell and the Quinsam rivers are close to the centre of the town of Campbell River. In fact, a main road runs within a stone's throw of the two rivers for what is very much an urban rather than a wild setting. Just look at the number of cars parked there every day during the season.

For all that, the Campbell and Quinsam lack nothing in terms of popularity with local and out-of-town anglers, among them a large number visiting from Europe who drew the attention of television crews from the Netherlands and Germany.

Both rivers are subject to extremely heavy fishing pressure, especially on the Campbell below its junction with the Quinsam, where the 37-year-old hatchery is into the second year of a four-year modernization program costing C$14.6 million, an expenditure of public funds made possible by the value of its long-standing contribution to the economy.

In addition to pinks, the hatchery also raises chinook and coho salmon, steelhead and cutthroat trout. Six of the last seven years saw the hatchery report annual releases of over six million pink fry and more than eight million in 2000 and 2002. It's little wonder the return numbers are so good just now with improved ocean survival a definite factor over the past decade.

While some fishermen tend to dismiss the pink as a less worthy challenge than, say, the chinook or the coho, that's definitely not a widely held view. On the credit side they are very readily available, come well to a sunk fly or lure and, for their size, are strong and stubborn fighters. That said, they are definitely much smaller than the other Pacific species, with an average weight of around three to four pounds. A six-pound pink is a good one and double-figure weights are out of the ordinary, with the world record just over 15 pounds.

Not so long ago, in early August, I spent two days on the lower part of the Adam, below its junction with the Eve, fishing with my usual partners, retired teachers Glenn Di Georgio and Harvey Stern. Following a three-hour, early morning drive on all but deserted roads, we quickly established an overnight forest campsite close to the confluence of the two rivers, with the tidal portion of the Adam only 10 minutes away.

The fishing had been strong for some time and continued for the following weeks. We made the most of our opportunities, fished floating lines with short intermediate or type two or three sink tips and a selection of flies in smaller sizes (No. 6 and No. 8) with pink the predominant colour. That was our choice, and also that of the majority of fishermen we encountered, but I am sure other colours, green, blue, purple and even white, would have been just as acceptable, for the fish were present in large numbers and willing takers for most of the time.

Not surprisingly, the fishing pressure was greater downstream of the boundary marker above which catch and release is the order of the day. While allowed to take their four-fish limit, many anglers kept only a couple for the table and returned the rest with admirable care and respect, a tactic that can only help ensure the continued good health of this most bountiful fishery.

Summer and early autumn beach fishing for both pink and coho salmon along the coastline of east Vancouver Island, either wading or from pontoon-type boats, has been gaining steadily in popularity over the past decade.

The estuaries of the Keogh, the Quatse and the Cluxewe rivers, all north of the Adam and Eve system and convenient to the town of Port Hardy, have a fine reputation as has the area around the mouth of the Oyster River, to the south. Further south again, and less than an hour's drive from my home city of Nanaimo, a community-run hatchery at Nile Creek, on Qualicum Bay, is the key to excellent opportunities along extensive, easily waded beaches on either side of where the seemingly insignificant stream meets the ocean.

In Nanaimo, a net pen project, with young, hatchery-produced pinks held for a short time to imprint, has developed newly established runs into Departure Bay, within sight of the main ferry terminal, and to the harbour itself with urban fly anglers meeting plenty of fish at the mouth of the downtown Millstone River. Interestingly, all the pink fisheries south of the Campbell are based on stocks originating from the Quinsam hatchery.

Popular pink salmon fly patterns include: Pink Handlebar, Kathy's Coat, Micky Finn, Pink Fuzzy, California Neil in green and pink, Harvey's Pink Shrimp, Blue Streak,

Pink Eve, Pregnant Shrimp and Pink Euphasid along with various minnow and fry patterns in green and blue. By law only single, barbless hooks may be used on flies and lures.

←———

Vancouver Island coho recovery

FEBRUARY 2014, *Chasing Silver Magazine*, FINLAND

Salmon fishing comes in many different guises. One salmon species is found in the Atlantic and five species – six if you count steelhead – are found in the Pacific. Atlantics are most usually taken in fresh water, in rivers and lakes in the United Kingdom and Europe, and on the east coast of Canada, by fishermen using both flies and lures.

The Pacific salmon species are more readily available in salt water but are also caught in rivers, although they do tend to lose condition and their ocean-bright appearance fairly quickly as they approach their time to spawn. Unlike Atlantics, all Pacific salmon die following the spawning ritual.

Pacific salmon sport fishing extends north from California to Alaska by way of Oregon, Washington and British Columbia, and it is the ocean fishery that attracts the most attention. Trolling from boats of all sizes, close to shore and well out to sea, using both lures and natural bait, is far and away the most popular approach of fishermen targeting chinook and coho salmon, the principal sport species.

Sockeye and pink salmon are also popular with the trollers at certain times of the year, and in specific locations, while the chum appear toward the end of the season and are generally less likely to be taken on lures while still in the ocean. Once in fresh water it's a different story, and a 10-pound chum hooked on fly or lure is one of the strongest fighters of them all.

Among all this activity the saltwater fly fisherman pursues his passion in comparative obscurity. It's not that Pacific salmon cannot be caught in the sea on a fly; they can and are, but in nothing like the numbers that the trollers expect to land. And that brings me to the beach fisheries of east coast Vancouver Island, where first pink salmon and then coho salmon hold the attention of a growing number of fly fishermen each year.

The pinks – and in a good year, such as the one just past, the runs are counted in millions – arrive in late June, July and August; the larger coho come later, at least to our island beaches, and never in the same numbers. September and October are the peak months, with 2013 providing some of the best results in years, a welcome change not yet fully explained but most likely linked to improved marine survival rates.

In the 1970s the Strait of Georgia, lying between the east coast of Vancouver Island and mainland British Columbia, the continent of North America if you like, provided coho in abundance, sufficient to support an extensive sport fishery and a commercial catch as well. Then the numbers began a steep decline, leading to a continuing ban on the retention of all wild coho, along with historically low numbers of chinook. Overall, recent catches in the Strait have been estimated at less than one-tenth of past levels.

It's far too soon to be speaking in terms of a significant, ongoing recovery where the Georgia Strait coho are concerned, and we will have to wait until well into 2014 to see whether, in fact, a corner has been turned and stocks really are starting to rebuild.

In the early months – that's May and June – of 2013, trollers, while fishing for chinook, were catching and releasing wild coho weighing between three and five pounds, something to my knowledge last experienced a good 20 or more years ago. This led on to expectations that beach fishing for coho later in the summer might be well worth the effort, and so it proved.

With easy road access to the numerous Vancouver Island beaches that lie between the towns of Nanaimo and Campbell River, a distance of just over 150 kilometres, the fisherman, local or visitor, is spoiled for choice. And there are more opportunities further to the north, in particular in and around the Eve River.

We all have our own special favourites and will often check out three or four locations over the course of a morning. Island traffic is generally light, especially early in the day, and the original coastal road, not to be confused with the newer, faster inland highway route, often runs within casting distance of the water.

It's a simple matter to stop and scan the water for signs of fish, with binoculars a useful but not essential aide. The coho, and to a lesser extent the pinks, will often give themselves away by jumping clear of the water's surface. They may not always, and that's so often the case, be fish that are prepared to come to a fly or a lure, but at least the fisherman can be confident that, at worst, he is not casting into barren waters.

Fishing at first light and again in the evening is always popular as is the one-hour period before and after a tide change. My own preference is to fish an incoming tide, more especially when I am using, as I often do, my little seven-foot fibreglass dinghy. With wheels fitted to the stern, it's easy enough to drag down to the water, even over some pretty uneven terrain. Then it's a matter of spotting the fish and rowing out quietly to within casting distance.

I have three or four valued and regular fishing companions – and that's one of the best parts of the whole experience – who all rely on pontoon boats using both paddles and fins to manoeuver. The fins leave their hands free to cast and retrieve, and that's an advantage when I am occupied with the oars.

When an adverse tide or wind is a problem, I simply drop anchor in a likely location and hope the fish will come to me. Sometimes they do and sometimes they don't. We are always looking for telltale signs of fish, jumpers or nervous water as they move quickly just below the surface, and even indications of action being enjoyed by other anglers.

The shore fishermen, and they are in the majority, obviously do not enjoy the same level of mobility, and we boaters have an implied obligation to give them room and not to crowd their opportunities by coming too close.

We also have to remember that anglers using spinning tackle on two-handed rods of up to 13 feet in length can cast a weighted lure on light lines a very considerable distance, far further than could ever be achieved with the shorter, single-handed spinning rods that were the norm until very recently.

It seems to me as though the local spin fishermen have taken a leaf out of the books of the fly casters who have been making increasing use of double-handed rods over the past five years. With no obstructions to their back, the traditional overhand cast works well and, combined with a stripping basket, allows long casts to be made and managed. Calm seas are never guaranteed and the stripping basket means loose line can be kept clear of the water and the current as well as the inevitable, tangle-causing floating weed.

For fishing from a boat, fly rods need be no more than a six or seven weight in the nine- to 10½-foot ranges. Slightly longer switch rods are also becoming increasingly popular, with a combination of floating line and intermediate tip more than adequate since both coho and pink are seldom more than two or three feet down in the water column. Indeed most beach fishing takes place in locations where the depth ranges from two or three feet to 20 feet and, generally speaking, no more than a quarter of a mile from shore.

Barbless (by law) flies, fished on 10- to 15-pound breaking strain leaders of between six and 10 feet in length, will always be a matter of personal preference when it comes to patterns. For example, some years ago Glenn Di Georgio, a 1970s rugby-playing and now fishing partner, devised a tying I later named the Nanoose Bay Special.

This fly has since become a particular favourite of mine. It dates back a good decade to a time when it accounted for a significant number of fish, mostly coho but also a few chum, when they were holding in Nanoose Bay, near Nanaimo, waiting for the fall rains to draw them into one or other of two adjacent creeks. The fish, many weighing double figures, would move in and out with the tide, and we would be waiting for them, enjoying quite amazing sport for the better part of a week, wading and casting whenever they came within reach of our flies. Glenn again found fish in numbers from the shore one day in October of last year, while on that occasion, I had much less success fishing from my small boat.

There are two or three other beaches not too far away from home that are always worth a look in September and October, in particular those on either side of Nile Creek, an insignificant little stream to the north of Qualicum Bay where a small, locally run hatchery has had great success in building up a very strong, annual run of pink salmon. Fly fishing from the shore is both popular and effective at this location, and for a good mile on either side of the creek as well, with easy parking and access to the shore for wading anglers and for those who prefer to launch small boats from the water's edge.

The hatchery-enhanced Big and Little Qualicum Rivers, to the north of the towns of Parksville and Qualicum Beach, undoubtedly contribute to the quality of the local beach fisheries and are themselves popular if often crowded destinations when the coho and chinook salmon appear in September and October. Both also support stocks of wild cutthroat trout that tend to be less heavily fished than the salmon.

Hatchery coho are easily identified by their missing adipose fin, and two a day can be retained. Up to seven million smolts are released each year from a number of hatcheries on both sides of the Canada–US border. Anglers are encouraged to return the heads of any they keep because a small proportion (less than 5 per cent) of them carry a coded-wire tag. These tags provide the scientists with valuable information on abundance, distribution and survival.

There was a time when sport fishing was an important economic asset for the tourist industry on the east coast of Central Vancouver Island. Motels and tackle shops, fishing guides, restaurants and boat rental businesses all stood to gain when coho and chinook runs were strong. When the salmon were no longer there in numbers, the visitors looked elsewhere for their sport, but now the hope is that better times are ahead, that the improved results enjoyed in 2013 will be evident again this year and in the years to come.

SALMON STAMP FEES TO REMAIN IN BC

The improved numbers of coho in the Strait of Georgia in 2013 wasn't the only positive development for local and visiting salmon fishermen. In March it was announced that the Canadian government had decided to return all revenues from salmon conservation stamp sales to British Columbia.

The six-dollar stamps, attached to saltwater fishing licences, allow the angler to retain one or more salmon depending on local size and catch limits. Each year some 220,000 stamps are purchased by sport fishermen, but since 1996, only about 20 per cent of that revenue has come back for investment in the fishery with the rest going into general federal government revenue.

Announcing the government's change of direction, Dr. Brian Riddell, chief executive officer of the Vancouver-based, non-profit Pacific Salmon Foundation, said the funds would be directed to benefit community salmon conservation, restoration and enhancement activities.

Commenting on the decision, Dr. Riddell said: "This change will result in significant investments in our fisheries that will be looked upon favourably by recreational and commercial fishers, First Nations, coastal communities and conservationists. It has received broad support from a range of stakeholders who care about Pacific salmon, including business leaders, recreational and commercial fishing interests and volunteer stream keepers."

2014 Georgia Strait coho chronicles

MAY 2015, *Chasing Silver Magazine*, FINLAND

Recovering coho salmon stocks in the Strait of Georgia, between Vancouver Island's east coast and mainland British Columbia, were at their highest level in 20 years, and with the 2014 regulations amended to allow retention of one wild fish a day, in addition to one hatchery fish, our expectations were laced with optimism as we embarked on another beach fishing season.

Over the past 10 to 15 years, late summer and early fall beach fishing for Pacific salmon, both by wading and from small boats, has been gaining steadily in popularity from Nanaimo north to Campbell River, a distance of some 150 kilometres.

The following diary extracts tell the story of our combined efforts, the highs and the lows, as we searched for fish through the month of October 2014. The notes were compiled by four longtime fishing friends, Bryce Olson (Cedar), Harvey Stern (Nanaimo), Glenn Di Georgio (Parksville) and myself.

OCTOBER 2: A quick stop on the northward journey at Nanoose Bay found a rising SE wind but also saw several fish showing in the usual spot opposite the railroad tracks. Decided to head to Deep Bay, where the wind was negligible. Immediately noticed several larger coho jumping about 300 feet offshore and that was all it took to launch. However, it took a while before more rises (jumps) were noted and I was able to get a fly, a green Mickey Finn streamer, in place. Had two strikes on two casts then a solid hit from an estimated 8-pound or more salmon that immediately did the coho streak for the end of the fly line and then a quick reversal toward the boat, where it casually jumped and returned my fly. A great first shot at these hot dogs of the Pacific Coast. —*Bryce*

OCTOBER 3: It's just before 6:45 a.m. and still dark, with the

Nanoose Bay tide dropping to a low of 4.2 ft at 7:19 a.m. First Nations clam diggers' lights were winking in the distance, and the tide was much, much further out than I anticipated, so here I am, back home for an early breakfast. —Peter

OCTOBER 4: Could see some fish in Nanoose but tide too far out so decided to come back later and headed north ... checked all usual haunts seeing just a couple of fish in each spot ... did not launch boats. Returned to Nanoose and a rising SE wind and no sign of fish, although someone had filleted two coho on the beach. It's got to happen soon. Will return to searching on Sunday. —Bryce

OCTOBER 5: A tour of the "hot spots" saw us back at Nanoose later in the morning. The tide was way out but plenty of fish showing in very calm water. I hooked up right away and landed a decent-sized wild coho. Great start but also an ending as I landed no more but had several brief takes. Good friend Philippe Herve du Penhoat, from France, landed one, and then a breeze came up and it became hard to locate the fish as they move around a lot and don't show themselves. Glenn started to list to starboard due to a leak in one of his pontoon boat valves and departed but caught a nice coho on the way in. —Bryce

OCTOBER 6: Finally got the little boat in the water at dawn this morning at Nanoose Bay. Few fish showing on the right of the railway tracks, pretty well opposite the snag where the bald eagles perch. Harvey also on the hunt and soon landed a nice coho on a Green California Neil. Then he noticed fish jumping far out and headed off. I followed after a bit and was fortunate to get a perfect shot at a finning fish just after admiring three that jumped in unison ... all bright and of decent size. Played my fish, also on a Green California Neil pattern and five-foot intermediate tip, for a good 10 minutes and then saw the hook pull out as I went for the net. —Peter

OCTOBER 7: Beautiful fall afternoon, full flood tide and calm waters just begging to be fished. Left home at 3:00 p.m. and did the tour. After over an hour of observing different pieces of water – at least 10 minutes at each location – Sunny Beach twice and Nanoose for 25 minutes, I did not see one jumper. Talked to various fishers just leaving the water at several places and all had the same report. As Glenn says: "We need rain." Until that happens I'm going to place my efforts on hold. —*Harvey*

OCTOBER 7: A trip to Nanoose today had almost no coho showing. By chance when I was rowing I noticed some fins and on third cast with a Red California Neil one of those fins turned and attacked my fly. That is literally what happened ... I could see the turn of the fish, and it literally dove at the fly ... what a rush! A leap and a searing run with several jumps well into the backing. The speed was indescribable! At the end of the run it turned, and a race to retrieve line and the slackness indicated it had come off. Then a large chum – around 15 pounds – jumped about 50 feet away. It had a fly in its mouth, and the fight was on again with another race to the backing! Finally landed it after about 10 minutes. Without a doubt this was the most excitement I have had on a fly rod. —*Bryce*

OCTOBER 8: Gentlemen, looked, launched, left.... that sums up this morning's Nanoose Bay trip. Had the boat in the water at 6:45 a.m. and was on the way home by 8:30 a.m. There were a few fish showing off the bible camp with two fly fishermen wading for them plus a kayak fisherman who arrived as I departed. Nothing showing when I was there off the railway tracks and nothing out in the middle either. —*Peter*

OCTOBER 9: On the water at dawn and home by 10:00 a.m., empty-handed but satisfied having had an opportunity to cast at numerous fish, both jumpers and finners. However, only one gave me the courtesy of a decent tug. High tide was at 7:12 a.m. and the fish started to show strongly around 8:00 a.m. By 9:15 a.m. they had moved away, and as I packed up, they started to show again on a consistent basis well out into the bay.   —*Peter*

OCTOBER 9: Just back from Royston. We arrived there in fog around 8:30 a.m. and saw fish jumping. Just a few strokes from shore and I am into a beautiful coho, landed and all of 10 pounds, a fin-clipped hatchery fish. Two more searching casts and I am into a second and larger salmon which proceeded into backing in a roaring run: Landed him – about all the net will handle. The bay is very shallow and I caught the fish in about two feet of water. The fog lifted and the fish simply quit biting. There were a lot of them all up the bay, both coho and chum, and a few fishermen. I saw only one other caught until Philippe hooked and landed one around 2:30 p.m. about 5 or 6 pounds. We were in and among fish the entire day, but they had lockjaw despite numerous flies tried. The successful patterns were the Red Coho Bugger and a Bead Head Neil for Philippe   —*Bryce*

OCTOBER 10: Morning #4 at Nanoose and nothing to show for another dawn start. But the fish are now there in significant numbers. They just would not bite for me ... and I covered my share of finners and jumpers with the usual range of flies. It will be interesting to get Harvey's take on the situation since he was just heading out when I called it a day around 10:45 a.m. Started out down the tracks and found fish in the same place as yesterday. They showed for a while at first light and then vanished – or went down – so I moved across toward the creek mouths where two boats were on station. They each hooked at least one fish around the time of the high tide change (8:12 a.m.). Then I noticed a school of coho in four or five feet of water opposite the car parking area and fished that for a while, again without any offers. These were nice bright fish and of a good size   —*Peter*

OCTOBER 10: I arrived late and the action had halted. Maybe

saw a dozen jumpers over the course of an hour and a half. One small school of bright, silver fish moved in and a wading fisherman took one on the fly. Talked to one other rod and he had two for the morning so they were biting. 　　　　　　　　　　　　　　—*Harvey*

OCTOBER 11: Back to Royston where the same conditions prevailed as last time with fish very active close to shore. The difference being that they had developed lockjaw. Glenn hooked into a big coho but lost it after a couple of great runs, a really large fish. After that the whole area went quiet with no fish showing, so we headed home. 　　　　　　　　　　　　　　　　　　—*Bryce*

OCTOBER 11: Interesting how it can change day to day. Will give Nanoose first throw and then perhaps think of an alternate location if that fails to live up to expectations. I think a lot will depend on what the weather holds for us over the next two or three days. There are certainly enough fish at Nanoose, but like Royston, that's no guarantee that they are going to bite on a consistent basis. 　　　　　　　　　　　　　　　　　　—*Peter*

OCTOBER 14: Off to the beach before first light and completed the "grand tour" as follows:

- ‹ SUNNY BEACH: No fish showing after a half an hour and no one fishing.
- ‹ NILE CREEK: No fish showing in 10 minutes and no one fishing. Nile Creek was up from the recent rains and flowing nicely.
- ‹ POWER LINE: No fish showing in 20 minutes and no one fishing.
- ‹ HENSON ROAD: No fish showing in 20 minutes and no one fishing but two others showed up looking. One had come from Courtenay and had spent a half-hour at Deep Bay without seeing a thing. The other fellow had just come from the Shady Rest, where he said there were a few people fishing and he saw one fish taken but none showing.

< DEEP BAY: Had to check it out for myself. No fish showing in 20 minutes and no one fishing.
< SUNNY BEACH (again): One person looking. He had been there for a half an hour and hadn't seen a fish.
< SHADY REST, north viewing site: One spin caster, one beach fly fisher, and one belly boat fisher. No fish showing in 20 minutes and horrendous water and wind conditions.
< FRENCH CREEK: Two spin fishers and one fly fisher fishing from the rip-rap and one fly fisher who had just launched his pontoon boat. Several lookers. No fish showing in 20 minutes.
< NANOOSE BAY: Several lookers, half a dozen beach fishers, mostly spinning, and two boat fishers. A few fish showing sporadically along the railroad tracks side. Watched a guy in an inflatable take two fish. Launched and fished for over an hour, during which time the inflatable took another and left. I left also as the waves built to three feet and capping with strong SE winds. —*Harvey*

OCTOBER 16: High hopes unfulfilled ... looked at Blood Creek and Holly Farm beaches on the way to Nanoose Bay. Arrived some three hours before high tide, around 2:30 p.m. and was joined for chat and eyeballing by first Glenn and then Bryce and Philippe. We saw nothing. Launched into the wind and slowly rowed up along the tracks. Saw some fish jumping at the first houses with two spoon fishermen in place. Anchored and bounced around at the end of a long anchor line but nothing interested. Bit more wind than ideal and was back in the truck by 2:30 p.m. —*Peter*

OCTOBER 20: No fish in the net but certainly worth the Nanoose Bay effort today. Conditions well-nigh perfect with a comfortable wind from the SE. Launched around 1:00 p.m. and finished in a heavy shower at 4:15 p.m. just as Harvey was launching after a fruitless up-Island survey. Rowed across to the far side, where two or three boats were already in place. Found a spot upwind of them, dropped the anchor and covered fish for the next

40 minutes. Eventually changed flies, from blue and silver to one of Glenn's new bead-headed Nanoose Bay Specials, and promptly hooked and just as quickly lost the first of two fish. The second one gave great play for a good 10 minutes and was close to the boat when the hook came out – again. Definitely a good-sized coho, possible double figures, but that's how it goes. The thrill is always in the take. Bryce and Philippe arrived just as the action died but Bryce later took a very bright fish well out in the bay on a Bead Head California Neil pattern with a hungry seal adding to the suspense.   —Peter

OCTOBER 21: A day for the windsurfers. As one of them remarked: "A bad day for fishing is a good day for kiting." I spent three hours on the church side of Nanoose Bay, the last hour with Harvey, but saw only the occasional fish jumping in the waves, not enough to encourage us to launch. At 3:00 p.m. when I headed home, it was blowing SE 19, down from SE 23 at 1:00 p.m.   —Peter

OCTOBER 21: You left too soon. After you went the winds died down and the fish returned to the area in good numbers. Had one on for about 10 seconds, after changing from a sand lance pattern to my Nanoose Bay Special. Wish I had done so sooner.   —Glenn

OCTOBER 22: Perhaps it was the aftermath of last night's heavy rain and strong winds, for the majority of the Nanoose Bay fish were either lying low or had moved away into the two local creeks. Whatever the reason, there were very, very few to be seen over the course of the afternoon. The wind started as a challenging SSE 18 but then died completely to flat calm an hour before the 5:15 p.m. high tide. Perfect spotting conditions but scarcely a fin in sight. Bryce came and left after a cheerful hour's on-shore conversation as did kite surfer and local doctor John MacMillan, bemoaning the absence of strong winds, while Glenn headed off to wade the incoming tide.   —Peter

OCTOBER 23: Went to Nanoose about 1:30 p.m. in the middle

of a deluge, which then ended and the bay went dead calm. Tide was about low. Noted one school of coho about 100 feet out in about two feet of water. Tried casting to them but they moved off, the only action I saw. I'll take a look tomorrow but am losing hope.

—*Bryce*

OCTOBER 23: Don't know whether there will be many more opportunities this year for us to catch coho on the beach. At this point the season seems to have been a bit of a washout. Even though the fish are still showing they appear to have lost the need to strike. Could it be the season is coming to a rapid close? —*Glenn*

OCTOBER 25: When they came, the fall rains were relentless. Rivers and creeks filled to their banks and the salmon moved in from the sea. How much rain? Well, our local Nanaimo River, on the east coast of Vancouver Island, increased its flow from 20 cubic metres/second to 240 cubic metres/second between October 17 and 22, while the famous Cowichan River, further to the south, went from 4.6 cubic metres/second, dangerously low, to over 90 cubic metres/second by month's end. On the west coast of the Island, Port Alberni recorded a staggering 434 mm (17+ inches) of rain for the month compared to just 26 mm for the same month in 2013. Definitely our beach fishing season was at an end. It was time to tidy fly boxes, put away rods, clean and oil reels and dress lines for the last time. —*Peter*

A birthday wish on the Kitimat

NOVEMBER 2015, *Chasing Silver Magazine*, FINLAND

Mid-June and expectations are running high. And with good reason, for we know the Kitimat River, in northwestern British Columbia, has already produced its first chinook salmon of the year, fish that will be holding in some deep pool or run, waiting to intercept our gaudy Intruder-style flies, fish of a size sufficient to satisfy the wildest, most outrageous expectations of any angler.

Chinook are the largest species of Pacific salmon and were originally known in BC as spring salmon, presumably to mark the timing of the first runs. In more recent years the name *chinook* has gained increasingly widespread Canadian acceptance, with the *tyee* salutation saved for sport-caught fish of this species that weigh over 30 pounds.

These are most certainly not fish to be taken lightly and probably not to be challenged with even a powerful single-handed rod unless it is being employed with a serious level of big fish expertise. Anything less has to be an invitation for an expensive disaster, a heartbreaking failure to eventually subdue a brute of a salmon that could quite easily weigh from 30 to 40 pounds and more. Specimens of even half that weight are every bit as obstinate, as tenacious in their efforts to achieve freedom.

This six-day trip to the Kitimat River had been planned well in advance with Doug Machuk, one of my regular fly-fishing companions over the past decade. It had its origins in previous years' pursuit of the spring-run steelhead that arrive in the Kitimat in March and April, often with snow still on the ground and cold water conditions that are demanding for fisherman and guide alike.

Doug, from Banff, Alberta, broke new ground on the Kitimat with a June chinook trip in 2014. He came home with reports of big fish, big water and excitement aplenty. It was enough and more to start us planning together for a return visit in 2015. Once again we would make our headquarters at the Steelhead House in Terrace, with Darren Wright as our guide and Missy MacDonald, his partner, ever present to look after everything else, including comfortable accommodation, pre-dawn breakfasts and ample riverbank snacks and lunches.

For the visiting fishermen there was nothing else to do but eat, sleep and get ready for the next day on the river. And those days called for the earliest of early starts. Our guide held firm to the conviction that the early bird was most likely to catch the worm, or in this case, the chinook.

It takes about 40 early-morning minutes to drive along the almost-deserted Terrace to Kitimat highway to the chosen launching point, where the drift boat slides easily off its trailer and into the river. With boots and waders already on and the rods rigged, it's only a matter of minutes before we make our first casts and switch into serious fishing mode.

Between June 21 and June 26 this year, six days of pretty intense fishing effort, we were fortunate enough to see the Kitimat at close to its early summer best. The winter had been one of record low snowpacks across the province, and the threat of high summer's subsequent forest fires, urban drought and unprecedented river closures further south was already on the horizon.

Only on the second to last day did we encounter any significant rain, rain that came overnight and persisted through the morning to bring the river level up by a good six inches. The rain also left us in the right place at the right time, with chinook showing strongly – and taking.

Earlier in the week we had fished hard, launching the drift boat at first light and working our way downstream to cover all the known pools and runs with our double-handed 9-weight Spey rods and big showy flies, Intruder-style patterns in a broad range of colours armed with the sharpest of barbless hooks.

My 80th birthday was just weeks ahead, and it was my ambition to mark the occasion with my largest-ever salmon on a fly. Another life in Northern Ireland, more than 40 years ago, had produced its share of Atlantic salmon from the Strule, the Mourne and the Finn, and other rivers too, but most of them were sprightly five- and six-pound grilse with the occasional larger fish, perhaps up to 13 pounds. Here on the Kitimat, we were hoping for a fish on an altogether different scale.

After the first couple of days our enthusiasm level was still high, but the outcomes to that point had fallen well short of expectations.

I had lost what felt to be a good fish on the first day, a solid "take" along the turbulent edge of a high rock face followed by two ponderous head shakes and then nothing. The next morning Doug hooked and just as quickly lost two before eventually landing a salmon of around 12 pounds to open his account on our third day.

It was a lot of work for one fish to hand but we were far from discouraged, and we felt that a forecast for a change in the weather toward the end of the week would make all the difference.

Each day we would see salmon, and some were most certainly very large fish, showing and rolling in the long, broad pools, pools where you could cast and step for an hour or more, covering fresh water each time. Bright sunshine and early summer heat provided most pleasant fishing conditions, but they were far from ideal for our campaign. Water colour and visibility were good. The river running at around 10C (50F) made for pleasantly cool wading in the heat, regardless of a persistent and hard-to-trace wader leak.

The anticipated rain came on the Wednesday night and continued on through Thursday morning. All of a sudden our expectations were being realized in a most impressive way. The last of eight salmon raised during the morning – and we usually finished our day around lunchtime before heading back for a deserved rest – came to my rod. And what a fish it was.

In the high 20s for sure, maybe even a little more, but without a suitable scale, and thus risking more stress on the fish, it's hard to tell when they are that big. The so-strong hookup was full of conviction as the fly came around and the fish was immediately on the move, off on an unstoppable run that took me a good 90 metres downriver. And this regardless of all the pressure I could manage with a 14-foot, 9-weight rod and a Hatch reel with a drag that would surely have subdued a lesser opponent in a matter of minutes.

In passing, a word of thanks to Bend, Oregon, steelheader Loren Irving for the generous loan of the reel, an essential step up from my more traditional and much, much older click and pawl versions, veritable antiques and adequate for steelhead and Atlantics, but hardly sufficient for these immensely strong Pacific salmon. In planning for this project we had left nothing to chance.

Everything mechanical worked perfectly under immense pressure and now I knew for sure why Darren insists on leaders with a 25-pound breaking strain. I also understand why he comes equipped with a 50-inch landing net, for there are fish in the Kitimat that are twice the size of mine. No matter, my 80th birthday wish had been answered in the best possible way. Time to light the candles.

Our final day started with a bang, or a bust, depending on how you look at it. By the time we had finished we had touched 11 fish but only managed to land and release two, including one of around 30 pounds (38.5″ x 25″) that Darren saw move just at his rod tip and was able to cover immediately with a flick cast that saw his fly grabbed as it landed in knee-deep water.

The river had come up a good foot with the previous day's rain and was falling back all morning. I managed to hook and play two very large fish for a considerable time. Both went far out into the backing and both were then lost as the hook pulled free. The second one was the bigger of the two by some way, and I had it on for at least 10 minutes while on the run down the riverbank desperately trying to regain at least some line.

Quite honestly there is simply nothing that I have ever encountered in a lifetime of fly fishing that matches the pulling power, the energy, the stamina of these heavyweight Kitimat chinook.

The rain had most definitely made all the difference, and the fact we landed fish with sea lice still in place on our two final days was confirmation a fresh run was incoming from the ocean, not that many kilometres away, and that those fish already in residence were becoming a lot more interested in our offerings.

How soon we forgot the long, hot days earlier in the week when we could not muster a single touch between us as we completed an ever-mounting count of casts. That, of course, is so much a part of the joy of fly fishing, whether for modest-sized trout or huge Pacific salmon, never knowing, or at least being sure, of the moment when fish and fisherman will come together.

Later, looking through my notes while waiting for my late evening, 100-minute flight back to Vancouver from Terrace, I pondered on how best to summarize my experiences on the Kitimat. The fishing had been quite wonderful, reaching its climax over the last two days, and the setting very different, and widely available to all resident and visiting licence holders, to anything associated with the Atlantic salmon rivers of Eastern Canada, Iceland, Europe and Ireland.

The town of Kitimat (population 9000) was just a small fishing village at the head of Douglas Channel before 1950. Today it is an important and growing industrial hub with a long-established aluminum smelter and the potential for the possible development of a massive and controversial liquid natural gas terminal to serve Asian markets.

It was that relationship between town and river of the same name that led me to make the connection between the residents, many of them workers in the local resource industries, and the excellent salmon and steelhead fishing that is so readily available to them in their leisure hours.

"Blue ribbon sport on a blue collar river" seems to sum it up nicely, I thought, as I prepared to travel back to Vancouver.

Tackle notes

Our rods, borrowed from our guide, were both by Sage, a TCR 9140-4 Graphite 111e and a 9141-4 Graphite 1V. Hatch Plus 9 reels were filled with 540 and 660 grain Skagit Compact line, Rio Gripshooter running lines and ample backing while the sink tips were 15 feet of T 17 finished off with 3 feet of 25-pound Maxima Ultra Green tied with a Bimini twist shock leader. At no time did we feel we were outgunned, but had a fish of say 40 pounds come along, it might have been a different story. Perhaps next time.

CASTING BACK V ...
to steelhead

←——┤

Steelhead are special

OCTOBER 1971, *Nanaimo Daily Free Press*

I suppose you could call it a conspiracy of three. Composing room colleague Gerry Smith had presented me with a box of new Spin-N-Glo lures and wasted no time in extolling the virtues of the Nanaimo River later in the year. Then Steelhead Society enthusiast Mike Pray dropped by the office by to tell me all about the Stamp River.

I was hooked good and proper but then that was a foregone conclusion for no angler in his right mind would turn down a chance to go steelhead fishing on a clear and frosty Vancouver Island morning in late October.

In fact we nearly didn't go, for Mike took to his bed Tuesday feeling anything but well and then changed his mind when he woke up much improved yesterday morning. There was a misting of snow on the hills and more on Mt. Arrowsmith with a real nip in the air and it was good to be on the move, to be out after steelhead for the first time since Victoria College student days in 1954.

Memories of the Cowichan and the Sooke long ago, and of one grand fish from the Campbell, came flooding back as we bowled merrily along. Mike's cold and cough were improving all the time in anticipation of what might lie ahead. I just couldn't wait to get started.

The upper reaches of the Stamp, beyond Port Alberni, must rate with the most attractive fishing country in BC. The river flows broad and strong, the tall trees reach for the heavens, often crowding to the very water's edge. There a man can lose himself entirely, mentally and physically, and yet know that company is not that far away.

So it went through the day to remember, one to savour in the months ahead, one that provided a word-perfect introduction to a form of freshwater fishing that will always command a special place in my affections.

Catching fish is part of the sport, but it must never be allowed to become the dominant issue. The true angler should derive just as much satisfaction from the beauty of his surroundings, from the absolute sense of freedom always associated with fishing in wild places.

To be honest I did not expect to catch anything on this first time out since my recent arrival in Nanaimo from Belfast. After all, in terms of experience, I was the novice and Mike the master. He knew the river, I didn't. He was familiar with his tackle and his lures. I was trying to recall techniques forgotten for 16 years.

Working upstream from the famed Money's Pool, we came across an unsuspecting pair of Canada geese, their startled music filling the air as they beat away on hurried wings. Still no fish until Mike's reel shrilled and a silver shape threw itself clear of the water and was gone.

He fished on. So did I. Then it happened. A boil in midstream indicated a mighty boulder and a possible lie to the left where the river's flow eased perceptibly. One cast was all it needed. The take was quick and sure and immediately the fish ran downstream, jumping as it went.

This was no record steelie. Rather a typical little summer-run fish of slightly under five pounds. Perfect in form and game to the end. In addition to being a dedicated angler I also happen to enjoy eating all kinds of fish, and this particular one, now safely frozen, will welcome my family on their arrival from Northern Ireland at the weekend.

Later another fish of almost identical proportions was brought to the bank and then released, giving equal pleasure as it recovered its balance and made off toward a deep glide where massive spring salmon were engrossed in the annual spawning ritual, a spectacle in its own right.

A third and larger fish made good its escape during the afternoon, leaving me to reflect on Mike's words of caution as he regularly checked his own leader against the risk of any fraying between lead and lure. Had I followed his advice I would have finished the day with three steelhead rather than the pair that went down in my fishing diary.

Still, I have no complaints. Rather an overall sense of satisfaction and of relief that rivers like the Stamp continue to flow as they have since time began. They have changed, of course, since the first loggers came to the Island, and I am told that the density of the steelhead run, both summer and winter, has declined over the past 15 years.

For all this the Stamp remains a river of unquestioned quality, one that must be preserved at all costs as indeed must every wilderness area in British Columbia.

Too much has been lost, has already been ruined beyond recall, but here on the Island there is still hope and much that is worth saving for future generations. Few places in the world can match Vancouver Island's visual appeal and the superb opportunities it offers for those of us who truly love the outdoors.

Before the deluge a great ripping steelhead

APRIL 2001, *www.ariverneversleeps.com*, VANCOUVER

When it rains on Vancouver Island, off Canada's west coast, it really rains. Serious rain, sweeping in relentlessly from the Pacific across and around cloud-shrouded, densely treed mountains, fills creeks and rivers to the banks and more.

The previous March day had been pleasant enough, mild with just the right mix of cloud and blue sky. Then came the overnight deluge that was to bring the Gold River up a good four feet. The water was still on the rise as we took our late afternoon leave.

What memories son Conor and I took with us to enliven the three-hour homeward drive to Nanaimo, over fast-flowing creeks and larger tributaries, winding through the forest grandeur of Strathcona Park and past the ranks of unsightly stumps that edge the shores on the hydroelectric-harnessed Upper Campbell Lake. Low water and cleared, barren slopes were a visible reminder of the unusually dry and mild winter of 2001–02. Little wonder there are already concerns about increased risk in the summer fire season ahead.

Acclaimed Canadian author Roderick Haig-Brown's riverside former home, now restored as a heritage bed-and-breakfast, was next before we left behind his beloved Campbell River, and its namesake town. Then came the Island Highway, its multi-million dollar construction having replaced for most drivers much of the previously tortuous but scenic coastal route to Victoria by way of Courtenay, Parksville, Qualicum, Nanaimo, Ladysmith and Duncan.

Along the way we spoke of the distant past, and I told Conor the story my early May, 1954 steelhead, which weighed around eight pounds and was taken on a small spoon and light line from the Campbell. For me, then a teenage college student not long from Northern Ireland, it had been a fish to treasure, one cooked and partially eaten before a restless night spent in the chilled back of a small truck. Changed times indeed but even now so easily recalled.

Our first sight of the Gold River had been all the more encouraging for the knowledge that steelhead numbers were reportedly up on last year with an increase in the average size as well. In the riverside café, beside the main highway bridge, the coffee shop talk had been notable for the English accents as a party of six fishermen, all the way from Ipswich, mapped out plans for the rest of their day. Steelhead are like that, a challenge for which no journey is too long.

The Gold has long been rated one of British Columbia's most reliable steelhead producers, a river where these magnificent migratory fish are caught in still significant numbers on both fly and lure but no longer on bait following the introduction of new regulations by the provincial government on April 1. These are wild fish so catch and release is mandatory, and the mortality rate is negligible, according to our guide, Mark McAneeley.

A full-time professional who works from a home base in Campbell River, he should know. He regards the new Vancouver Island ban on the use of any form of natural bait as a "very important" step forward. "Too many fish, especially with inexperienced bait fishermen, end up deeply hooked, and the mortality is inevitably much higher," he says.

Of course there will be those who argue against the ban, but how can they discount the rationale put forward in the synopsis of the 2001-2002 BC Freshwater Fishing regulations?

"In an effort to address steelhead, sea-run cutthroat and Dolly Varden conservation problems, the use of bait in most Vancouver Island streams is prohibited. A small number of streams will remain open to the use of bait, either seasonally or year-round. In addition, temporary stream closures and catch-and-release requirements are in place for several east coast Vancouver Island streams."

Thirty years ago, when we came as a young family to live and work in British Columbia, the Gold was rated the most productive of all Vancouver Island steelhead rivers, with an annual take of just over 2000 fish. Angling pressures were considerably lighter then, with access to the more remote rivers and lakes a major challenge. In those days, catch and release was simply not an issue, and the occasional fly fisherman was heavily outnumbered by bottom bouncers and float fishers using bait and lures fashioned from both plastic and metal.

Since then we have seen relentless and continuing growth in the popularity of fly fishing, its techniques and equipment, along with the growing realization that no fish stock, no saltwater or freshwater species, can be expected to survive unrestrained exploitation. Single, barbless hooks have long been the rule for most of the province's freshwater fisheries, and it's not that many years since the ocean salmon fishermen were also directed by law to use barb-free hooks.

The mountain-ringed community of Gold River, population now around 1,700 against a peak of 2,300 according to the municipal office, has its origins in the coastal forest industry. While recently reduced for a variety of political, economic and environmental reasons, the industry continues as a major employer.

That said, hundreds of forest-related jobs have gone over the past decade, leaving tourism and all aspects of outdoor recreation to gain significantly in appeal and importance. Steelhead fishing has to be a prime example, for it attracts devotees from all over North America and from further afield.

Our day on the Gold started well before daylight with the early-rising robins in full song while the rain cascaded down as it had through the night. Like all good guides, Mark was confident of success on a river where he spends between 30 and 50 days after steelhead each year.

The successful guide has to be knowledgeable, experienced, enthusiastic, flexible and a good communicator. Mark is all this and more. He enjoys the companionship of his guests and the opportunity to be close to the water as much now as he did in 1987. That was when he decided guiding would be his career in preference to his previous accounting-based positions.

Now his year starts by working on the Gold and other north Vancouver Island rivers including the Nimpkish and the Eve, along with helicopter outings for big cutthroat trout. In May he moves on to guide for massive chinook salmon at Langara Island Lodge, on the northern tip of the Queen Charlotte Island, now better known as Haida Gwaii.

Then comes his final change of scenery, an annual nine-week stint, starting around September 4, when he guides out of Silver Hilton Steelhead Lodge on the Babine River, a major tributary of the immense Skeena system in northern British Columbia.

As the name and location suggests, the Silver Hilton is a remote, fly-in destination for fishermen who have the resources to focus all their energies on taking, and releasing, big steelhead on a dry or waking fly. These are fish that will run into double figures, steelhead that come to large flies worked across and downstream on double-handed rods with floating lines and hefty tippets.

The rest of the year, basically December and January, is Mark's own time, set aside for family and what he describes as "personal fishing," confirming that, for him, fishing is much more than a job.

More time spent in his company would most certainly have enhanced my own limited casting abilities, would perhaps have unraveled the basics of the Single Spey, Double Spey and Snap-T casts that we watched him execute with effortless precision. On the day, he was using a 15-foot, 10-weight, four-piece Winston rod matched with an FR4 Islander reel, 10/11/12 Rio Windcutter floating line and 15-foot sink tips weighing between 200 and 400 grains, depending on flow and pool depth.

The need to get the fly down, well down, is paramount with winter-run steelhead, and for a time I felt my own equipment, a four-piece, seven-weight, 13.5-foot Sage rod, Hardy Marquis reel, floating line and 160 grain sink tip, was not up to the task. Mark was more optimistic, acknowledged that my mainly overhead technique was just about adequate for the occasion and went off to help Conor with his casting. That instruction quickly gave the steelhead learner the encouragement to start moving his fly out and across with new-found confidence.

Later I asked Conor to reflect on his first-time steelheading experience. "Casting while close in to the bank was akin to tying knots with frozen fingers," he said. "More fumbling about than getting the line to move in the right direction. Like a well hit golf ball, the casts that sail with ease and perfection seem effortless, as fluid as the stream running beneath them."

With the river rising but still fishable and with Mark's inflatable river raft giving us easy access to the pools downstream from the launching place, we settled into the rhythm of the morning. We fished two good-sized pools carefully and then, further downstream, we saw half a dozen steelhead already in position and preparing to spawn, fish that should never be disturbed by anglers.

Then on down to another holding pool, convenient to the road. This pool gave me the long-awaited chance to hook and play my first Gold River steelhead. The big moment came after both Conor and I had touched fish that came tentatively to our large flies, mine leech style and purple, Conor's one of Mark's distinctive orange-hued dressings.

Mark ties them on heavy 1/0 hooks, certain they are far more likely to provoke a response than any of the smaller, more traditional Atlantic salmon patterns in my fly box. "Perfect for summer-runs," he judged, "but useless here. You have to have a big, showy fly with lots of movement and then fish it on a level leader three or four feet in length. Anything longer and you lose the advantage of the sink tip."

When it came, the take was nothing less than a violent, slashing assault on the fly, halfway down the run and well across toward an outcropping of rock. One minute I was wading waist deep, contemplating the continuing rain and the indignity of the pinhole leak in the crotch of my waders, focused on my casting and the proximity of a tree-crowded bank to my back. The next moment there was the steelhead, jumping and jumping again as fly line and backing spun off the reel.

This was an immense fish, not in terms of its size but in the manner it came to the fly, the way it played, cartwheeling into the air at least a dozen times, and the overall power of the fight it offered in heavy water. Such heart, such determination, such a truly noble adversary.

The hook hold, in the corner of the mouth, looked to be impregnable. Eventually, the fish came into clear view at our feet, a darkening male of between 10 and 12 pounds. Mark counted it as caught, since he twice had his hand on the leader, but the camera was never out to record fish and smiling fisherman. Instead one final plunge saw knot and fly part ways at the eye of the hook as the fish made off. Too bad, but it was a great experience while it lasted.

It was time to break for lunch, for hot coffee and soup at Charlie's Family Restaurant, where the always welcoming, Turkish-born Charlie Gumustas was ready to prepare a special prime rib dinner had we been staying on for a second night.

The rest of the day was spent on the upper reaches of the river, clambering down the steepest of sodden slopes on our way to pools where the water proved to be already on the high side for the fly. Then back to the tail-out behind the golf club, but even there the chances of a taking fish were limited as the Gold, like an incoming tide, thrust itself ever further out and across the sand.

Throughout, the fishing was never easy, for this is a powerful, surging river running over a bed of boulders of all shapes and sizes that demand cautious wading. Little wonder its steelhead are of such superb quality. Anything less than perfection could not hope to survive let alone prosper.

Most certainly our day had lived up to every possible expectation. The opportunity to hook and play a wild steelhead on the fly was more than enough to encourage advance planning for a return trip next year, perhaps in March, when the chances of encountering bright fish are better. As to the rain, it was long overdue and badly needed at that.

Afterwards Mark reflected: "I reckon the best of the best of the fishing on the Gold comes between the middle of January and the end of April. I like big flies that have long, flowing hackles with plenty of action in them. The fish see them as intruders and come at them very strongly. In low water, I tie sparser dressings.

"I use a lot of marabou and rabbit strips in various colours, purple, orange, red and black, in sizes from 1/O to No. 2 and a lot smaller, down to No. 12s for the summer-runs on the Gold and the Heber. I also include a few strips of Flashabou for increased visibility. My leaders will range in length from three to four feet in winter with a breaking strain of 15 pounds. With full floating lines I use tapered leaders up to 12 feet long with 10/12-pound tippets.

"The majority of my winter steelhead are taken on bright orange flies, but it always pays to go through a pool trying two or three different colours. In high water, the fish will be lying mid-pool and down to the tail. When the water is lower, look for them in the runs at the head of the pool. In winter fishing, you have to use a sink tip, and it's important to have very sharp hooks. I like Eagle Claw Lasersharps with a downturned eye. These sink well and are strong enough to hold a big fish. I also like Tiemco heavy wire hooks with upturned eye in sizes No. 2 to 2/0."

←———

The steelhead – BC's most noble fish

FEBRUARY 2006, UNPUBLISHED PAPER FOR *The Greater Georgia Basin Steelhead Recovery Program*, NANAIMO

"No other fish chooses a better meeting ground for himself and the angler than does the summer steelhead. The young streams of Vancouver Island and the mainland coast are incomparably, heroically beautiful clear water between tall trees, lost from sight at a little distance, yet world filling when one is by its side."

Roderick Haig-Brown – *The Western Angler*

They come home in the dark of a winter's night or in the early dawn of a warm summer's day. Each year their arrival is awaited and welcomed in small towns and cities across the province as well as by expectant visitors from afar. Their contribution to our provincial tourist economy is significant, especially in many smaller communities, while their relationship with our environment is a key indicator of its continuing health and well-being.

They are found from Haida Gwaii, previously known as the Queen Charlotte Islands, south to the Fraser and its tributaries, in a multitude of rivers and streams along the length of our North Pacific coastline and all around Vancouver Island. They make their way deep into the heart of the chilled northern regions of the province and through the desert country that defines the southern Interior.

These are the steelhead of British Columbia, to many sport fishermen the most precious, most highly regarded of all our game fish. More than any other single species, the steelhead – *Oncorhynchus mykiss* to the scientific community – represents the very best of sport fishing in this province.

The angler marvels at the steelhead's wide distribution, its strength and stamina and its impressive size. Some of the rivers of the incomparable Skeena system are famous for producing occasional steelhead weighing in excess of 30 pounds, superb specimens three feet and more in length from nose to tail. No other country, anywhere in the world, can make a similar claim, for these are the largest of them all.

To the fisherman, and in particular to the man or woman who uses an artificial fly to deceive his or her quarry, they are trophies beyond any price, fish that in this more enlightened era are quickly photographed and then released immediately, hopefully none the worse for the experience.

They are native to the wildest of rivers, pass through deep canyons, surmount foaming falls, undertake spawning journeys that can extend over hundreds of miles and, in some cases, set aside the need to feed for months on end.

When it comes to measuring incomparable beauty, the mature steelhead, bright from the sea, is truly a treasure. It represents the finest possible example of Nature at her brilliant best, without question the most noble of all this province's many fish species.

The visiting angler envies the resident British Columbian for the diversity of opportunities the steelhead provide, from the remote streams of Haida Gwaii to the more convenient watersheds of the Lower Mainland and Vancouver Island. These are easily accessible rivers, open to all legal forms of rod and line fishing and to anyone with the required provincial freshwater licence and conservation surcharge stamp.

Of course, the steelhead rivers of British Columbia have been famous around the world for well over 100 years. The bigger waters have reputations in keeping with their size and the quality of fishing they can provide. The Bulkley, the Morice, the Kispiox, the Babine, the Copper and the Sustut are the pride of the Skeena system.

The summer fishing on the more remote Dean is special to many, while farther south, the mighty Thompson demands respect for the physical challenges it presents and the so-powerful fish for which it is renowned. Sadly, its numbers have dwindled to the point where there are valid concerns for the very survival of the species in that particular watershed.

Fishermen in the Lower Mainland place much emphasis on the Vedder-Chilliwack, while on Vancouver Island, the Cowichan, the Stamp, the Gold and the Campbell hold positions of pride in British Columbia angling lore. The Campbell was made world-famous by the writings of Roderick Haig-Brown, and his friend, retired Brigadier General Noel Money, cherished a broad pool on the Stamp that bears his name to this day. No fisherman could ever ask for a better remembrance.

As for those anglers who look to the smaller, less well-known streams for their sport, they tend to cherish their secret spots in the hopes that they will remain largely unknown and unspoiled.

In many other countries, and even elsewhere in Canada, with some of the Atlantic salmon rivers of Quebec a case in point, freshwater fishing of this overall quality and variety would not be available to the general public. Instead, private interests would have the controlling rights.

Through the years, established fishing writers, among them Haig-Brown, John F. Fennelly, Trey Combs, Barry M. Thornton, Mike Cramond, Lee Straight, Art Lingren and Karl Bruhn, have all paid homage to the steelhead trout of British Columbia. Their words provide a lasting tribute to this marvellous fish, one that surely deserves more formal recognition by a province of Canada already famous for the sport fishing opportunities it provides.

While past reputations are of importance there are now pressing concerns about the overall health and future of certain fisheries. For a decade or more there has been a marked decline in the number of steelhead counted each year in many rivers that empty into to the Georgia Basin, both on the mainland side and on Vancouver Island's east coast.

Programs are in place to address the issue and remedial actions are being undertaken through the Greater Georgia Basin Steelhead Recovery Plan, launched in 2002, and supported by an annual investment of approximately $1.2 million from provincial government and other sources – notably the Habitat Conservation Trust Fund. But this is not nearly enough. We must do more!

More than half a century has passed since Roderick Haig-Brown, passionate fisherman, conservationist and inspired author, voiced the concerns of his generation when he wrote: "I know that neither hatcheries nor biologists, nor all the thought and ingenuity of man can put them back when once they've gone."

Even then, the steelhead of British Columbia were facing daunting pressures on all sides. Pressure came from the commercial salmon fleet, from thoughtless logging and mining practices, from damaged and polluted urban waterways and from a steadily increasing number of sport fishermen who had yet to recognize the value of today's catch and release ethic.

Times have changed. While the original problems are being

addressed, it is now widely accepted that some wild steelhead stocks face a new and perhaps more uncertain future. For reasons still not fully understood, ocean survival rates for the immature fish have declined significantly for the province's most southern stocks since the mid-1990s.

Instead of 10 to 15 mature fish coming back to spawn from every 100 smolts entering the ocean two to three years before, only two to four have been returning to complete the cycle of renewal. At this level of ocean survival many populations are now judged at conservation risk. Climate change is the probable cause, and it is affecting freshwater habitats as well.

For this reason, the primary objective of the Georgia Basin Recovery Plan is: "to stabilize and restore wild steelhead stocks and habitats to healthy self-sustaining levels. Wild stocks in most systems will not recover unless their freshwater productivity can be significantly increased to compensate for cyclical reductions in marine survival."

In total, 58 high priority watersheds have been identified on the east coast of Vancouver Island and in the Lower Mainland. Plans are in place to ensure that individual steelhead runs in these watersheds, each one significant to the province's rich biodiversity, are given every possible opportunity to survive and thrive.

Making the viability of these watersheds and stocks a priority can generate widespread public support. We all must recognize both the steelhead's value as a sport fish icon and sentinel of environmental quality and the need for enhanced stewardship at a time of extreme conservation challenge.

Recognition of the steelhead as British Columbia's official fish emblem would be a significant step forward in the drive to guarantee not only its long-term future, but also the future of all the other creatures that share the streams and rivers of British Columbia.

No refusing Babine invitation

WINTER 2006, *Fly Fusion*, CALGARY

Fly Fusion *Editor's note:* "Fly Fusion *normally refrains from pub-lishing articles that are destination specific because we are an instruction and information-based magazine. Even though this piece focuses on British Columbia's Babine River, it is far more than a destination piece. It reveals that if various individuals and groups are willing to work together toward a common vision, fly fishing for steelhead will not be something we merely tell our children about, but will be an activity that we can continue to participate in with our grandchildren.*"

It was one of those experiences blessed from the outset in so many different ways. In hindsight it seems my stars were in perfect alignment, for Pierce and Anita Clegg's invitation to spend time on the Babine River was something very special.

After all, this famed Skeena tributary, one of only five Class One rivers in British Columbia, is numbered among the world's truly great steelhead waters. To this day it's capable of producing fish weighing well over 30 pounds and just possibly over 40 pounds. It also has limited access and conservation-based catch and release regulations that attract the most discerning fly fishermen.

The second week in September saw the Cleggs' Babine Norlakes Fall Steelhead Camp open again for the nine-week 2006 season with ten rods in residence, all but myself hailing from south of the border, a representative group from across the continent, the majority with fly-fishing pedigrees as long as your proverbial arm. The fact that many are regulars, returning year after year, only served to heighten the sense of anticipation, confirmation that this could be a week to remember.

Before the two-hour early morning drive from the pleasant, Alpine-themed community of Smithers to our pickup point on the river, Pierce had warned of low water conditions. His view was that another 18 inches to two feet of water would have made for near-perfect fishing prospects, but he was confident the first steelhead of the year had already journeyed over 270 miles up the Skeena and into the Babine on their way to their spring spawning destinations not that far from the camp.

The majority of these wild, summer-run fish will have spent three years in fresh water and another two years at sea before returning to spawn for the first time in their sixth year. Many will weigh well into double figures and others will be smaller. Some, on their second and even third spawning run, are much larger, a mixed age population that speaks well for the overall health of the stock. They will overwinter in the chilled upper reaches before spawning in April and May, in the river below Nilkitkwa Lake and in a number of its tributaries, many of them the tiniest of streams.

In early September over the past five years, the river, backed by the 110-mile-long Babine Lake, recorded discharges from 2165 cubic feet per second in 2002 to 1398 cubic feet per second in 2005. In the same week in 2006, the flow, from a drainage area extending over an area of 2610 square miles, was between 841 and 739 cubic feet per second, the lowest for many, many years. Happily, the Babine still presented itself as a river of considerable proportions with more than enough water to satisfy the needs of some pretty serious fly fishers.

This was my first surprise, for Pierce's talk of low water had left me drawing comparisons with my local Vancouver Island rivers in the summer of '06. They had shrunk to a point where they were no longer attractive to fishermen let alone inviting to the salmon waiting offshore for the fall rains. The Babine, with more and more big rocks starting to show, presented an increasing challenge to our guides in their jet boats, but the steelhead were still well served in terms of flow and cover.

The warm weather (and there was no hint of the frosts, and sometime snow, that can enliven the angler's daily mix in October and early November) did influence the fishing in another way. The Nilkitkwa River, which is not linked to the lake of the same name, joins the Babine just upstream of the camp. It's glacial in origin, and unseasonably high temperatures had led to a thaw and reduced water clarity in the main river for the first few days.

At times I could hardly see my wading boots in less than three feet of water, but this proved no deterrent to the steelhead. And yes, they had arrived on time and in sufficient numbers to keep us all fully focused. Not everyone's expectations were realized in terms of fish caught and released, but interest and effort never flagged. Some 100 steelhead were brought to hand during the week.

This was actually a below average return, based on previous years' records, with the blame laid at the door of an even longer than usual commercial net season that saw 44 active days out of a possible 71. Imagine what the fishing would be like on the rivers of the Skeena system if a way could be found to spare all steelhead from the ravages of the annual sockeye fishery.

We soon found most if not all the early run was spread out over the more than 50 named pools, runs, glides, and riffles that lie between the camp – where the so-convenient Ejnar's Pool can be a popular and often productive start and finish point – and the aptly named Bill's Last Cast, some 14 miles downriver. Along the way lies a quite wonderful assortment of superb fly-fishing opportunities and challenges.

It's picture-perfect steelhead habitat with pools of all shapes and sizes, ranging from the huge to the intimate, runs that are easily waded and boulder-rich streams where every cautious step forward is an adventure. There are places where the ever-present, fall-coloured forest of spruce, pine and cottonwood crowds the shoreline leaving the expert Spey caster in his element. Then there are the more open spots where even the most wayward back cast will go largely unpunished.

This is wild, uncrowded, wilderness country. Jet boats are the only practical means of transportation, both for the visiting fishermen and for the day-to-day needs of the rustic and welcoming Norlakes camp, then in its 45th year, and of the Babine Steelhead Lodge, some three miles further downstream. During the short season the two operations work to an agreed daily routine, making the best use of all the available water with no sense of crowding or overfishing on any particular stretch.

As it happened, we were fortunate to have the river to ourselves for that first week. The other lodge opened just after we left. Not that the presence of another dozen rods would have been a problem. The scale of this fishery is such that there is ample room for all, while its remote location means very limited opportunities for the casual visitor. A jet boat is almost an essential, as is precise knowledge of the river and its many hidden hazards, and few relish the prospect of pitching tent in a watershed famous for a healthy and often visible grizzly population of between 75 and 100 animals.

While some of my fellow fishermen enjoyed multiple sightings of both adult grizzlies and cubs, I had to be satisfied with fairly frequent encounters with fresh and impressively large overnight tracks in the damp sand at the water's edge. They left me acutely aware of my surroundings, more especially on those occasions when I was fishing by myself. As a precaution, everyone carries bear spray and bangers, all returned unused at the end of the week.

With guiding duties entrusted to Pierce, Darren Wright and Paul Robinson we never lacked for expert advice. We fishermen were rotated on a daily basis to the upper, middle and lower stretches, with the details posted outside the camp's spacious dining area at the start of the trip. This is a fine way to meet new friends, to savour the pleasures derived from unspoiled surroundings, a great river and its famed steelhead.

Over the course of the week I saw not one piece of garbage, no discarded line, cans or plastic packaging: overhead no planes, no throbbing helicopters, no vapour trails etched across the mainly blue sky. When the jet boat moves away, the silence is broken only by the sounds of the river, while moulted eagle feathers and decaying salmon carcasses are Nature's acceptable discards.

We fished long and hard, for seven and more hours each day, and I count myself fortunate to have been able to release at least one steelhead every day, from 25 to 33 inches with one even larger, along with perhaps half a dozen good-sized but dark, red-flanked chinook. The salmon, discounted by some, came strongly to the fly, a thrill in itself each time, and fought with admirable vigour on a seven-weight, 13 1/2-foot double-hander.

You may question why I would be so satisfied with a one-fish day, and I'll give you a simple answer: It was a steelhead. I need say no more, for to hook and play a steelhead on a fly has to be as good as it gets. Compared to my previous experiences in Ireland and Scotland, these Babine fish are definitely stronger, more resolute, than like-sized Atlantic salmon caught on identical tackle in similar water conditions.

My first one, from Lower Trail, was something of a fluke, for it fell to an ugly Pink Leech at the closest possible quarters, the take coming just as I was starting to lengthen line in readiness for the next cast. In retrospect, I think the fly must have dropped straight into the unfortunate steelhead's mouth. Afterwards, I had three almost successive and deliberate touches from the same spot in mid-river, but never once did the loop of floating line in my right hand draw tight to signal a likely hookup. Later, Paul suggested a change of fly and from then on through to the last morning, I fished only one pattern on a 15-foot clear intermediate sink tip and six feet of 12-pound test leader.

That fly, a #2 Edgebrite Boss, served me well. I landed three fish on two different days and lost four more through the week when the hook pulled out after an appreciable time. The best of them came two days after I had the good fortune to be drawn with two other guests for an overnight stay at the camp's quaint satellite cabin, hidden in the forest beside the long, deep pool that is Beaver Flats.

The evening was prolonged and social, with red wine to accompany fine steaks cooked over an open fire as the sky filled with stars, but we still made an early start the next day. Around mid-morning, after time well spent on the Flats while the others ventured further downstream, I was dropped off at a pool called Lower Chicken with directions to fish it slowly and carefully down and through the breaking water at the tail-out.

I did just that and was soon rewarded with one of those epic, crashing, spray-flying takes for which steelhead are rightly famous. In a second the big fish was across to the far bank jumping, jumping as I watched in awestruck admiration. Eventually patient pressure told and it was on its side in the shallows, safely photographed and released. A bright, impressively proportioned hen with characteristic pink-blushed gill covers, it measured 36 x 19.5 inches, or a little over 18 pounds by the long-established Babine weight vs. girth and length formula.

In a lifetime of fly-fishing opportunities, few if any fish have given me greater pleasure. Had Darren been on hand with his landing net, my steelhead would have been on her way a few minutes earlier. Instead, I had the satisfaction of starting and finishing the job by myself before standing back to reflect quietly on a priceless fishing moment.

On the final morning, with much improved visibility and the water temperature still in the high 50s F, I had my introduction to fishing a very large, waking dry fly, a pink-tailed, deer hair Bomber tied on a #5/0 hook.

The first fish must have followed halfway across Allen's Pool, for it showed right below me with an audible and visible surge just as I was lifting off. The second boiled beneath but did not take the fly on the dead drift further down before a third came with a rush at the swinging fly and was as quickly away. Exciting beyond words and enough to show me why so many steelheaders use no other tactic and believe this to be the most appropriate approach to these cherished fish.

Through the week there were tales of fish hooked and fish lost. "I just held on with both hands and hoped," said Bob Mason at one point as the new Babine season gathered momentum. Some of the regulars did well on dry Bombers. Loren Irving, from Bend, Oregon, released one 39-inch beauty, while others relied on sunk patterns with the Green Butt Skunk a particular favourite. Three of us swore by our identical, four-piece double handers, and we admired some great Spey casting, for our guides were true masters of this popular and graceful technique.

Perhaps all this helps explain why ardent fly fishermen from across the world travel every year to the rivers of the Skeena system. It also explains why the people most closely involved with the Babine hold such a deep affection for all it represents that they work tirelessly to ensure it is protected from various and diverse threats to its long-term well-being. These threats range from expanded forestry and road-building to commercial fishing; from proposed Skeena estuary fish farms and the associated threat posed by sea lice to migrating smolts to the continuing illegal hunting of grizzlies.

Four years ago, the owners of the three lodges that operate on the river came together to establish the Babine River Foundation with the theme "There's only one Babine." In support, guests gladly pay a $250 surcharge that helps fund the continuing work of the Smithers-based Babine Watershed Monitoring Trust. This was established early in 2005 as a partnership between the foundation and the provincial government, which contributes one dollar for every two dollars raised by visiting fly fishermen, who already have contributed well over $100,000.

The Babine Trust monitors the government's land use plans for the area's natural resources, taking into consideration the best interests of the river, its fish and wildlife and the surrounding environment. The five unpaid trustees are governed by the trust agreement and do not represent the stakeholders or settlors. These include three government ministries, the local forest industry, the foundation and the community, all now committed to work as one in the best interests of the watershed.

In 2006, the foundation funded projects that included studies of stream crossing impacts, water quality in relation to stream crossings, the wilderness values of the Babine River Corridor and the development of partnership proposals. The foundation has also been able to support local First Nations with territories in the watershed.

Pierce, a vocal and effective advocate for the river, took over the Norlakes trout and steelhead operations in 1986 and makes the point that without stewardship and responsible conservation, the future will be bleak. "The tragedy of the commons is a tough legacy to fight in our human existence but I prefer to go down fighting even if the fight is not winnable," he says.

It's a fight that has to be won, for steelhead numbers across British Columbia are far removed from what they were 30 and 40 years ago. The Babine is a provincial and a national treasure, a river where fishermen's dreams become realities, where a true wilderness experience is still there to be enjoyed, where the steelhead and the salmon, the grizzlies, the wolves, the moose, the beavers, the eagles and all the other abundant wildlife live as they have always lived. Why would anyone do anything to deny them that right?

←————┤

Steelheading in heaven

NOVEMBER 2010, *Chasing Silver Magazine*, FINLAND

Skeena system steelhead, stunning in appearance, impressive in size and always resolute in their resistance to the fisherman's fly, were increasingly well-distributed throughout the watershed by late August of 2010.

On the Babine River the stock was as good as, or perhaps even better than, it has ever been at the start of the season, which runs from early September until British Columbia's harsh northern winter closes in again around mid-November.

I can't speak from personal experience, but as the season progressed, I am sure the story was the same from rivers like the Morice, the Kispiox, the Bulkley and the Sustut, all well-regarded parts of the same system, all with their own dedicated following. I do know the Kispiox was very, very low in September, while the Bulkley suffered from a flood that brought high, dirty water and limited mid-month fishing opportunities.

It was my good fortune to be on the upper part of the Babine for the second week of September along with five other guests at the famous Norlakes Steelhead Camp, built by the pioneering Ejnar Madsen more than 40 years ago. (See "Strom's letters from Ejnar," page 283.) Over seven days we experienced steelhead fishing of a quality that has to rate with the best of its kind anywhere in the world – a pristine wilderness watershed, an abundance of fish, perfect river and weather conditions and more water, miles and miles of it, than six fly rods could ever hope to adequately cover in seven days.

Then there was the wildlife: bald eagles everywhere, and two grizzly bear families, mothers with well grown two-year-old cubs, fishing for dying salmon within sight of camp, and a huge male out in mid-river as we started out one morning.

For current camp owner Pierce Clegg, guides Darren Wright and Josh Nowlin and camp cook Larry Hartwell – "we don't do small, Peter" – and his right-hand man Joel Nowlin, it was the perfect start to the Clegg family's 25th season at the riverside camp and rustic cabins.

My cozy home for the week was Steelhead Paradise, and second-year cabin partner Doug Machuk, from Banff, Alberta, was quick to agree that the very name had to be a positive omen. We both knew it was back in 1963 that John F. Fennelly, the American author and investment banker, wrote his now seminal book of the same name. *Steelhead Paradise* (1963, Mitchell Press Ltd., Vancouver, BC) is generally credited with establishing the reputation and future potential of the then largely unknown Skeena River system.

Fennelly's verdict on the Babine, following his own early season disappointments but balanced by enthusiastic reports from friends, indicated: "I am ready to agree that the Babine must be a magnificent steelhead river if fished at the right time of year." That judgment most certainly holds good today, and it's worth adding the estimated Skeena escapement numbers in the 10 years to 1965, the period encompassed by Fennelly's writings, were significantly below those of more recent times, with only 1962 approaching 25,000 fish.

Four previous visits to the Babine, all during the same opening week, had left me with an excellent sense of the present-day fishery and the heights it can achieve given optimum conditions from arrival to departure. Named pools easily recognized and remembered, successes and setbacks recalled. Each previous trip had its highlight moments but none can ever match those of 2010.

We live in an era when the importance of and need for conservation is widely recognized and valued, and steelhead fishing is increasingly accepted as being more about the totality of the experience than the exact number of fish brought to hand.

The week's results, in terms of fish landed, were quite outstanding, all the more so when you consider that as many fish again were raised without making contact or hooked, played and then lost, either at the very outset of the contest or after a prolonged encounter. My own experiences on two different pools attest to this. In both cases I had a substantial steelhead on for a time before the hook hold simply let go. We quickly discounted such disappointments as the next opportunity came along. It was that sort of unforgettable week.

This was the year when all the pieces so essential to the fulfillment of any angler's dreams came together in one glorious, extended steelhead fishing festival. We seemed to encounter fish in every pool we fished, the majority of them of double-figure stature and a few running close to or exceeding 20 pounds.

For the Babine, that's not an exceptional size. Specimens much closer to and over 30 pounds are recorded every year. Not very many, for sure, for these are indeed hard-won trophies, but their presence is beyond dispute and a magnet that helps bring fishermen back again and again.

The level of the river, running at around 1130 cubic feet per second and dropping back a little every day, was judged to be as near perfect as makes no matter, while the visibility was all that a steelheader could ever wish for, with just enough colour in the water to offer the recently arrived fish some added sense of security.

Add to the mix seven days of perfect weather with just one brief thunder shower, mild enough to get down to shirt sleeves in the middle of the day but not warm enough to prompt the Nilkitkwa, a major tributary that joins the main river just upstream of the camp, to add any extra colour from a thaw high in its glacial origins.

The discerning fly fisherman could ask for nothing better. Floating lines, long leaders tapered to 12 or 15 pounds, and flies fished on or just sub-surface were the preferred approach throughout the week. The steelhead, too, were on their best behaviour, often visible holding in surprisingly shallow water as the jet boats idled their way downstream, giving us opportunity after opportunity to fish a succession of pools for the first time that day.

The boats, incidentally, are used only to move the anglers from place to place on the river. The actual fishing involves wading and casting with, for the most part, double-handed rods and a single fly tied on a barbless hook. It's all catch and release for an entirely wild stock, and the two lodges on the upper river follow a self-imposed fly only policy. The second lodge was due to open a week later, so we had the entire upper river to ourselves.

The traditional daily routine, unchanging over the years, sees morning coffee and hot chocolate brought to the cabins by Pierce and his colleagues at 7:00 a.m., with the next hour featuring

Breakfast by Larry, always superbly hearty, along with lunch box preparations from a well-laden table of cold cuts, fruit and a variety of high calorie delights.

Then it's time to tackle up, pull on waders, boots and jackets ready for another day on the upper, middle or lower reaches. The rotating fishing arrangement works well and gives each fisherman the opportunity to fish as much water as possible and to learn from the personable, knowledgeable guides.

Pierce and Darren Wright can reflect on many years of Babine and more general steelhead experience, while Josh, a lifetime angler from a family of fishermen, is enjoying his first professional guiding season. He previously worked in camp with Larry, looking after the guests and making the most of whatever fishing opportunities might come his way.

Toward the end of the week as I prepared to fish down a pool just one more time, Josh made my day when he offered good advice and what he described as a "trouty looking" home-tied fly on a smallish hook, certainly no larger than a No. 6. Earlier, he knew, I had parted company at the same spot with a good, hard-running fish after it had grabbed one of Darren's special Intruders, a much larger offering.

Perhaps what followed had something to do with the fact that there was an ongoing hatch of small mayflies and sedges just then. Maybe the fish, and we have to assume there are times when they do feed in fresh water, were keyed on the mayfly nymphs or perhaps they were simply reminded of their earlier years as always-hungry smolts.

Whatever the explanation, Josh's suggestion was precisely the right fly and the right moment. I hooked four steelhead in the 10- to 14-pound range, landing all but one in the space of a magical hour.

The first two came in mid-river to a conventional swung fly worked through deep, streamy water, the others from a slower moving seam on the right with the fly allowed to drift naturally on a slack, floating line that only straightened on the take. In both these instances the hook set was deep in the mouth of the fish, suggesting, to me at least, a very deliberate feeding response.

We live and learn and all credit to Josh for his perceptive, possibly instinctive, reading of the situation. I also took note of his "wait for the weight" and "think outside the box, think inside the stream" advice. Sound words of wisdom for any steelhead fisherman.

In a sense those four fish came as redemption for what had happened to me on the same pool a year before. The steelhead on that occasion was much, much more than I could manage, a really massive buck with a double red stripe along its flanks, clearly seen as it came into view in deep water near the tail-out. How big was it? My guide's estimate was in the high twenties to low thirties. To me it was simply huge, an image that will be with me for as long as I go fishing.

It was, by a long way, the largest fish I have ever hooked on a fly and one that promptly turned and raced far downstream before the inevitable parting of the ways. Reeling back all that line and backing was indeed a humbling experience. More backing, a lot more, might have helped but I doubt it. It was simply not to be, but at least I know I had my one chance at what was a truly great Babine steelhead.

On later reflection, the 2010 trip approached steelhead fishing overload. The true worth of the experience came into focus only after the passage of time. I know this had to be my week of weeks, one where brilliant mental images will serve to brighten the longest, darkest days of winter. Pierce was right when he described this year's fishing as "steelheading in heaven."

Dave Hall: American angling treasure

MAY 2011, *Chasing Silver Magazine*, FINLAND

In conversation one day, Dave Hall described himself as "a blue collar artist who gets up in the morning and throws paint around," but he is much more than that.

Relaxing with his teacher wife Lisa in their cozy two-storey log home, within sight and sound of Oregon's captivating North Umpqua River, he is a man at ease with himself. His is a life that has brought him considerable personal satisfaction as a family man, respected fishing illustrator, expert fly fisherman and most knowledgeable guide on a truly famous steelhead watershed.

The North Umpqua, translucent green and inviting the previous day but now heavily discoloured and on the rise after a night of pounding rain, has been Dave's home river for years. He knows it with a rare level of intimacy.

As our host, friend and guide he was anxious to reveal to Pierce Clegg and myself some of the river's secrets and perhaps even a sight, even a fleeting contact, with a cherished winter steelhead. It was not to be, but no matter. We were there and going fishing, regardless.

Thirty miles of forest-clad, fly only river are easily accessible from his home by way of a narrow, winding climbing road. It had all seemed so hopeful the previous evening as we once more toasted Dave's wonderful artistic contribution to our recently published book *Babine*.

The acclaimed British Columbia steelhead river had brought us together in the first place, Pierce and Dave more than a quarter of a century ago, Dave and myself in the mid-2000s when we shared a rustic cabin and a memorable week's fishing on the Babine at the Clegg family's historic Norlakes Steelhead Camp.

Not for the first time we all agreed there is nothing better than when old fishing friends come together after a lengthy time apart. Email contacts, however frequent, can never take the place of dining table stories to be told and plans to be laid' while family and fishing news is shared.

An opportunity to experience one of the most highly regarded of all American steelhead rivers had been an added incentive for me to undertake the 1100 mile (1770 km) road trip from Vancouver Island, south through Seattle and Portland and on along the thunderous urgency of the mile-a-minute I-5 freeway. Pierce, in turn, took a flying detour on his way home to Smithers and winter-gripped northern BC following a family visit to San Francisco.

We met up at Eugene Airport and drove on toward Glide and the Halls' hospitality. Once off the freeway, we took our time and enjoyed a peaceful back road along the lower river, through rolling cattle ranch land and past clumps of still leafless oak trees hung with trailing moss and mistletoe. We encountered just three or four vehicles over the last 20 miles of our journey, in sharp contrast to the hectic three- and four-lane pace of the freeway. We were truly entering an altogether different, more relaxed world.

Glide, with fewer than 2000 residents, holds its famous river in high regard, and the first-time visitor has to be impressed with the way the fishery is managed. Highway pull-offs and trails are clearly marked, and interpretive signage is provided at all the most popular locations.

When the time comes to put a fly in the water, the accepted North Umpqua tradition is to give precedence to the angler in possession of a particular pool or run. There are always other accessible spots to fish further along the way, and crowding is simply not how the game is played by those who respect the traditional niceties of fly-fishing etiquette.

In fact the Steamboat Inn, a historic riverside watering hole, even goes to the lengths of printing a card on Stream Fishing Etiquette for its guests. It notes: "A true angler goes fishing not only to catch fish but also to enjoy Nature's gift of pure, clear water, the forest and all the creatures who live in them." The message concludes: "A true angler practises catch and release in order to conserve the fishery." We need more of this thinking across North America, both to the north and the south of the border between our two countries.

As it happened, that weekend we were able to join more than 80 members and guests of the local Steamboaters steelhead conservation organization at their annual winter get-together in nearby Roseburg. Bill McMillan, longtime outspoken steelhead advocate and author of the classic *Dry Line Steelhead and Other Subjects* (1988, Frank Amato, Portland, OR), was the guest speaker and left us all with much to think about when he described steelhead populations in the USA today as "merely a remnant." I could only reflect on my good fortune to be a resident of British Columbia, where at least some of our river systems still support healthy runs of these magnificent fish.

We knew the North Umpqua had been running at 1400 cubic feet per second over the previous week, but overnight it came up to around 1900. Not too high to fish by any means but spoiled by the colour of the snowmelt and rain runoff, quickly limiting visibility to a matter of inches in all but the distant upper reaches. Dave drives his veteran "fishmobile" with the relaxed confidence of a man who has travelled the same road a thousand times and more, so he took us far upriver on both days.

Despite the rain and the chilling sleet, the scenery was spectacular. It did not take much to imagine the North Umpqua in its lush summer finery, its pools and runs clear as glass, its shading vegetation in full leaf, its summer-run steelhead poised mid-water, waiting to pounce on a skated dry fly or perhaps a sunken nymph presented on a floating line and long, tapered leader.

Looking back to the 1980s, to the days when Dave was guiding for upwards of 120 days a year on the river, Trey Combs, in his wonderful book, *STEELHEAD Fly Fishing* (1991, Lyons and Burford, New York, NY), explains how our good friend came to rely heavily on "buggy" patterns when the standard, more traditional tyings weren't working.

He goes on to quote Dave as saying: "The Hammerdown October Caddis and the Golden Stonefly are patterns I have been using for trout for years with great success. I just enlarged them to accommodate steelhead and varied some techniques in their presentation.

"The Flashback Nymph was a fairly standard, all-purpose nymph pattern. As with the Hammerdowns, I enlarged it and used some pearl Flashabou to give it sparkle.... all the flies use a soft hackle that, when wet, makes for a lot of movement and a great silhouette. The silhouette is the key. It is far more important in clear water than colour."

Combs's book has to be required reading for any aspiring steelheader or indeed for any fisherman with an interest in the still-developing history of steelhead fishing. The book runs to almost 500 pages, with 15 chapters devoted to specific and highly regarded steelhead watersheds, both in Canada and the USA. His 21-page North Umpqua chapter provides fascinating insights into its history, its biology and its personalities, and these include such famous American fishing names as Zane Grey and Clarence Gordon.

While we Canadians had come to explore and enjoy all aspects of one of America's finest steelhead streams, we had also come to learn more about Dave Hall, the fishing artist whose work and reputation is known from coast to coast.

This is his story, in his own words: "I was born in Los Angeles in 1948 and lived in the San Fernando Valley until I was 14 or 15. In 1964 the family decided to move to Oregon, and I have been here ever since. We came from Los Angeles, and you know what a huge city that is, to a small town on the main Umpqua River called Elkton with a population of 143 people.

"I have lived all over the state, on the coast and in the central part as well. I eventually came back to the North Umpqua in 1980, met my wife Lisa, settled down in Glide, started a family and went to work guiding. In 1983 I began on a part-time basis with Umpqua Feather Merchants, world-famous in fly-tying circles.

"I had been pursuing my artistic career in the winter and guiding on the river in the summer. Later the work became full-time and I stayed around until 2008 when they moved the business to Colorado. We had two children in school and did not want to leave our home.

"The quality control supervisory job with Umpqua led to a number of opportunities in the artistic world. My fishing art finally had a market as I had access to all kinds of manufacturers, magazines and publishers. As soon as they got to see my work, things kind of snowballed.

"When I got out of college I had a Bachelor of Fine Arts degree from the University of Oregon and immediately started to go into contemporary art, entering various competitions and doing things around the state and in Washington and California. At that time I was doing a lot of representational art and a lot of abstract art.

"That went on for approximately ten years. Then I decided I would try something different for a change and I wound up doing a small set of watercolours of rainbow trout. I fished all the time and thought *Why am I not doing with my art what I am experiencing almost every day?*

"It was a set of three trout and my brother was absolutely enamored with the pictures and bought them. Then a friend of his saw them and it went from there. Somebody else wanted a set and another set sold and so on. At that time I was still doing my contemporary art and some abstract work, but I was trained as a realist painter too.

"Once you start doing outdoor work a deer has to look like a deer and a steelhead has to look like a steelhead. Soon I found I was selling a lot more work than when I was doing the abstracts, so the change in direction was for both economic and artistic reasons.

"One of the things you learn as an artist, whether you are a writer or a musician or a dancer, or anyone in the creative field, is that you mature and, if you are on the right track, you realize how much work you have to do to be successful.

"It's a 40 to 50 hour a week job. I get up at six in the morning and sit down to work at seven. Some days I have really good days and some days I don't paint particularly well for whatever reason, but you have to stick with it. You have days when everything is great and a week later you are cruising along and nothing is working.

"There is a reason I have diversified so much, and my work includes watercolours, oils, acrylics and pen and ink. Some artists don't work like this, but you have to remember I live in a very rural area and my career would probably be a lot further along living in a metropolitan setting where I would have a much bigger market.

"My problem is that where I live, everything I do, I have to ship out to other places. I can't just walk into a publisher a mile away and say 'here I am.' Everything has to be packaged up and sent off by mail.

"I have been very fortunate to be able to do lots of different things. The very first book I illustrated I did for nothing. It was for an established publisher and it was a book by a well-known author on terrestrial flies and fishing patterns representing beetles and ants and so on. They had two illustrators for the book and their budget was gone.

"I had become good friends with the author Harrison Steeves, and at the end of my letters to him, I would add little drawings of insects and bugs. He told the publisher that he thought I would be able to do the job, drawing crickets and ants and grasshoppers and the like. The publisher called me up and said 'my author would really like you to do some insects for the book.'

"I thought it might lead on to something else, and 27 books later I have been blessed not only with opportunities to work on all these books but also for many different fishing magazines, for various book publishers and art directors as well as for local and distant art galleries and private buyers.

"It all has to be done professionally. It has to be on time and each piece has to be what the client expects. You can't turn anything down. Once you refuse one job you are toast so I have taken on everything, from how to prepare smoked meat to how to tie Bimini Twists for a book by Lefty Kreh on fishing knots. One of the things to my advantage is that for a lot of these books, I was one of the first illustrators who is actually a fisherman.

"The publishers didn't have to explain it to me. My knots were always right, my river scenes were always right, my fisherman's arms were always right. Sometimes illustrators, who aren't involved in these activities, do it so that the fish don't look like fish and the anglers don't look like anglers. That has allowed me to lend credibility to what I have done because I am a fisherman.

"That's really important. You may have seen my fishing work and my passion for it. It's simply what I know. I remember I had an art teacher who always recalled a great line from Pablo Picasso: 'You paint and draw what you know, not what you see.' You have to know what you are doing and you have to know your subject.

"I remember an illustrator that had to do a picture of an American football running back for a really exclusive sports magazine. He did a beautiful painting but he put the wrong number on his jersey. That was because he did not know anything about football. The number was that of a lineman and not a running back; the magazine was appalled and simply could and would not publish the illustration.

"I am so lucky to have been able to fish the North Umpqua for more than half my lifetime and also to be an artist. I was single for a long time in my life, and I don't say this sarcastically. I was almost 35 when I was married, so I have fished a lot and I have painted a lot and seen a lot of rivers around Oregon and up on the coast. But I have always had a special affiliation with the North Umpqua because it was the first river we came to visit, and the small towns along it, and I have never lost my original visions of the most wonderful watershed.

"My dream was to someday live on the North Umpqua and it's all worked out perfectly for me. Visually it's a marvellous river to fish, both in summer and winter. It's a river by itself and it does not have a lot of traffic. It can be difficult and the fish are hard to catch.

"Not a lot of people work the North Umpqua. I have taken out visitors from all corners of the earth, and from just about every continent, and I have never had one of them that did not at some point remark to me: 'this is a really quite beautiful river.' And it's a wild river with wild steelhead, both summer and winter. We also have a small run of hatchery winter and summer steelhead for those interested in keeping a fish. Our wild fish are catch and re-lease only on a single, barbless hook. There aren't a lot of rivers left like that in North America today."

He should know. He lives on the water and fishes it through the seasons, picking his pools and days as only a local resident can, and he delights in sharing its secrets with old friends and casual visi-tors. The North Umpqua has to be an American angling treasure. The same can be said for Dave Hall – artist, fisherman and very good friend. Thanks for everything, Dave.

Finding the needle on the Kitimat

NOVEMBER 2011, *Chasing Silver Magazine*, FINLAND

A young moose browsing fearlessly in a leaf-bare thicket beside the highway that runs 73 kilometres between the communities of Terrace and Kitimat; thrusting through crunching, waist-deep snow to reach the river's bank; a bronze-backed fish surging to the surface to snatch fiercely at a swinging Intruder pattern. Three vivid and typical memories from days spent in pursuit of spring-run steelhead in northwestern British Columbia.

Here, on Canada's far western coast, we tend to pigeonhole our precious steelhead under two predictable headings, summer-run and winter-run. The summers start to arrive in late June and July, whether it be to the rivers on the west coast of Vancouver Island or to the tributaries of the rightly world-renowned Skeena and Nass systems, hundreds of miles to the north, or to a multitude of other rivers between those far-apart locations. How fortunate we are who live and play in this part of the world.

The winters begin to appear in late November and keep hardy Vancouver Island and Lower Mainland fishermen happy until the calendar comes round to spawning time in March and April. Further north, at least on the mainland, snow, ice, sub-zero temperatures and well-defined close seasons see even the most determined fishermen not too far from the comforts of home.

Then there are the true spring-run steelhead of March and April, which are drawing increasing numbers of fishermen to rivers like the Kitimat and the Copper *aka* Zymoetz, the Zymacord, the Ishkheenickh *aka* Ksi Higinx, the Kitsumkalum *aka* Kalum, the Dala and the Lachmach along with an impressive number of other watersheds in the huge Skeena Region of British Columbia. Many of the Skeena Region place names are traditional names used by the area's First Nations. The province has nine distinct fishery areas, from the Skeena and the Peace in the north to Vancouver Island in the southwest and the Kootenay in the southeast.

The main stem of the Skeena, a massive but rewarding challenge in itself, can fish exceptionally well in March and April for both steelhead and early chinook with upwards of 80 kilometres of water available to anglers between Copper River and China Bar. However, fishing opportunities are always dependent on the timing of the breakup of the winter's ice floes.

Further upstream, the various Skeena tributaries, rivers with such world-famous names as the Bulkley and the Kispiox, the Babine and the Morice, are off limits between January 1 and June 15. That still leaves lots of choices for the spring steelheader in other parts of the sprawling, lightly populated region.

In 1996, guide and lifelong outdoorsman Gill McKean came to

learn his trade in Terrace, 1355 kilometres north of Vancouver and in the very heart of Skeena country. He and his complement of six guest fishermen are located within easy reach of the Skeena itself, as it runs majestically toward the North Pacific minutes from his front door, and of more than a dozen large and small Skeena and Nass watershed rivers. The richness of opportunity here can be overwhelming to the visitor unfamiliar with the sport fishing scene in Canada's most westerly province.

Without a guide, it's all a bit of a "needle in a haystack" situation. However, in this, the age of the Internet, even the complete stranger can quickly amass enough information with its multiple search engines to guarantee at least some reasonable hope of success. Fish with Gill and his team for four days, as I did, and action – often lots of action – is almost a certainty.

By the time winter's icy grip begins to ease across BC, and it's obviously later in the north than the south, the summer- and winter-run steelhead have spent many months in fresh water. While waiting for their time to spawn, they have lost the early brilliance in appearance that is the hallmark of a fish fresh from the ocean. By contrast, the spring-run members of the clan are often bright as a newly minted coin and bursting with energy. Hook one and see what it means to be in touch with one of the fly-fishing world's most exciting challenges.

That's the life enjoyed by Gill and his fellow guides at Westcoast Fishing Adventures, a family owned and operated business based on his large and comfortable Terrace home. The welcome is warm and the rooms spotless. The kitchen and larder are more than adequate. Fishermen are hearty eaters, and the dawn to dusk catering is such that even the most demanding appetites are satisfied at the end of the day.

And they are demanding days, especially for the guides as they move their fishermen from river to river and from pool to pool using an extraordinary range of transport. A couple of high end trucks, three drift boats, two jet boats and two large inflatable rafts together with a couple of snowmobiles and an all-terrain vehicle, commonly known as a "quad," add up to a substantial investment. These various modes of transport ensure the fishermen who come to stay with Gill have the best possible chance of being in the right place at the right time.

As the year progresses they will target not only spring-run and summer-run steelhead but also three species of Pacific salmon, chinook, coho and chum. It's the chinook that attract the most attention, for the Kitimat River produces some absolutely huge fish in the early summer months, monsters that can weigh 50 pounds and often a lot more. (See "A birthday wish on the Kitimat," page 149.) These chinook can be hooked on the fly, but landing fish of this size in a fairly large river is another matter altogether, so it's more usual to rely on sturdier tackle, lures with strong hooks, multiplier reels and powerful rods that would not be out of place on the ocean.

All that's for another time, perhaps for those who have yet to be tempted by the prospect of a spring-run steelhead, not long from the sea and willing to engage with the angler wielding his double-handed fly rod. The Kitimat River was our principal destination on this trip, which was undertaken during a later than usual spring that made access to most of the other local rivers seriously difficult if not impossible on account of the yet-to-thaw deep snow.

Even on the middle reaches of the Kitimat we had to make our way through a couple of feet of snow as we hiked down from the main highway and along Humphrys Creek on our way to a stretch of water that, on the day, failed to live up to its visual promise. Not to worry, there were plenty more places to try.

That's one of the great attractions to river fishing in British Columbia. For the most part it's readily available to all holders of the appropriate licence. The Kitimat is a good example, and while the boat angler enjoys countless opportunities over mile after mile of prime steelhead and salmon water, there is also lots of room for the bank fisherman. It's a matter of knowing the access points to the trails leading from the main road.

On our travels, and in excellent weather and water conditions, we encountered only very occasional walk and wade anglers and then in places where it was easy to give them lots of room to fish as we continued with our drift, always anticipating the scope of what was to come around the next bend.

There is a year-round ban on the use of powered boats on the Kitimat, so drift boats and inflatable rafts are the usual means of transport. The rafts are easily launched where the Terrace-Kitimat road runs close to the river. As it happened, my first spring steelhead came not far from our starting point on the second day, from a tail-out fished carefully without success the previous morning. The contact came in mid-river, minutes after a tentative pull had straightened the line for an instant. This time the hook hold was good and the resistance strong, providing a most satisfactory start to the day.

That mid-teens fish, quickly released as all wild steelhead have to be in BC, was the first of three of a similar size I encountered on the Kitimat. The other two, one landed and one lost, came later in the day from a broad, boulder-strewn stream that lies between where the Big and Little Wedeene rivers join the main flow from the right. Again the takes were powerful, one just below the surface with the fish showing for a heart-stopping moment as it turned, in much the same way as a summer-run steelhead will come to a waking dry fly.

With time a constraint and the more distant rivers difficult to access on account of the lingering and heavy snow pack, we decided to spend another day drifting the Zymacord, a smaller river than the Kitimat and a tributary of the Skeena, which it meets not far from downtown Terrace. Here too there was still deep snow, and we struggled through it to reach the water's edge after parking the truck and trailer on an adjacent and well-used logging road.

From there on, the day, while fishless, was an absolute delight.

The river, which could well have been approached with a single-handed rod, wound through a heavily forested valley between banks still blanketed with snow. The raft made it easy for us to move from pool to pool and to cover all the likely holding water. We had only one half-hearted take and a couple of handsome cutthroat trout to show for our efforts. But the wild and majestic forest scenery more than made up for our lack of success.

The Kitimat, by contrast, flows through a wide, glaciated valley that was heavily logged in the past. This makes for an ever-changing watercourse, one that sees pools and runs altered significantly year by year during periods of high water. At the same time, the removal of the ancient, old growth forest has opened up a succession of vistas that were totally magnificent on a bright spring day. Although not a true wilderness river by any means, the Kitimat is well worth a visit by fly fishermen anxious to add spring-run steelhead to their fishing diaries.

GILL McKEAN: A LOGGER'S GUIDING DREAM

Gill McKean, now in his late 30s, has come a long way since the days when, as a 10-year-old, he lived for the moment he could slip away from home to fish for rainbow trout in Nanaimo's urban Millstone River.

The boy who started fishing with a branch of alder tree as a rod and green wool as a lure went on to survive two serious accidents while working as a tree faller in the notoriously dangerous forest industry. He could just as easily have been killed when he was hit by a flying log and ended up in hospital with a fractured skull, broken ribs and a broken shoulder. Three years later another injury ended his career in the woods.

"When I was working in the forests, everywhere I went I saw rivers. They were my passion and I could never fill my craving for fishing," he recalls.

In 1996 he decided to move to the town of Terrace "to get my feet wet guiding and to learn my trade. I bought an old truck with a camper for 400 dollars and lived in that and went to the laundromat for a shower."

Today he has his own busy guiding business and reckons he spends between 220 and 230 days a year on the water. He remembers going float fishing with his father as a boy, but now he places his greatest emphasis on meeting the needs of his fly-fishing clients, making the most of the many exciting opportunities available to Skeena Region locals and visitors alike.

For Gill, his partner Mandi McDougall and their children Austin (12), Koltyn (6) and Maci (18 months), fishing is a way of life. Their spacious home, Mountainside Guest House, is also the focal point of their livelihood. For the fishermen, whom they know as both clients and guests, he comments: "We live in a perfect place as far as the fishing is concerned and our spring steelhead are really special, big, strong and beautiful."

Steelhead for every season

MAY 2013, *www.ariverneversleeps.com*, VANCOUVER

We talk and think a lot about steelhead here in British Columbia, but we seldom acknowledge the remarkable diversity of the species. For example, how many countries can say with certainty that Atlantic salmon can be caught on the fly every month of the year within their national borders? Few, if any.

Here in BC the immediate answer has to be in the affirmative although you will rack up a good few miles meeting the 12-month steelhead challenge. It starts, for me at least, on Vancouver Island in January, February and March in pursuit of winter-run fish in rivers like the Stamp, the Cowichan, the Gold and the Salmon. These are the ones I know best and there are others too – smaller, more intimate island streams and lesser known for that reason – which still produce more than the occasional fish.

Back in the 1970s I did well with gear on both the Nanaimo and the Cowichan, a river I first experienced as long ago as 1954, but the Nanaimo River, for whatever reason, has failed badly over the past decade and more as have the returns to such formerly productive east coast waters as the Big and Little Qualicum and the Englishman. Now only remnant stocks are left, and these should be cherished in hopes of recovery. Happily the Cowichan has proved to be the exception to the east coast malaise and still definitely holds its own.

These winter-run fish are not easily taken on the fly. Water temperatures are well down, and flows can be high and strong, adding to the difficulties facing the angler determined to do it the hard way with a swung fly on a fast sink tip rather than with a bottom-bounced lure fashioned from metal or plastic. Using roe as bait is simply not a subject to be discussed on these pages – smelly stuff that I for one would ban completely but then what right have I to impose my view on so many others for whom it is the only recourse? To each his own, as it were.

I have nothing against pink plastic worms or Spin-N-Glos, or spoons for that matter, but in recent years I have become more and more enamoured with the mystique associated with seeking winter fish on the fly in the early part of the year. I have been successful on the Cowichan and the Gold in February and March but have still to manage a hookup in January.

April, the first month of spring and the long-anticipated changing of the seasons, is another story altogether, especially if you have the opportunity to head north to those rivers of the Skeena system that are open to angling at that time of the year. I am thinking in particular of the Kitimat and its run of spring fish, shining bright steelhead that move in from the nearby Douglas Channel in March, April and May to spawn and quickly return to the sea.

So different from the summer-runs, for which the Skeena system has garnered international fame. These start to arrive in July and August – that is if they can avoid needless, wasteful death in the nets of the sockeye fleet – and only spawn the following spring, often after travelling hundreds of miles.

The summer-runs are the steelhead that have brought fame to rivers like the Kispiox and the Babine, the Morice and the Bulkley, names well known internationally and so important to the local economy in terms of the income generated by tourist anglers from the USA, the UK, Europe and Asia.

The name and potential of the Kitimat is less well known, at least where the spring-run steelhead are concerned. It's seen more as a river for the fisherman who wants to come in the early summer to fish for huge chinook and the other salmon species. My focus is steelhead, and over the past three years, I have fished hard there during the course of an early April week.

The first year, 2011, was a useful introduction to a river that flows through a broad and sometimes braided valley that must have been one of the most beautiful places in the world before the loggers had their way and decimated the forest and its huge cedars. Now the new growth, with lots of cottonwoods and alders, has become well established along with the moose, the wolves, the bears, the beavers and other typical wildlife.

That first year I caught three double-figure fish on the fly and went home well pleased. In 2012, I fished with Doug Machuk, from Banff. Ignoring the deep snow, we put in our time on both the Skeena and the Kitimat and came up completely empty-handed.

This year Doug and I met up again in Terrace for what proved to be a most successful week, perfect water and weather conditions, fresh-run fish in the river and opportunities to hook, and land, some really substantial steelhead. In fact it was the overall size and vigour of the fish we met that will stay in my mind for a long time. For whatever reason Doug had fewer hookups but managed to finish with a rare 100 per cent record and the three largest steelhead of his career, two in the high teens and the best of them a formidable male of 21.5 pounds that measured out at 40 x 20 inches.

My own hooked to landed (and of course released) record was a lot less impressive, but three in a row caught from the same pool on the last morning helped to ease the pain. Then, in the last 30 minutes I made contact again, this time with one of those fish we all dream about.

The fish took the fly, a Pink Intruder, with a thump at the edge of the seam, and while I felt I played it well, following my guide's directions to give it no quarter, the hook eventually came back. The estimate was "definitely as big as Doug's," and I know I have only once before, on the Babine a few years ago, been in touch with such a powerful and determined adversary.

And so the year goes on. Month after month somewhere in BC we can expect to fish for and catch our steelhead: summer-runs in the rivers of the Skeena and Nass systems, and on Vancouver Island too if you know where to look, and then back to the Island for the first of the winters as they build numbers into December. No mention, you say, of all the other BC steelhead rivers, especially those of the Fraser system, but that's another story and one for another time.

A steelhead love affair: A book review

FEBRUARY 2014, *Chasing Silver Magazine*, FINLAND

Wild steelhead is a species near and dear to the heart of every fly fisherman fortunate enough to live on or travel to the Pacific coast of North America. So too will be the striking new two-volume book of the same name, *Wild Steelhead* by Sean M. Gallagher (2014, Wild River Press, Mill Creek, WA).

A simple blue slipcover holds the companion volumes that run to a total of 675 pages, including an essential and detailed index. *Wild Steelhead* is the latest addition to a distinguished family of fishing books from Wild River Press produced under the direction of publisher, editor and fisherman Thomas R. Pero.

In the past he has impressed us with *A Passion for Steelhead*, *A Passion for Tarpon*, *Atlantic Salmon Magic* and *100 Best Flies for Atlantic Salmon*, but I have a feeling both he and his readers will come to regard *Wild Steelhead* as his pièce de résistance.

He tells me that this beautifully written, superbly illustrated tribute to an iconic fish – the book's subtitle is *The Lure and Lore of a Pacific Northwest Icon* – was a project that took almost three years to the day to complete, from original concept to Seattle launch in early December.

The initial visual impression is almost overwhelming, for this is a book of exceptional quality, in both its overall appearance and page-by-page presentation. Then there is the physical impact of a matched brace of books that weighs in at a little over a solid seven pounds. Think large trout or small but perfectly proportioned steelhead.

Publisher and editor Pero sets the scene with his introduction, "Romancing the Steelhead," and in a sense you know right away what to expect when he concludes: "This book is our tribute and your treasure." And immediately he draws you into the book by writing that author Sean M. Gallagher, a retired Washington schoolteacher, "may be the best steelhead fisherman you have never heard of. For 50 years he has waded, hiked, biked, rowed, paddled, rafted, boated, float-planed and helicoptered to the fish."

With an introduction like that, the reader is compelled to turn the pages, to relish what is to come, to admire the scenery, the stories, the people, both men and women, and the fish and flies that bring the pages to life through both words and more than 1,000 images. This is a book for all thinking anglers but especially for those who, one way or another, have come to live the life, with all its ups and downs, of what can only be described as a steelhead love affair.

The balance of strong design combined with the striking work of lead photographers Adam Tavender and Greg McDonald, means the "look of the book" is of the highest possible order. Biologist John R. McMillan, son of the renowned Bill McMillan, contributes the incredibly informative "Special Foreword, Swimming with the Steelhead," leading us on to chapter after chapter of personal recollections, in-depth "Around the Campfire" interviews, thoughtful essays and river profiles that bring us to the banks of the "spectacular" Thompson and the "incomparable" Dean and many other rivers in both the United States and Canada.

The book introduces to a wider audience some of steelhead fishing's most distinguished names, among them the late Harry Lemire – the author's mentor and friend, to whom he dedicates the book – Bob Clay and Bill McMillan. The fact that all the principal players responsible for *Wild Steelhead* are also personal friends and veteran accomplished steelhead fly fishers in their own right gives their work added legitimacy. These are men to whom "going fishing" is second nature, men who seek steelhead in all weathers and in every month of the year in the rivers of British Columbia, Washington, Oregon, Idaho and California.

Atlantic salmon have long had their own distinguished literary tradition, dating back at least as far as the early 1900s; the steelhead is less well served in this regard but is now catching up fast thanks to a strong field of American and Canadian writers and editors.

In *Wild Steelhead* Sean Gallagher and Thomas Pero present a book concept that will appeal to all steelheaders, from eager teenagers just learning what's involved to the diehards who have seen and done it all to the old-timers, no longer able to make it down to the river but happy to have treasured memories once again refreshed. Truly this is a book for all ages, a very special addition to any fishing library.

←——————|

Steelhead vs. Atlantic salmon: Steelhead have my vote

MAY 2014, FIRST PUBLISHED IN *Fly Fishing and Fly Tying*, UK

The happy lady angler from Japan put it so well to her guide: "So much difference between one steelhead and zero." We all know the feeling. Whether it's wild steelhead on the Pacific Ocean side of North America or Atlantic salmon in the rivers of Eastern Canada, Europe and the United Kingdom, that first fish of the day, the week or whatever, always lifts the spirits sky high.

It was the same for me in April on the Kitimat River in northern British Columbia, Canada's sprawling, most westerly province. Spring-run steelhead were moving in from nearby Douglas Channel, and my fishing partner Doug Machuk was enjoying a hot streak. Every fish he hooked came to the net. Good for him, of course, but it would have been nice to have had one or two of my offers stick instead of either just a quick tug, yank, grab or pull, call it what you like, or worse, much worse, the fish throwing the hook after a few or more minutes of high energy contact.

I have long regarded steelhead as a superior sporting fish to the Atlantic salmon, and I have caught my share of both species over the years. True I have never had the good fortune to meet up with a really big Atlantic, but I have hooked a couple of very large steelhead.

By *large* I mean fish weighing in excess of 20 pounds. One such, on the Babine River a couple of years ago, took all my line and backing and eventually broke off far down the next pool, "kicked my ass" as they say in these parts; the second one capped an otherwise memorable final morning on the Kitimat, and fought with the heart and strength of a champion.

With a 12-foot 9-inch Sage eight-weight, double-handed rod, 570-grain Airflo Skagit Compact line, nine feet of type three sink tip and three feet of leader, tested to 15 pounds, I was able to hold my own and apply plenty of side strain only to have the unweighted fly pull free after a good 10 minutes.

That was that, the last chance on the last morning with our 90-minute flight back from Terrace to Vancouver, 840 miles to the south, due to leave in less than three hours. There could be no complaining. Doug had finished with his admirable 100 per cent hooked and landed record intact while I had earlier accounted for three successive fish to 16 pounds from the next broad pool upstream.

Angling for spring-run steelhead, fish that come into fresh water from the ocean and spawn in a matter of weeks, is growing in popularity in British Columbia. Only a minority of rivers support such runs; the majority of BC steelhead are either summer-runs, appearing in July, August and September and spawning the following spring, or winter-runs, also spring spawners, that arrive in November and on through to March – different rivers, different life cycles.

A steelhead, for those who have not yet had the good fortune to experience these wonderful anadromous fish, is just a very, very big rainbow trout, one that, like the Atlantic salmon, starts life in fresh water, drops back to the ocean as a smolt and returns one to four years later as an adult ready to continue the cycle.

Biologists now classify steelhead as a salmon, but unlike the other five species of Pacific salmon (chinook, coho, sockeye, chum and pink) a fair percentage of steelhead will survive spawning and recover to return a year later as even larger fish.

As with Atlantics, steelhead can be caught on sunk and on skated and dead drifted dry flies – a hugely exciting moment when you consider the size of the fish – on the usual array of lures, everything from pink plastic worms to spoons and plugs, as well as on bait, most often cured salmon roe, illegal on many systems.

Back to the Kitimat adventure and our opportunity to fish for six and a half days on a river that also supports resident cutthroat trout, Dolly Varden and, in late spring and summer, chum, coho and chinook salmon, the latter in sizes that attract much attention. After all, who would turn down an opportunity to do battle – and battle it is – with a salmon that could weigh anything from 35 to 50 pounds?

The Kitimat, flowing through a wide, glaciated valley, is one of those northern rivers where access is made easy by the proximity of a paved road, in this instance the highway that runs between the towns of Terrace and Kitimat. River and road travel together in close proximity through the valley, and there are a number of spots where it is possible to launch a traditional drift boat or inflatable raft.

These places also offer a starting point for the walk and wade fisherman. Unlike many of the Skeena system rivers, the Kitimat does not allow jet boats, so the anglers walk and wade their way downstream while stopping to fish all the likely pools and runs. Some do bring their own pontoon boats and inflatable rafts,

From the orange highway bridge that crosses the river a few miles from Terrace there is mile after mile of perfect fly water, and the steelhead are often holding, not in deeper pools but in riffles and streamy runs only two and three feet deep. For the stranger, that's where the guide earns his keep, for he knows from experience where the fish are most likely to lie at a particular height of water.

My first fish, on only the third cast, was a hen of around nine or ten pounds, a perfect example of a spring steelhead, feisty and bright as a new coin, a fish that jumped and jumped again and again after a first mad upstream dash that left me struggling to keep a tight line. In the net and held up quickly for a photo she was soon back in the water, back on her way to fulfilling her destiny.

In terms of the long-term future of the species, catch and release makes nothing but good sense. The Kitimat also supports a federal government-funded salmon and steelhead hatchery that has been operating for salmon since 1977 and for steelhead since 1984. It was established to address concerns over the impacts of overfishing and habitat destruction, in particular extensive logging of the Kitimat valley.

Although marked steelhead are more often encountered in the river's lower reaches, where the hatchery is located, it so happened that my second released fish that day, a male in the mid-teens, was both clipped and badly scarred on one flank from an encounter with a seal. Unfortunately this is now an ongoing problem on a number of BC rivers. Seals wait to ambush the incoming steelhead where fresh water meets the tide and even follow them upstream for a considerable distance.

We did meet a seal in a pool well up from the ocean the previous year, when our four days of solid fishing failed to produce a single offer, but this time the only wildlife we saw were bald eagles and beavers, two swimming and one young one that amused with a most inelegant dive from a five-foot-high bank. The valley also supports wolves and moose, their tracks evident in the damp sand. Along with the grizzly bears, these make the fishing environment that little bit different.

The taking of a fresh hen steelhead followed by a big male made for interesting comparisons. The female was much more active, moving fast and jumping frequently, whereas the buck simply stopped the fly in its swing and then fought stubbornly subsurface almost all the time.

Water conditions for the week were just about perfect, with rain on the third day producing an 18-inch rise in levels as an incentive to attract more fresh fish from the ocean. The river did colour up the following day but cleared again just as quickly, leaving optimal conditions for the fly. Pink is always a good shade for steelhead, and Intruder-style tyings now dominate most fly boxes, my own included, although I am sure more classic, named patterns would have worked equally well as they have for me in the past.

Just as the river itself was at its best so the weather also cooperated with only the occasional snow shower and no overnight frosts. We were also fortunate in that the snowpack over the winter of 2012-13 was significantly less than in previous years. The riverbanks and access trails were completely clear. In all regards it had to be the perfect trip, one to showcase BC steelhead fishing at its very best. Roll on, 2014.

The Kitimat is among the top 10 from some 50 rivers that make up the Skeena Region. Statistics covering the years between 2000–2001 and 2007–2008 show total annual catches ranging between 460 and 3546, with the average around 1900. Between 2006–2007 and 2012–2013 the annual catch ranged from 480 (06–07) to 1952 (2012–2013).

There is no privately owned steelhead fishing in British Columbia. All anglers must hold a valid freshwater licence issued by the British Columbia Ministry of Forests, Lands and Natural Resource Operations. For a visiting resident of another country, the cost is C$80 (annual), C$50 (eight day) and C$20 (one day) plus an additional C$60 steelhead conservation surcharge. Extra licence fees are involved for rivers in the Classified Waters category, but these do not apply to the Kitimat.

All wild steelhead must be released unharmed in BC while a total of 10 hatchery fish, those with a clipped adipose fin, may be retained over the course of a year.

Visiting fishermen also need to be aware that flies for steelhead can only be tied on single, barbless hooks – the doubles and trebles popular for Atlantic salmon in other countries cannot be used. Also, only one fly can be fished at a time – no droppers.

←———|

Last day steelhead one to remember

AUGUST 2014, *Chasing Silver Magazine*, FINLAND

The dismal early April 2014 diary extracts tell their own story, or at least for the first three days:

DAY ONE: Very heavy overnight rain led to high water conditions on rivers in the Terrace, British Columbia, area. The flow on the Kitimat went from 100 cubic metres/second, which is more than acceptable, to just over 600 cubic metres/second in a 24-hour period – big, dirty, even dangerous and quite obviously unfishable.

DAY TWO: No steelhead on offer today, although the river was back in nice enough order, coming down from 613 cubic metres/second to 279 cubic metres/second in 24 hours and still dropping when we called time in the late afternoon. Visibility was in the three- to four-foot range for the three days, perfect for what we had in mind.

DAY THREE: Another blank day. Where are the steelhead? This time last year we were into double figures in terms of fish hooked although not always landed. Others on the river this year tell a similar tale. Some are inclined to blame the low water temperatures, 4/5C and most definitely chilly when it comes to wading and casting Intruder patterns on sink tips with a double-handed rod hour after hour into a biting wind. But that's steelheading: much effort, high expectations and always a promise around the next corner.

DAY FOUR: What a way to round out the four-day trip.... only one steelhead hooked between the two of us but a truly great fish.... 41 x 21.5 inches which, according to the historic formula (length x girth x girth $/750$ = weight) comes in at 25.29 pounds, my first steelhead to hand over 25 pounds. Huge is the only word for it – most definitely a fish to remember and the one that prompts this story.

For the past four years this trip has been our annual early April ritual to mark the start of another steelhead season in British Columbia. I make my way some 1280 kilometres north from Nanaimo, on Vancouver Island, to Terrace while regular fishing partner and innovative fly tier Doug Machuk travels almost as far west from Banff, a town forever associated with Alberta's famous national park of the same name.

After another long, hard Alberta winter he's no stranger to snow, ice and sub-zero temperatures, while I say little about the profusion of spring bulbs and blossoms we are already enjoying on the mild West Coast. Canada is truly a country of amazing climatic contrasts. Terrace is snow free this time, although when the clouds lift, we see the surrounding mountains are still deep in the white stuff.

The Kitimat in spring is a medium-sized river with easy access from the 38-mile highway that runs between Terrace and Kitimat. A small, isolated community, Kitimat is fated to suffer boom town growth if and when it becomes the marine terminal for the proposed and very controversial pipeline from the Alberta oil sands. We watch anxiously from afar as the politics unfold.

Seven- and eight-weight Spey rods from 12 feet to 13½ feet in length are the obvious choice for the Kitimat steelheader, with the rest of the gear a matter of personal taste. Leaders (15-pound test) are usually no more than four feet in length fished on medium to fast sink tips, with the fly, on a single, barbless hook, most often tied Intruder-style in a kaleidoscope of colours.

In 2013 we found pink to be far and away the most successful hue, and Doug stuck with it again this year. I opted for blue and black having been gifted two new flies tied by Gordon Shead, a Vancouver Island fishing companion, incorporating the rubber legs made popular by Oregon guide Scott Howell's Squidro patterns. Not a traditional steelhead fly to be sure but one that was to make all the difference between a fruitless, fishless expedition, at least in terms of steelhead contacted, and one with a very special outcome.

That outcome was all it took to banish the blues, to raise our spirits, to make worthwhile all those hours spent casting and swinging, always hoping that the next step downstream would be the one to produce that long-awaited contact between fisherman and fish, the electric moment when the line draws tight between the fingers as the hook takes hold and the reel starts to make its own special music.

A DISTINGUISHED OLD REEL

Which brings me to another twist to this particular story. My new old reel, a vintage four-inch Scottie by Sharpe's of Aberdeen, arrived in the New Year from Keith Wilson, its previous owner in Abbotsford, BC. For a while I had been seriously considering the purchase of an older Hardy Perfect, but the cost, between 800 dollars and well over 1000 dollars, was and still is hard to justify. Then I located the Scottie and it was love at first sight.

As a gentleman of a certain age I just happen to like both the looks and the sound of traditional click and pawl fly reels. I have never had reason to covet any of the more modern versions with their carbon fibre and cork type disc drags. The Scottie, for all its years, comes with still strong springs and a tension adjuster while two fingers pressed hard on the fast spooling line serve their purpose well when the big moment arrives.

Better still, I learned from Keith that it already has a rich history. Over some 30 years in his possession, it had subdued Atlantic salmon on Newfoundland's Humber River and steelhead on the Skeena, the Thompson and the Dean. Before that, it had passed through the hands of a noted Scot, one Jamie Maxton Graham, of Peebles, described in his 2001 obituaries as one of the UK's leading authorities on antique fishing tackle.

Provenance means a lot when it comes to antiques, and I have since learned that this particular reel was almost certainly made for Sharpe's sometime between 1945 and 1953 by Ernest Dingley, son of the famous English reel maker William Dingley, who had spent some 20 years with Hardy up to 1911. Now a fresh chapter is unfolding, with a 25-pound steelhead providing the best possible introduction to its latest owner.

To fish for spring-run steelhead, we keep coming back to the Kitimat. Although it's not one of British Columbia's blue ribbon streams, not like the Dean or the Babine, the Thompson or the Bulkley, it can be fished by visitor and resident alike on regular British Columbia freshwater licences with no requirement for the extra expense of an additional Classified Waters permit.

This friendly river for the fly fisherman has easy access from the highway and no major obstructions to impede the passage of inflatable rafts. There is unlimited access to many kilometres of inviting fly water and ample opportunity for walk-in fishermen too, although we encountered none this time.

On our fourth successive visit to the Kitimat, we were now covering familiar runs and pools, recalling the outcomes from previous years: a fish of more than 20 pounds that Doug took after an epic give-and-take battle; another very large one that I played and eventually lost a year ago just before we finished on the final day; a spot where I had three smaller fish on – and 12/15 pounds is not really small – and landed two, all in the space of half an hour.

We know from experience that the Kitimat has the potential to produce very large steelhead, perhaps as big as 30 pounds or more, and this at a time of year before the arrival of the more numerous summer-run fish in the many famous rivers that comprise the nearby Skeena system. They can be busy for locals and visitors alike in the autumn months, whereas the Kitimat in spring sees significantly less angling pressure until June and July when the emphasis switches to the annual run of huge chinook salmon.

That's a fishery that I have still to experience. Until recently, it has been largely the preserve of the gear rods using plugs, spoons and various other spinning lures on their heavy-duty reels loaded with strong, braided lines. With fish that can weigh in excess of 50 pounds it's not exactly friendly territory for seven- and eight-weight Spey rods, even with fish half that size. But the challenge remains, and chinooks definitely can be hooked – and eventually landed – on a deeply sunk fly. Then it's a matter of holding on and waging a patient battle, using tackle suitable for the occasion.

The year 2013 brought a very large run of pink salmon, many millions of fish, into the Kitimat. The presence of their emerging fry in April 2014 probably accounted for the increased number of plump, sea-run Dolly Varden, a char, and cutthroat trout that intercepted our steelhead flies. They came from both soft water and strong streams, with the best of them a shining bright, silver blue Dolly Varden that weighed a good three pounds. All showed a preference for the Black and Blue Intruder.

The big fish came from a familiar pool that will remain nameless for obvious reasons. It had produced for both of us in previous years and was as good a place as any to start our final day. From the fast run at its head it opens out into a strong, wide flow with the only obstacle a substantial fallen tree root and trunk grounded in midstream above the tail-out. The next decent flood will surely move it on.

Nothing special happened for the first part of the morning, and when it came at last, the take was more of a decisive tightening than one of those sudden steelhead grabs that can set the heart pounding. From the start it was obviously a fish of some stature, no jumps or dramatic dashes, just power and more power. Sudden surges with back awash and spray flying in mid-river announced the presence of a significant adversary.

Duly measured, quickly photographed and returned to the water, this great steelhead, a male, left behind a single scale in the net. The scale was subsequently read by provincial government senior fisheries biologist Mark Beere, and from him, we learned the fish was probably six years old. By its appearance it had likely been in the river for two or three weeks, no longer ocean bright and clearly showing the deep scars of a previous life-or-death encounter with a seal or perhaps a sea lion.

We can only hope its progeny are made of equally stern stuff and that they will survive the many challenges that lie ahead, thus enabling us to continue to enjoy all the traditions and pleasures of spring steelhead fishing on British Columbia's Kitimat River.

For readers interested in specific tackle, I use as my first choice for spring steelhead, a Sage Z-AXIS 8129-4 rod matched with a Scientific Anglers 560 grain Skagit Extreme Taper with integrated tip, one that combines running line, head (23 feet) and tip (12 feet) with no connecting loops. Later in the season, for summer-run steelhead, I will switch to a 34-foot 510 grain Airflo Scandi Compact head combined with either a floating or an intermediate tip. Partner Doug Machuk went with an 8-weight, 13 foot three-inch Echo Spey rod, 570 grain Airflo Skagit head and 13 feet of T11 on a Hatch Plus 9 reel.

CASTING BACK VI ...
to New Zealand

←————|

B & Bs and big browns: 2001 reflections on New Zealand

FEBRUARY 2001, *www.ariverneversleeps.com*, VANCOUVER

As spring gives way to summer in the Northern Hemisphere, so the seasons are reversed south of the Equator. My wife Daphne and I had the good fortune to experience this reversal when we spent the month of February and an all-too-short first week of March in New Zealand. That Southern Hemisphere, late summer/early fall expedition was a very special trip for many reasons.

Just as at home, the overseas angler should be prepared for days when the fish fail to co-operate or, more likely, the fisherman's skills are found wanting. This fact did not in any way detract from the overall quality of the experience of fishing in New Zealand. The range of lake and river opportunities freely available was enhanced by the universally warm welcome extended to overseas visitors, the many home-cooked meals and the very favourable exchange rate.

Like so many fly fishermen, I had waited a long time for this trip to become a reality and had taken considerable pleasure from the advance planning. From the outset we had decided to go the bed-and-breakfast route, to make our reservations well in advance, so we knew exactly where we would be on any given day. Admittedly this meant we were working to a fixed schedule, with minimal flexibility, but we never had to worry where we would end up for the night.

B & B in New Zealand can easily become dinner, bed and break-fast by arrangement with the host families, and these evening meals remain a cherished highlight as hosts and strangers quickly became friends. Our stays were usually of two or three nights' duration, which gave us time to get to know our hosts and to see something of the local scenery, as well as opportunities to sample the local fishing.

Taupo provided a perfect example of great hospitality and new-found friends. John Read, now in his early seventies, was a truly superb New Zealand test cricketer and national team captain in his day and continues to serve the game on a worldwide basis as a respected official. He and Norli, his wife, also find time to wel-come guests to their home just across the road from the lake. From there it took me less than 10 minutes to drive to the mouth of the Waitahanui. Talk about convenience.

At first light on my first morning at the river mouth I ran across Graham Moeller. He too runs a B & B home, and as an accom-plished fly fisherman, delights in taking visiting anglers to the best locations. He is also a fine cook, as we found on being invited to lunch next day, to dine on freshly caught Taupo trout washed down with an excellent bottle or two of local white wine.

Canadians still continue to enjoy some great fishing, often on our very doorsteps. For an overseas experience, there are many places in the world where one can expect to find outstanding trout fishing. Some of the South American countries are prime exam-ples, but can any of them match New Zealand when it comes to value for money, ease of access to the water, light to negligible traf-fic on all roads except those close to the major centres, pleasant climate and an English-speaking population?

New Zealand is at the bottom of the world, but with jet age travel, we are not that far away from North and South Island des-tinations. What to expect for the fly fisherman visiting New Zea-land for the first time? The following notes may prove helpful for those fortunate enough to be preparing for that long-awaited trip to the "land of the long white cloud."

LAKE ONSLOW: Spent three days on the Clydesdale farm of Trish and Alan May. The Clutha, New Zealand's largest river, borders their 200-hectare property and is home to some very big trout, including sea-run browns. The Mays raise upwards of 2,000 deer. They export venison to Europe and velvet from the stags' antlers to Korea for use in countless medical remedies.

I spent one day fishing with Alan and Jack, his 86-year-old father, on Lake Onslow. Located at an elevation of 700 metres, and reached only after a 90-minute drive over a long, uphill gravel road, the lake provided us with memorable fishing to a strong stock of brown trout. Nymphs and dry flies worked equally well for fish to three pounds, all in prime condition and beautifully marked with small heads and robust bodies. Access to a boat was essential, for this is big water with an extensive shoreline, bounded on all sides by rolling, tussock-covered hills with not a tree to be seen in any direction.

MATAURA RIVER: One of the South Island's most famous destinations, the Mataura remains for me a complete enigma. The trout are there in numbers, to be sure, and the fly life is abundant, but this particular fisherman made precisely nothing of them. This despite a strong afternoon rise in streamy water and lots of spent duns, floating and largely ignored in the back eddies. Dry fly, wet fly and nymph – the fish spurned them all and were still moving, presumably to nymphs or emergers, as we took our leave. The only consolation was that Alan May, knowledgeable and experienced in such matters, was limited to a couple of fish and then only after a very concentrated effort.

WAIAU RIVER: Flowing from Lake Te Anau, and within easy reach of the town of the same name, the Waiau is a considerable river in terms of size and flow. Clear as gin, like all the New Zealand waters I had the good fortune to visit, it fished brilliantly at dusk, when there were plenty of sedges in evidence, and again for an hour or so on either side of first light. Wading was comfortable if challenging with good-sized rainbows showing at dusk and dawn and fighting powerfully, at times well on to the backing, in the swift currents. One visiting fly fisherman I encountered had just seen his wife off on a five-day mountain hike to Milford Sound and was settling into his comfortable motor home just yards from the river. "I'm not sure how I will manage without her," he remarked, without much conviction.

LAKE WAKATIPU: New Zealand's third largest lake presents yet another vast expanse on quite magnificent, crystal-clear water ringed by mountains, some still capped by snow, with Queenstown as its hub. Fran and King Allen have built their own dream farm, Bridesdale Charolais, above the Kawarau River, a few kilometres downstream from the lake. Thanks to them, we had an opportunity to travel by boat almost the full 80-kilometre length of the lake and to fish twice at the mouth of the remote Von River. What an experience that was. On the first occasion, mirror calm and in bright midday sunshine, a three-pound brown trout took my first cast almost at my feet, much to the great surprise of all concerned. We later released and lost rainbows of a similar size. As an onshore wind built up the waves, we were able to watch trout move across in clear view as the flies swung where the current swept over the drop-off and into the lake. For King Allen it was a picture-perfect introduction to the charms of fly fishing. He, for one, will be back at the same spot sooner than later. I can only envy him the opportunity.

LAST WORD: Five weeks spent in New Zealand were totally memorable in every sense. Our bed-and-breakfast hosts were kindness personified. We dined like royalty, enjoyed our share and more of excellent red and white wines, revelled in the largely deserted roads, marvelled at the ever-changing scenery as it unfolded over more than 2,000 kilometres of driving and, above all, cherished the countless fishing opportunities we were able to experience.

You have never been to New Zealand? Then you'd better start planning right away. It's too good to miss.

←————|

The magic of Moonglow

MARCH 2001, *www.ariverneversleeps.com*, VANCOUVER

Lake Taupo, North Island, New Zealand: The inscription on the well-thumbed book's flyleaf reads: "If you can't fight 'em..." Little did I or my wife Daphne, who wrote that note in July 1964, ever imagine that 37 years later we would be fishing in the very boot prints of the late O.S. "Budge" Hintz, former editor of the New Zealand *Herald* and author of *Trout at Taupo* (1955, revised 1964, Max Reinhardt, London) and its 1975 sequel, *Fisherman's Paradise* (from the same publisher).

All those years ago *Trout at Taupo* was a fly-fishing classic, a book to treasure for its vivid and very personal memories of a still legendary fishery, one that continues to attract its devotees from all over the world. I re-read it as essential homework for a four-week journey to a country where the quality of trout fishing is still beyond compare, and it raised my long-held expectations to boiling point.

Throughout its 239 pages, Mr. Hintz's emphasis is on the incomparable sport he enjoyed to the downstream wet fly on the major rivers that flow into Lake Taupo and, in particular, on the beautiful, spring-fed Waitahanui. He also spent many productive years on the estuary streams at the point where rivers and lakes merge to form what could well be the world's most productive brown and rainbow trout fishery.

In his time, the rainbows averaged five pounds with a daily limit of 10. Now the average seems to be between three and four pounds and the limit is down to a more reasonable three. There is also an ample stock of fish that go twice and three times that weight and considerably larger from time to time. It all takes some believing, for to this day, the lake and its rivers produce an annual rod catch in excess of 300 and perhaps close to 400 tons of trout.

Just now, as the Southern Hemisphere summer gives way to autumn, the fishing effort is concentrated on the lake, where streamer flies and lures are trolled deep behind slow-moving boats for an annual catch in the regions of 70,000 trout. In expectation of a very special fly-fishing moment, those locals and visitors not trolling on the lake gather each dawn and dusk at the river mouths, the famous New Zealand rips.

Later, in April and May and on into winter, the mature browns and rainbows, averaging over five pounds, move out of the lake on their annual spawning pilgrimage. The fisherman now has an opportunity to challenge really big fish on fly only streams, clear as Irish crystal and flowing with a vigour certain to test both angler and his tackle to its furthest limit. Many see this as the essence of the Taupo experience.

The Waitahanui, beloved of Mr. Hintz, is a case in point. A sunlit afternoon's effort with small dry flies, fished both blind and to the occasional riser, brought me half a dozen released rainbows, each one a picture-perfect example of the species, direct descendants of the original Taupo stocking from California's Russian River more than a century ago. The largest of the six, a good two and a half pounds, ran and jumped with the energy of an Atlantic salmon before slipping away into the shadows of a deep pool beneath the high, lush bankside foliage.

While the locals tend to rely on the upstream nymph, often fished below an indicator, and downstream attractor patterns for both resident and migratory fish, the dry fly clearly has its place on what can be likened to a super-charged English chalk stream, one where the strength of the current is such that a wading stick, the New Zealander's "third leg," is an asset if not an essential.

A five-day January visit was only enough to whet the appetite, to leave me with a determination to return someday to see what it's like to fish such famed rivers as the Tongariro and the Taurango-Taupo when the autumn and winter runs are at their peak.

Not that I have any possible reason to complain. In fact I could never have imagined what was ahead as I took my place on the shore in the so-called "picket fence" close to where the Waitahanui enters Lake Taupo. Our dinner-bed-and-breakfast base was five minutes' drive away, and even with 20 or more other rods on duty, there was never any sense of overcrowding.

On that first morning, with all the traditional emphasis on the still dark minutes between 5:00 a.m., the legal starting time, and the onset of early light, just after 6:00 a.m., we could both hear and sense big trout plunging at close quarters, sometimes almost at our feet.

My fly was a Taupo traditional, the Red Setter, and it eventually fooled one rather lean rainbow of around two and a half pounds that was quickly released. Each time the single fly, fished on a nine-foot, nine-pound breaking strain leader, swung round in the deep current – which draws away to the right from the river mouth for some considerable distance – there was the expectation of contact with a fish of real substance.

Later a chance lakeside encounter with local fishing host and artist Graham Moeller –the title "fishing guide" does not begin to describe what this genial companion brings to his vocation – prompted a change to a luminous fly pattern, the Moonglow.

This one fly went on to account for a dozen trout in all, including three notable browns of between nine and a quarter and eight pounds, the two largest coming in less than a dozen casts between 5:00 and 5:30 a.m. on Saturday, February 17, 2001. The word spread fast, and on the day we left Taupo for South Island waters, George Blake and Tom Ruru, at Waioranga Sports and Tours in Taupo, told me they had sold out of that particular pattern.

I had waited for the better part of 50 years for my first chance at a brown trout worthy of its place on the wall. To take two such trophies at one all-too-short session makes this a day of days, one that perhaps owed something to an earlier decision to add a 15-foot intermediate tip to my floating line.

Whatever the explanation, and I can make no possible claim to expertise in terms of Taupo trout, I accept that this was an outcome I can never, ever, reasonably expect to repeat — at least not unless I return to the rip off the mouth of the Waitahanui. Thank you, New Zealand, for this lifetime fishing highlight.

←————

Mental stuff on the Mararoa River

JUNE 2001, *www.ariverneversleeps.com*, VANCOUVER

Sometimes it's the fish we don't catch that leave the most indelible images. Like the formidable chinook, 40 pounds at least, dark and with a great, hooked kype, that slipped the barbless hook with net poised one evening last September as we trolled off the North Arm of the Fraser River.

Old friend, fishing partner and net man Glenn Di Georgio was beyond consolation; my own feelings were mixed, recognizing this great male was on the final leg of a lifetime journey and deserving to complete the cycle in the weeks ahead. No hard feelings, no regrets, perhaps even a sense of relief that the life and death decision had been taken from my hands as the huge fish dropped back and out of sight.

More recently, on New Zealand's South Island, with the images in my mind still as clear as the startlingly pure water, we came upon a substantial brown trout holding in a challenging lie in the middle reaches of the Mararoa River. We were totally alone, in wide-open country, 40 minutes driving time from Te Anau, a lively South Island resort town and prime fly-fishing centre. My host was local guide Lex Lawrence, his offer of a morning's sight fishing to round out the overseas experience accepted with delight.

He and his wife Lyn call their farm-stay, bed-and-breakfast

home Rose 'n' Reel, a name that caught my eye as I scanned the Internet for suitable resting spots on our 2001 New Zealand journey. With a full six years' big trout background, the sturdy, retired sheep farmer proved to be the ideal tutor for what lay ahead, an advanced level lesson in an aspect of fly fishing that New Zealanders see as very much their own. Judged by the catch and release photo display on his dining room wall, and in the garage too, Lex is most certainly a practitioner with senior faculty status.

Today and tomorrow, and who knows for how long into the future, the fleeting moments that we were to share remain in sharp focus. His description of the virtues of the Mararoa was succinct: "Not that many fish to the mile, like so many of our Southland rivers, but they can be big."

He crouched above me and to my right, his silhouette all but obscured by the clumps of tussock grass and other dry, bankside vegetation, and began to talk me through the process. Perfectly positioned to stare through the surface glare and along the margins of a hurried flow where the stream narrowed, he had spotted two large browns. The better of the pair, he suggested modestly, could well outrank my recent near double-figure catch from Lake Taupo.

Both fish were within moderate casting range and the light crosswind and high cloud cover presented no additional problems. But then there was the mental stuff, the inevitable sense of expectation and the thoughts of what could lie ahead. The tension, the enhanced adrenaline charge, just had to be contained.

Concentrate, concentrate, try to stay calm, hold back momentarily on each cast to ensure the best possible presentation. Nothing in my past had prepared me for this test of nerves.

The first half-dozen casts swept past and well over the intended quarry. I switched to a weighted, Bead Head Nymph, fished on some three feet of six-pound test leader, tied directly New Zealand-style to the bend of the hook of an indicator dry fly.

The scenario has to be familiar to all who have read, heard or dreamed about fly fishing at the bottom of the world. The reality, with all its attendant challenges, was a very different proposition.

Lex was a wonderfully patient mentor. "Up a bit ... give it another couple of feet ... he's still there but staying down ... that time he moved to your right ... he's definitely a good one." Each cast ramped up the anxiety level in concert with my own growing sense of inadequacy. The telltale indicator dry fly, an Adams, kept vanishing in the broken water at the head of the run, while Lex continued to call out the underwater action.

Inevitably, perhaps, this is a story with no happy ending, except of course from the point of view of that particular Mararoa River brown trout. There was to be no thrilling climax as it deftly came to the No. 14 nymph and immediately turned away to give battle from the sanctuary of the deepest lie.

Lex's warning call came at the instant the fish finally moved to my fly. At that precise moment the indicator fly again disappeared from view. The signal registered as my floating line straightened tantalizingly out and across the current. Fractions of a second had to count as I responded, lifting into the fish only to feel the nymph come back with just the slightest hint of resistance from below.

"He definitely had it and then let go. I saw the flash as he turned and his body shook. It was a big one, no doubt about it," my teacher reflected as we walked on upstream.

His business, since retirement from full-time farming in the mid-1990s, is to bring visiting fly fishermen to resident trout, to offer guided instructions and then hope they can make music together. Once you try it you realize this is tough fishing and humbling too.

Another day for the memory bank, not so much for the big trout that remained uncaught as for the excitement of the pursuit and the introduction to a very different approach. That's the essence of fishing far away from home: new faces, new waters, new approaches, all adding fresh elements of knowledge to the essential lore of our wonderful sport.

Return to New Zealand: 2013

MARCH 2013, *www.ariverneversleeps.com*, VANCOUVER

What better place to spend the month of January than in New Zealand. While British Columbia is dreary, wet and cold, the Southern Hemisphere is warm and welcoming. The mythical "Land of the Long White Cloud" is just as appropriately called "the Shaky Isles," tragically so in light of the deadly Christchurch earthquake that took 181 lives in February, 2011.

Early in 2001 Daphne and I enjoyed five great weeks in New Zealand's North and South Islands, fishing, touring and settling into a dinner, bed-and-breakfast itinerary that proved the perfect way to see the country and meet the people. We found both to be quite wonderful, and the fly fishing, in numerous rivers and lakes, more than met expectations.

This year, with both of us a decade older, we decided to settle for a full month in one place, a location we knew well, as it happens, and enjoy all the comforts of home. In this instance it was a fully furnished, modern two-bedroom cottage on what was, until very recently, a spacious, working cattle farm set between the South Island's Queenstown, a major and thriving resort centre, and the more exclusive and much smaller Arrowtown.

Fran and King Allen, now planning for at least semi-retirement, were our hosts in 2001 and have since visited with us in Canada, and it felt good to pick up where we had left off last time. Generous in the manner of all Kiwis we have met over the years, they made us most welcome. They offered us the use of an elegant, vintage 1971 Jaguar saloon, all leather seats and polished wood interiors, for local fishing jaunts; fresh fruit and vegetables from a carefully tended garden and daily fresh brown eggs from seven friendly "chooks."

The Allens' Bridesdale Farm, at the end of a long and winding driveway where families of quail and rabbits of all sizes dodge among the grazing sheep, is set on high ground overlooking the Kawarau River. The river empties Lake Wakatipu, some 80 kilometres in length and the country's third largest. Nearby sits Lake Hayes, much, much smaller, really tiny by comparison, but with a solid reputation for its trout fishing, unfortunately not to be substantiated on this visit.

For those of us from far away, who came expecting the usual benign summer weather patterns, there were some surprises in store. Overnight, upper levels snow on January 2, unheard of for the time of year we were assured, drew even more attention to the towering and close-to-hand Remarkables range of mountains (2319 metres). Heavy rain, often accompanied by blasts of thunder, left its mark on all the local rivers and streams.

Early in the month the cycle path that borders the Kawarau, one of a number of such assets developed for the benefit of locals and tourists alike since our last visit, was under close to a foot of water where the Lake Hayes Creek meets the main river. The native paradise shelducks, together with a couple of black swans, made themselves at home on the adjacent flooded fields. The river was simply unfishable.

Not the best of outlooks for the visiting angler, but better times were ahead. It was never really all that cold and, by mid-month, the sun was out again and the thermometer was climbing back toward 30C.

As the rivers duly dropped back and cleared, the second critical element of our New Zealand adventure came into focus in the person of Craig Somerville, a Scottish-born fly fisherman, fly tier, new friend and founder of Castabroad, the New Zealand fishing travel advice and organization company.

Craig, in his early thirties, a trained chef and now luxury lodge manager after 10 years away from his native Glasgow, has his family home and office in Wanaka, about an hour's drive from our cottage. It's hard to imagine a more perfect location than this postcard-pretty lakeside town, small and caring enough to want to retain its original identity despite the fast-growing impact of tourism, and very convenient to a bewildering array of still water and river fishing.

In the main, Castabroad's business plan aims to meet the needs of overseas visitors who can afford to enjoy the best of what New Zealand offers in terms of fishing, guides and accommodation. Communication over the Internet enables him to suggest suitable itineraries, to fine tune plans to meet his clients' needs and then to make all the necessary arrangements using a selection of the best North and South Island lodges.

During our visit we had the opportunity to enjoy the hospitality of two of these outstanding establishments, Whare Kea Lodge and Chalet, on Lake Wanaka, and Silverpine Lodge, on Lake Hawea. Both were simply superb on all counts.

I have been keeping fishing diaries of one sort and another since 1951, when I was in my mid-teens, and I take great pleasure in the memories they provide, good and bad alike.

What follows is my day-by-day account of our most recent visit to New Zealand's South Island, a destination that should be on every angler's wish list, for the excellence of the trout fishing opportunities it presents, the absolutely stunning beauty of the countryside and the multitude of fishing locations it offers.

And since, by supplying too much detail, it would be all too easy to spoil some of the special waters I visited, in certain instances I have been deliberately vague as to specific locations. Should a trip to New Zealand be in your thoughts just now, then "go while you can" would always be my advice.

NZ fishing diary: January 2013

MARCH 2013, *www.ariverneversleeps.com*, VANCOUVER

JAN. 1: Long distance travel made easy. Direct 14-hour and 15-minute flight from Vancouver to Auckland followed by a two-hour internal leg to Queenstown. We left BC on December 30 and lost December 31 along the way as we crossed the Equator. Air New Zealand again provided exceptional service and meals at all levels and this despite a near-full Boeing 777-200 load of 345 passengers.

JAN. 2: Surprise, surprise.... overnight snow on the mountains that rise steeply from the river valley behind our cottage. Not at all what we expected to start a high summer new year so far from our Vancouver Island home.

JAN. 3: I had the use of the Allens' eight-foot dinghy for the month so tried Lake Hayes, 10 minutes away. Too much wind, and as I later discovered, the lake's usual clarity was being impacted by a summer algae bloom. So no fish seen or touched on a variety of flies fished on a sink tip.

JAN. 4: Drove to Wanaka (pop. 5000) over the Crown Range mountains on the highest paved road in the country. Met up with Craig Somerville, my Castabroad host, at the appropriately named Trout Bar with its fine setting beside Lake Wanaka. Thus we completed the first of a series of one hour, 120-kilometre round trips over the winding but never too busy mountain road. Many acute hairpins, quite spectacular views in both directions and, amazingly, hardy cyclists labouring up and over the 1120-metre summit.

JAN. 5: Lake Hayes flat calm but again nothing.

JAN. 7: To Wanaka for Craig to show me some favourite spots on Lake Wanaka, 35 km in length and fourth largest (192 sq. km) in the country, and the adjoining but completely separate Lake Hawea (141 sq. km). These are two very substantial bodies of clear, clear and very deep water offering good shoreline and creek mouth sight fishing for big trout when conditions are favourable. Not today, although we did work one decent but uninterested fish in Lake Hawea.

JAN. 9: Raining hard all day. Drove for a good hour along the shore of Lake Wakatipu to Glenorchy to find, not unexpectedly, both the well-regarded Rees River and Diamond Creek running high and dirty so no fishing opportunities there. As at everywhere we stopped to refresh in New Zealand, the coffee in a Glenorchy cafe was as good as it comes.

JAN. 11: To Kingston, at the other end of Lake Wakatipu, to see the still-working steam train, enjoy more coffee and a stop in tiny Athol, at Stu Tripney's "world famous fly shop." It was worth the effort just to see the amazing range of fly patterns he offers his customers. Also paused and looked at the famous Mataura River but it too was in brown flood – another opportunity denied.

JAN. 12: Walked down through the Bridesdale paddock and a herd of very curious cattle to the Kawarau, which borders the property. It's a good-sized river and was still running high and dirty, due to the influence of upstream runoff from the Shotover River and the high-water discharge from Lake Wakatipu. No fishing there today.

JAN. 13: Took a 20-minute drive to Jack's Point, outside Queenstown, where we found an 18-hole golf course, an up-market housing development and the attractive, open to all, Lake Tewa, stocked with rainbows and overlooked by the Remarkables. Noted for another day.

JAN. 14: Fished Lake Tewa. Again nothing although did see a few trout nymphing.

Now at the halfway point of the trip and still no trout to report. Nevertheless spirits remain high for this is New Zealand where a fly fisher's dreams do come true.

JAN. 16: Craig arrived from Wanaka after breakfast to fish with me on a spring-fed creek with a solid reputation for good-sized trout. A one-hour drive brought us to a small, intimate tributary with substantial weed growth and water of the utmost clarity. Time spent waiting for the mayflies to appear went quickly enough. Then, when the hatch eventually started in late afternoon, the trout keyed mainly on nymphs, often moving a considerable distance to complete the swirling intercept. We fished dry patterns through a heavy rain shower, talked to two energetic, wet-wading American seniors – in their mid-seventies and mid-eighties – and eventually had one good fish on and, just as quickly, off again. That was it for the day so still no trout to hand but definite progress in the right direction.

JAN. 17: A 6:30 a.m. pickup this morning with Craig accompanied this time by his good friend and professional guide Paul Macandrew, of Wanaka's Aspiring Fly Fishing. Our destination was a Central Otago river where I was told six- and seven-pound trout are accepted as the norm. Again hopes were high during the two-and-a-half-hour drive on highway and then unpaved sheep farm roads. When the river finally came in view, it was quite obviously rising and coloured by an unexpected overnight flash flood. Next stop, after superb coffee and muffins somewhere along the way, and then more driving, was another medium-sized river where the track through the riverside fields took us past two impressively endowed and possibly aggressive bulls. Talk about giving a threat a wide berth. At least half as big again as the previous day's destination, this river was in nice enough order, but we were promptly hit by foul weather conditions. Enduring rain, sleet and strong winds, we saw no fish despite much tramping and peering into deep pools and swirling pots. When it comes to fishing effort those two

Kiwis take no prisoners, and this Canadian visitor worked hard to keep pace with two men whose combined age is still a few years short of my own tally.

Finally, back to the vehicle and on the road again, to destination #3, another of those evocative New Zealand rivers with names that assume a lyrical quality when properly pronounced. It was there I finally managed a medium sized brown trout on a weighted Caddis Nymph fished New Zealand style, attached to the bend of the hook of the dry fly indicator. Not one of those double-figure New Zealand trophies so familiar from magazine photos but still a trout in the net at long, long last. I strongly and successfully resisted calls for a "kiss the fish" photo op before we headed for home, having covered a good 400 km. And Craig and Paul had still to drive another hour back to Wanaka. No doubt they recalled the very large freshwater eel that swam out from beneath a cut bank and right under Craig's rod tip before sinking back into the depths. It was all of three feet in length and must have weighed close to 10 pounds – totally unexpected.

JAN. 21: First day that was completely cloudless, sunny and warm.

JAN. 22: Lake Tewa in the evening ... one 15″ rainbow on a dry emerger.

JAN. 25: With Craig again as we fished together on yet another river in surroundings of stunning beauty, a broad valley with snow-covered peaks ahead and, all around us, the lands of a huge and historic 2000-hectare sheep and cattle farm owned and operated by the same family for four generations. This time the fisherman's expectations and the outcomes converged. The day's sight-fishing efforts produced a leaping brown trout of around six pounds on a dry Cicada Beetle pattern, and an even larger rainbow was lost after a prolonged dispute.

JAN. 26: An early start to Wanaka for an Aspiring Helicopters' pickup with Craig and Paul on our way across the Southern

Alps – sensational flying in every regard – to a totally remote, much anticipated and so beautiful river on the west coast of the South Island. Again much was expected but nothing materialized. The day was warm and bright, and had there been trout present in that part of the river, Paul would have found them. He is a complete master of all the nuances and techniques of sight fishing – spotting the trout from afar and then positioning his fisherman to cast to it with an upstream dry fly or nymph, or a combination of the two. Paul works as hard as any guide I have ever met, and his approach has much in common with that of a finely trained bird dog, always moving ahead of the guns in search of its quarry.

On the way back to Wanaka, passing Mount Aspiring (3033 metres) to our right, we stopped for champagne and ginger beer refreshments at the Whare Kea Chalet, an out-of-this-world mountain location built by the owners of Whare Kea Lodge. We spent the night at the lodge, where our hosts gave us the warmest of welcomes. A six star rating would not be an adequate accolade for the lodge, and the full moon rising over the lake, following our five-course dinner, was almost too good to be true.

JAN. 27: Off again with Craig to check out a river that flows into Lake Hawea and runs conveniently close to the road. There I managed a brown and a rainbow, both on dry cicadas and in the two-pound category, small by New Zealand standards, while Craig had a larger fish from a difficult lie hard against the far bank and under a mantle of overhanging branches. My trout came from open water situations, one sight fishing and the other from a blind cast with the fish dropping back from heavy water to take the fly in full view at the edge of a seam.

That night we were hosted by Michael and Susan Yates at their luxurious Silverpine Lodge, an exclusive destination located on a high bank site overlooking Lake Hawea, with easy access to a number of productive rivers and lakes. Together the Yateses have lived the most interesting of lives and their generous hospitality provided a wonderful finale to our New Zealand visit.

JAN.29: A last evening visit to Lake Tewa but no interest on the part of the trout despite perfect conditions.

JAN. 30: Back to the Kawarau River. It had dropped a good five feet from its mid-month level and was running almost clear. The result was two more rainbows on Muddler Minnow patterns, fished wet down and across. Not especially large but the best possible way to round out this New Zealand adventure. In 12 days of actual fishing, some of them less than a full day, I had the good fortune to experience 11 different South Island rivers/lakes. Three potential days' fishing were lost due to high water conditions.

A good guide is literally "worth his weight in gold" when it comes to making the most of what could very well be a once-in-a-life-time opportunity to experience the best of trout fishing in New Zealand. I was lucky enough to have some previous knowledge of the country and its fishing and to spend so much time with Craig and Paul, two men who really know what to do and where to go.

That said, the first-time visitor, as I was in 2001, can still find plenty of places to fish for brown and rainbow trout in New Zealand by asking the right questions and by studying, preferably in advance, the most recently published books – and there are some very good ones. These would have to include the latest editions of John Kent's *Trout Fishing Guides* to the North and South Island (2000 and 2002, Reed Publishing, Auckland, NZ) and Derek Grzelewski's lyrical *The Trout Diaries* (2013, David Bateman, Auckland, NZ), one of my favourite all-time reads. There are also the various fishing websites, in particular www.nzfishing.com and the New Zealand Fly Fishing Forum at www.flyshop.co.nz.

A sight-fishing tradition

MAY 2013, *Chasing Silver Magazine*, FINLAND

The wooden fly box, beautifully handcrafted from native New Zealand silver pine, is a lasting reminder of my recent visit to what has to be one of the world's most cherished trout-fishing destinations. The box was a gift from Craig Somerville, of whom more later, while the four flies came from South Island guide Paul Macandrew. Together the two worked tirelessly to re-introduce me to a quality of fishing and friendship that I will remember forever.

Not that this is to be another story about catching long-established brown and rainbow trout — their ancestors were introduced some 150 years ago — of mouth-watering proportions. For all sorts of weather-dictated reasons, the first month of the New Year proved to be a challenge for all concerned. Thus the flies in the box, three large, hairy and articulated, weighted Sculpin patterns and a fourth tied on what would be a respectably sized single hook for steelhead or salmon, never had a chance to show their stuff.

New Zealand trout can run to a very substantial size, double figures and more. I had discovered this on a previous 2001 visit with a matched pair of early morning browns, weighing over eight and nine pounds respectively and taken from the rip formed where the Waitahanui River meets Lake Taupo. Certainly the proportions of the flies in the box would not be out of place on any of the cherished steelhead rivers of Canada's British Columbia, and they may well face that test before the year is out. Popular Intruder patterns, you have been warned.

My wife Daphne and I had decided to exchange four of Vancouver Island's inclement mid-winter weeks for a similar length of time in a self-contained cottage, convenient to the popular South Island resort town of Queenstown. It was almost midsummer in the Southern Hemisphere; we had stayed there before, greatly enjoying the company of our Bridesdale hosts, Fran and King Allen, and knew we should be able to find good trout fishing close to hand.

Picking up an airport rental car with the registration letters FSH was surely a good omen, but then early January snow on high ground, near-freezing overnight temperatures and lots of thunder and heavy rain put a different complexion on the prospects ahead. The adjacent Kawarau River was out of the question, brown and swollen to the point a riverbank cycle path was under water. Travel further afield was no more rewarding.

All the rivers and lesser streams flowing into Queenstown's substantial Lake Wakitipu, among them the Rees River and Diamond Creek, near Glenorchy, were challenging their banks. The famous Mataura River, one of the country's best known fisheries, was running both high and with the rich colour of café au lait. These conditions were definitely not the best of outlooks for a visiting angler, but better times were ahead. It was never really all that cold and, by mid-month, the sun was out again and the thermometer was climbing back toward 30C.

Happily help was on the way in the person of Craig Somerville. Originally from Glasgow, Scotland, Craig now lives in the town of Wanaka, another attractive lakeside community and excellent trout fishing centre about an hour's drive from where we were based. Before leaving home, we had connected with Craig through the good offices of the New Zealand fly-fishing website www.nzfishing.com and had corresponded by email for some time prior to our arrival.

Craig is in his early thirties. He's a progressive young man with a vision, and it's all about trout fishing and satisfying the many needs of the visitor who comes to New Zealand full of enthusiasm but with little real idea of where to go or how to make the most of the amazing opportunities the country offers. And make no mistake about it: New Zealand remains a wonderfully inspired destination for the fly fisherman who has the time and the financial resources to fully enjoy the experience. Travel on a shoestring budget is also possible but will involve considerable effort, especially for the first-time visitor with limited time to spare.

Craig was introduced to quality trout and Atlantic salmon fly fishing in Scotland. He's a trained chef who has moved on over his eight years in New Zealand to work in a luxury lodge. This experience and background has led him to set up his own company, Castabroad. His business plan is simple enough, to be available to assist overseas visitors who are in a position to enjoy the best of what New Zealand has to offer by way of advice, fishing, guides and accommodation. His carefully planned itineraries are fine tuned to take the angler to the most productive rivers and to a selection of outstanding fishing lodges in both the North and South Island.

Craig, Paul and I fished together on an almost daily basis for the rest of the month, covering a lot of Central Otago ground, consuming our share and more of strong, early morning Kiwi coffee and muffins and meeting the challenge of rivers both large and small. Some days we would drive for a couple of hours only to have our plans dashed by an overnight flash flood. Other days our stars would be in the correct alignment and the trout would be in a co-operative mood.

Like all good hosts, Craig and Paul have their favourite rivers and streams, and while happy to share their secrets with me, they both asked that I respect their confidences when it comes to naming names. Not that the various locations we visited are all that far off the beaten track or, for that matter, especially difficult to identify for the intending visitor prepared to invest time and effort in some meaningful research.

And what of the fishing? There were days when we walked and walked in the worst of weathers, and in the best New Zealand fashion, searched the incredibly pure water for the telltale sign of a big trout, of a fish that betrays its presence by sipping a surface fly, or a sub-surface nymph. Sharp eyes are essential and patience too, as is the ability to distinguish between an underwater stick or stone and the shadowy shape of a large trout poised, alert and ready to feed at the next opportunity.

With high ground all around us, the mountains ahead in the Southern Alps still white with the snow of the previous winter and no traces of any recent fishing visitors, the river was all that I had long anticipated. Perfect trout habitat with a full, clear flow, chattering shallows easily forded by the curious cattle, and long, deep pools of great promise. I could not have asked for a more perfect setting, and Craig was confident, as he always is, that this would be my day, an opportunity to make up for previous disappointments.

Sight fishing is very much a New Zealand tradition, and while we put in lots of blind casting of dry flies in likely locations, hoping to find Mr. Trout at home and hungry, it was the sighted opportunities that made the day, and the whole experience if truth be told. Craig spotted the first fish almost immediately but it was definitely not for the taking despite a number of well-placed casts. We did not disturb it in any way. It simply was not interested in what we offered and that was that.

The story was altogether different for the second and third fish we found, further upstream. Each in turn was quite easily seen from our cautious, high bank locations, and with positions noted, the stalk was on. Using a dry Cicada Beetle pattern, representative of one of the local trout stock's most important food sources, I made contact with and duly landed and released the first fish, a strong brown in the five- to six-pound category. It was a moment to remember, both for the strength of the resistance offered and the sheer, raw beauty of the surroundings; simply put, this was New Zealand at its stunning best. The second fish turned out to be a rainbow of similar proportions, but it eventually came off. Not that we had any cause to complain.

On another day we spent a full afternoon waiting and watching on the banks of a spring-fed stream that had continued to run high but clean in spite of the recent downpours. Abundant weed growth and accompanying insect life suggested an excellent potential but this time the trout were not so easily deceived, even during a strong hatch of mayflies late in the afternoon.

Rising trout were easy enough to spot, although my sense was that they were keying on the insects' nymph stage rather than taking the dun. Eventually my only hookup was just as quickly lost, which would probably have been the case anyway in view of the sanctuary offered by the trailing aquatic growth.

Then there was the day when Craig and Paul brought me on an Aspiring Helicopters' flight across the majestic Southern Alps to a remote and highly regarded river on the west coast of the South Island. Mountain after mountain, a beautiful chamois bounding over a snowfield not that far below us and the unfolding panorama of glaciers and snow-capped peaks made for an unforgettable experience.

Set down at the edge of the otherwise inaccessible river, we proceeded upstream to search for resident large trout and for the chance to blind cast in the most beautiful setting imaginable. Such was the sense of anticipation that perhaps it would actually have been an anticlimax to find and hook a fish. To fly back empty-handed in no way diminished the experience, one greatly enhanced by the serving of champagne and ginger ale at the fly-in mountaintop chalet owned by our most gracious hosts at Wanaka's Whare Kea Lodge, where we stayed that night. Never before, and almost certainly never again, will I have the opportunity to arrive at my overnight accommodation by helicopter. Talk about living the dream.

Some of the rivers we fished were really easy to reach from well-paved roads while others required permission to cross a farmer's land and a drive along rough tracks. This was never a problem and it was also interesting to see so many well-signed public access points. British Columbia suffers badly by comparison. Access is made simple for the visitor in New Zealand but most definitely not in my home province.

I travelled with my own tackle, two six-weight rods and matching reels and dry lines along with a selection of dry flies, wet flies and nymphs, some of them Canadian, others dating back more than 50 years to my Northern Irish brown trout beginnings. Given the chance, they worked just as well as the modern Kiwi versions, although that said, the two-fly New Zealand-style rig, with a weighted nymph tied some 18 inches from the bend of a high-floating dry fly, definitely had its moments. The two-fly rig would not be allowed in British Columbia, where we are limited to a single barbless fly, floating or sunk.

Going fishing in New Zealand entails the online or in-person purchase, for NZ$161 (2016 fee) of a "whole season" licence from Fish and Game New Zealand. This allows the licence holder to fish in all North and South Island waters with the exception of those that fall within the Taupo Fishing District. Instead of a whole season licence, the visitor can buy a 24-hour version for NZ$20. For a month-long stay the more costly option made obvious sense. Catch and release is widely practised, and stocks, in the main, remain healthy, sustained by excellent water quality and the fact that the trout have no natural predators.

IN THEIR OWN WORDS....

CRAIG SOMERVILLE, Castabroad founder and managing director www.castabroad.co.nz:

"My elder brother and I grew up fly fishing with my father. We were born and raised on Loch Lomondside, just west of Glasgow. My grandmother has an old cottage on Lough Fyne, on the west coast, a tidal sea loch where we would go at Easter and for six weeks in the summer. We would also go way up the mountains to the hill lochs and chuck out our Alexandras and Black Spider patterns. We would create our own hatches by walking through the heather. Dad later got us into salmon fishing. We were most fortunate to be able to fish some really famous beats where fly fishing had started, for example at Castle Grant and Carron Laggan on the River Spey. Of course, as a young lad, I did not appreciate the history and how good it all was. I just took it all for granted. It was this experience, meeting the people fishing on the river and seeing how they lived that eventually led me on to the concept for Castabroad. It was the idea of getting people to very special places in New Zealand, lodges and rivers, to go fishing. I realized that no one I knew from my father's circle of friends had ever been here to fish. That represented a potential market so I introduced myself to as many people as possible in New Zealand and listened to their feedback. With my hospitality background they took my ideas seriously, understood me and supported me. I knew there were lots of overseas companies trying to sell New Zealand but, as far as I know, there was no one here on the ground. If I could work with 20 visiting groups a year that would keep me really, really busy."

PAUL MACANDREW www.aspiringflyfishing.co.nz, a professional South Island guide for the past 10 years, expects to be on the water for upwards of 100 days each year and describes Wanaka as a trout fishing mecca, adding:

"Most of our Southern Lakes regions have a mix of brown and rainbow trout and the scenery is nothing short of mind blowing, from ancient rainforests with gin clear waters to tussock-lined, alluvial riverbed valleys, each spectacular in its own way. I suggest to visiting fishermen that they bring sturdy walking boots, possibly waders depending on the time of year, a pair of light cargo pants for wet wading, a five-weight or six-weight rod, floating lines, good rain jacket and hat and polaroid glasses. They should also be sure of their casting ability, especially when it comes to their short casting game, say over four or five metres. It can happen that you only see one good trout all day so it's important to be able to make your best possible presentation."

DEREK GRZELEWSKI, acclaimed New Zealand fly-fishing author, photographer and magazine writer www.derekgrzelewski@me.com who now has his own *Trout Diaries* podcast and whose second book, *The Trout Bohemia*, will be available worldwide later this year:

"The fishing writing is a work in progress and the feedback I am getting is so good. People are really enjoying *The Trout Diaries*. I did not realize the power of the dream that people have to come fishing in New Zealand. We do get a little blasé about it. They come here and go dawn to dusk. We are a little spoiled and have a different level of appreciation. I have fished with these people and keep being reminded of how special this place is."

←———————|

The Trout Bohemia: A book review

SEPTEMBER 2013, *www.ariverneversleeps.com*, VANCOUVER

"Every trout fisherman must dream sometimes of New Zealand, where the great rainbow trout come up on the shallow bars in the big lakes, and everyone who knows and loves Pacific salmon must sometimes wish to see what Chinooks (sic) look like down there, so many thousands of miles from home in a country where winter is summer and summer winter and coastal currents do nothing to help the migration."

The writer, Roderick Haig-Brown, the book his beloved *A River Never Sleeps* (1946 reprinted 1974, Wm. Collins Sons & Co., Toronto), with the extract drawn from the chapter entitled "November: Before I Die." Haig-Brown's sudden death at 68, in October,

1976 meant he never did see New Zealand, never did have the opportunity in his later years to experience trout fishing that remains, by and large, as good as it can be to this day.

The challenge, as New Zealand author Derek Grzelewski knows all too well, will be to protect, to enhance those fisheries in the years ahead.

As it happens, I was just finishing yet another encounter with a well-used, early edition of *A River Never Sleeps* when the mailman delivered a much-anticipated package from overseas, in it my signed copy of Grzelewski's *The Trout Bohemia: Fly-fishing Travels in New Zealand*, the anticipated sequel to his widely acclaimed first book, *The Trout Diaries: A year of fly-fishing in New Zealand*, which appeared in 2011.

In January of this year (2013) I had the good fortune to meet Derek when we made our way to the South Island town of Wanaka. Publication of *The Trout Bohemia* was just around the corner and he was rightly excited at the prospect, at what the future might hold in store.

A professional in every sense of the word, with numerous prestigious magazine credits to his name, he has, in a matter of a few years, climbed to the pinnacle of the fishing writers' order of merit. There is a lyrical, thoughtful quality to his work that draws the reader along as his close companion on each and every adventure on rivers and lakes across the whole expanse of New Zealand and its two very different islands.

Derek, the seasoned journalist, provides his readers with wonderfully insightful descriptions of the kindred spirits he meets along the way, his bohemians. A thoughtful and expert fisherman, and also an accredited guide, he shares his knowledge, his understanding, of the brawling brown and rainbow trout he encounters in a way that can only ensure his reader is a better, more discerning angler at the end of the day.

Most certainly New Zealand Tourism, and Air New Zealand for that matter, should already have his name pencilled in for special recognition in the year ahead. If any one man has underlined the need for every trout fisherman worth his or her salt to see and experience New Zealand, it has to be Derek Grzelewski.

Haig-Brown's stories of fishing on Vancouver Island captured my imagination as a young man, encouraging me to bring my family from Northern Ireland to Nanaimo more than 40 years ago; Grzelewski's New Zealand narrative is just as powerful, just as evocative. He paints word pictures of a wonderfully scenic, fish-rich country where an angler and his fly rod are assured of both a warm welcome and the fulfillment of his or her wildest angling dreams.

He writes, too, of challenging personal relationships and of Maya, his cherished Airedale companion. The blend is captivating, the content, beautifully presented and illustrated, ever so readable, so enjoyable. Little wonder reviews of his book praise it so highly.

I have to admit fishing books have long held a special fascination for me. I love the look of them on the bookcase shelf, the memories they hold, the depth of information they can provide. The Haig-Browns, a dozen and more, are very special as are those by the likes of B.C's Art Lingren, New Zealand's O.S. Hintz, Ireland's T.C. Kingsmill Moore, Scotland's William B. Currie, the American steelheading trio of Lani Waller, Trey Combs and Dec Hogan, England's writer-artist Bernard Venables and the French writer, Charles Ritz.

Now, Derek Grzelewski has most definitely earned the right to be added to that distinguished list, a fisherman's fisherman if ever there was one, a writer whose first two books are quite simply as good as any I have come across, in recent times or indeed down through these many years.

The Trout Diaries: A year of Fly-fishing in New Zealand (2011) and The Trout Bohemia: Fly-fishing travels in New Zealand (2013) are published by David Bateman Ltd, Auckland, New Zealand. Together they are a pleasure to read and read again as another Canadian winter looms ever closer.

FAMILIAR FACES AND FAVOURITE PHOTOS

With literally hundreds of images from which to choose I found myself hard pressed to narrow down the final selection to a meaningful number. Those that made the cut are loosely arranged to follow the sequence of stories in this book. It's good to be able to include many familiar faces, some sadly no longer with us, along with a few personal favourites and definitely not too many deceased fish. Happily today we acknowledge the value of catch and release, both for the environment and for the fisherman's conscience, certainly not the case when I began my angling journey all those years ago.

← STOWE SCHOOL, FOUNDED IN 1923, IS LOCATED IN ONE OF ENGLAND'S MOST FAMOUS 18TH CENTURY HOMES. COURTESY STOWE SCHOOL.

← THE AUTHOR (L) AND OLD SCHOOL FRIEND PETER HOUGHTON-BROWN ON THE SOUTH FRONT AT STOWE WITH THE CORINTHIAN ARCH AND LAKES PAVILIONS IN THE BACKGROUND.

← IN 1950 I BOUGHT THIS ALREADY WELL-USED NOTTINGHAM-STYLE WOODEN REEL, THE FIRST OF MANY, FOR A FEW SHILLINGS IN A BUCKINGHAM TACKLE SHOP.

↑ TWO 1960S EARLY SEASON ATLANTIC SALMON FROM LOUGH MELVIN.

↑ MOORE ANKETELL WAS A CLOSE FRIEND AND REGULAR FISHING
COMPANION FROM THE MID-FIFTIES THROUGH THE SIXTIES.

← THE POOL BELOW THE WEIR
AT MOVANAGHER, ON THE
LOWER BANN, FISHES WELL
FOR BOTH BROWN TROUT
AND ATLANTIC SALMON.

← COMMERCIAL NETSMEN HAVE TO WORK HARD FOR A CATCH OF LOUGH NEAGH TROUT. COURTESY THE *BELFAST TELEGRAPH*.

← *BELFAST TELEGRAPH* ARTIST BILLY CONN PROVIDED THIS SKETCH FOR THE STORY ABOUT 'THE ONE THAT GOT AWAY'. COURTESY THE *BELFAST TELEGRAPH*.

↑ A SUMMER SCENE ON THE GLENDUN RIVER. COURTESY TOURISM NORTHERN IRELAND.

↑ MOORE ANKETELL (L) AND DOUGIE BARR ALL SET
FOR A DAY AFTER LOUGH SHEELIN TROUT.

LOUGH NEAGH TROUT CAN BE
CAUGHT ON AN ARTIFICIAL FLY. ↓

← A SUITABLY DECORATED PINT OF
GUINNESS CELEBRATES A FINE CATCH
OF SALMON FROM THE RIVER MOURNE.

← THE RIVER MOURNE LOOKING UPSTREAM FROM VICTORIA BRIDGE.

↑ A FAIRLY RECENT ANNIVERSARY PICTURE WITH WIFE DAPHNE ON THE ABERCORN ESTATE'S STRETCH OF THE RIVER MOURNE.

← DAVE LANE FISHING THE CHAPEL STEPS POOL ON THE RIVER FINN.

← HARKIN'S BAR AND RESTAURANT
PROVED TO BE THE PERFECT
RESTING PLACE FOR TWO
WEARY RIVER FINN ANGLERS.

← A ROADSIDE SIGN POINTS
THE WAY TO A POPULAR
COWICHAN RIVER TRAIL.

WAYNE DAVIDSON (L) AND GUIDE
KENZIE CUTHBERT WITH A
COWICHAN RIVER BROWN TROUT. ↓

← CHILLED WINTER FISHING ON SAANICH INLET IN JANUARY 1954.

A GOOD DAY'S SAANICH INLET SALMON FISHING IN THE SUMMER OF 1954. ↓

THE SCOTTISH SALMON SLAYERS AT LANGARA ISLAND, (L TO R) DOUGIE BARR, IAIN MILNE, ANDREW COWAN AND KENNY MILNE. ↓

← HARVEY
STERN PLAYS
AN EVE RIVER
PINK SALMON.

← THE LITTLE
WHITE BOAT
READY FOR A
DAY SEARCHING
FOR COHO
SALMON.

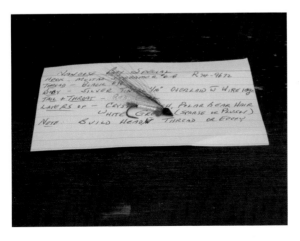

← GLENN
DI GEORGIO
CREATED THE
VERY EFFECTIVE
NANOOSE BAY
SPECIAL FLY
FOR COHO.

↑ READY TO RELEASE A BIG
KITIMAT RIVER CHINOOK.

← A SELECTION OF FLIES
THAT WORK WELL FOR
KITIMAT RIVER CHINOOK.

← A MORICE RIVER STEELHEAD
AND A VINTAGE FLY REEL.

← BABINE RIVER
STEELHEAD
FLIES.

← A GRIZZLY
BEAR FAMILY
VISITS THE
BABINE
STEELHEAD
CAMP.

← DAVE HALL,
BEND, OREGON
FISHING ARTIST
AND GUIDE ON
THE NORTH
UMPQUA RIVER.

← GILL MCKEAN,
TERRACE LODGE
OWNER AND GUIDE.

← TERRACE GUIDE
DARREN WRIGHT WITH
THE AUTHOR'S BEST-
EVER STEELHEAD.
COURTESY DOUG
MACHUK.

← PIERCE CLEGG, LODGE
OWNER AND GUIDE
ON THE BABINE FOR
MORE THAN 25 YEARS,
REVIEWS HIS OPTIONS.

↑ A PLAQUE AT THE MOUTH OF NEW ZEALAND'S WAITAHANUI
RIVER SALUTES FISHERMAN AND AUTHOR O.S. 'BUDGE' HINTZ.

← ONE TO REMEMBER
IN STUNNING SCENERY:
A SOLID NEW ZEALAND
SOUTH ISLAND BROWN
TROUT LEAVES THE
WATER FOR A MOMENT.

← HERRING FISHERMEN
IN THE IRISH SEA
PREPARE TO LAND THEIR
SILVER HAUL. COURTESY
THE BELFAST TELEGRAPH.

← IN 1967 THE AUTHOR AND HIS WIFE, DAPHNE, MET DON MCCARTHY, BAHAMAS TOURISM OFFICIAL.

VANCOUVER ISLAND-MADE ISLANDER REELS ARE EQUALLY POPULAR WITH SALMON AND TROUT ANGLERS. →

STABILIZING THE STOLTZ SLIDE ON THE COWICHAN RIVER HAS MADE A HUGE DIFFERENCE TO WATER QUALITY AND FISH HABITAT. COURTESY THE GREATER GEORGIA BASIN STEELHEAD RECOVERY PLAN. ↓

← SPRING
FISHING FOR
CUTTHROAT
TROUT ON
SPROAT LAKE,
NEAR PORT
ABERNI.

← FALL
REFLECTIONS
ON AN INTERIOR
TROUT LAKE AS
BRYCE OLSON
COMPLETES
HIS MORNING
ABLUTIONS.

← A CAMPFIRE
GROUPING OF
GOOD FRIENDS
(L TO R) BRYCE
OLSON, HARVEY
STERN, DICK
HIGGINS, GLENN
DI GEORGIO AND
PHILIPPE HERVE
DU PENHOAT.

↑ SUNRISE AT NILE CREEK AS GLENN DI GEORGIO PLAYS A PINK SALMON.

← A SELECTION OF FLIES THAT WILL CATCH BOTH COHO AND PINK SALMON.

↑ MY BEACH FISHING FLY BOX, SADLY LOST IN OCTOBER 2015.

← ALL SET FOR A DAY ON THE BABINE'S FAMOUS RAINBOW ALLEY.

CASTING BACK VII ...
to a mixed bag and other fish

←———————|

Herring for supper: The fishermen's story
AUGUST 1956, *Belfast Telegraph*

Eighteen hours a day, five days a week for a wage that can vary between 15 pounds and nothing. Add to this irregular hours, even more irregular meals and work that makes the average labourer look as if he is on a permanent tea break, and you have the life of the Portavogie, Co. Down, herring fisherman.

At the moment, the greater part of the Northern Ireland herring fleet is fishing the grounds off the Isle of Man, and I have just returned from spending three days on board the 62-foot *Gold Crest*, learning exactly what happens before you and I can have herring for tea.

I joined the *Gold Crest* at Ardglass, where she had just discharged the first herring for test processing by the new fish meal factory built there by the Ministry of Commerce at a cost of over fifty thousand pounds.

Jointly owned by the brothers Jim and George Young, of Portavogie, the eight-ton boat carries a crew of six, made up of the two brothers, their father and three relatives. Ulster fishing is nearly all a family business. I am told that this is necessary if the fishermen are to maintain the unity and fellowship that enables them to carry on under the worst of conditions.

The herring is a migratory fish, and the fishermen follow wherever it may go. At present the main fishing grounds are off Laxey and Maughold Head, north of Douglas, and it was here that we arrived just before dark after a seven-hour trip from Ardglass. On the way we had been joined by another Ardglass boat, the *Still Waters*, owned by the brothers James and John Palmer.

There are three or four different ways of catching herring, but the most common, and popular, is ring netting. That's when two or three boats work together in partnership, sharing both the profits and the work. The *Gold Crest* is a ring netter and its partner, or neighbour, is the *Still Waters*.

Herring fishing is a nocturnal occupation, and when we started to fish, the light had nearly gone. All around us were other boats, indistinct shapes pinpointed by their navigation lights, red for port and green for starboard. In the wheelhouse of each boat a fisherman, usually the skipper, was watching intently as a strip of paper fed out from the echo sounder. This device is both the eyes and the ears of the herring fisherman.

At short, regular intervals it sends out sound waves that, on striking the bottom, register an ink mark on a graph. Should something come between the boat's keel and the seabed it is also marked on the graph; by this means the herring are spotted.

At first all the fish we saw were lying close to the bottom where they are almost uncatchable. For the best results the fisherman likes to have his fish between the surface and 10 fathoms. "Anything deeper than that," Jim Young says, "we just scrape the scales off their backs."

After about an hour's searching we located what seemed to be a decent-sized school of fish and Jim decided to shoot the huge net. Like a long, brown snake it uncoiled over the stern of the boat until finally all its 350 yards length lay buoyed up behind us, rising and falling gently in the swell.

Below us the net, some 150 feet deep, was stretching to the bottom and forming an impassible barrier to the school of silvery herring. By now the *Still Waters*, signalled by a single flash of our lights, had picked up the loose end of the net, and the two boats were steaming slowly ahead.

Less than five minutes had passed before another flash of our lights had brought her toward us, towing the net in a wide semi-circle. As the two boats touched, bow-to-bow, four of their crew jumped on to our deck to help bring in the net. Ropes leading to its four corners were passed round the drum of the powerful winch, and the long haul had begun.

From this moment our deck became a scene of organized chaos. Ropes were stretched to the point of groaning tautness while the crew, impersonal figures swathed in dripping oilskins, dragged the weighty folds of the net from the sea.

All this time the *Still Waters*, her propeller just turning, had been holding us from drifting into the net. A heavy rope ran from her stern to a point just about in the centre of our deck rail.

When, at last, all was gathered in and the herring, a shimmering, moving mass of fish, lay trapped on the surface, she cast off the rope and came around to take up the loose end of the net. Now the two boats were lying side by side with the fish between them in what can best be likened to a huge, open-mouthed bag. From this the fish were scooped into the hold of the *Still Waters* by way of a braille net.

This particular "ring," as each sweep of the net is called, only realized about 10 cran of fish. A cran is 28 stone and there are about 1,000 fish to a cran, which meant we had taken over 10,000 herring. I learned that this was only a small ring, for the average one is usually about 20 or 30 cran. Some years ago a boat took 400 cran in a single set, providing enough fish to fully load four boats.

With the fish safely stowed we resumed our searching, but luck was not with us this time and we found no more that night. After a fruitless three hours it was time to make for Port St. Mary, on the Isle of Man, where the fish were to be sold.

The sale was complete soon after breakfast. The crew had the next 10 hours to themselves and took the opportunity to catch up on some lost sleep. They had fished the night before I joined them, and this was their first real rest in 40 hours.

By six that evening the boat was alive again and we were soon headed back to the fishing grounds. Although the wind had freshened it was not too rough to fish and, in three rings, we took 70 cran of herring. If all had been well these would have been sold at Ardglass but, as the *Still Waters* was delayed by an engine problem, we instead had to take the catch to Portpatrick, in Scotland.

The Herring Industry Board has set certain fixed minimum prices for the various grades of herring. The top price of four pounds four shillings per cran is paid for fish destined for the fresh market. For canning, the price is two pounds seventeen shillings and sixpence per cran; for fish meal, the destination of the majority of the catch, the price per cran is two pounds and two shillings.

In addition, the main ports are classified in three grades, A, B, and C. At B and C grade ports the price of herring for fish meal is reduced from forty-two shillings per cran to 35 and 28 shillings respectively. This reflects the distance these ports are located from the fish meal factory. There are only two Grade A ports on the Irish Sea, at Ardglass and Peel, in the Isle of Man. However, as the Ardglass plant is not yet fully active, the Northern Ireland market is very limited.

For years now, the absence of a fish meal plant in Northern Ireland has caused great hardship to our fishermen. It means that if they arrive back in port too late to sell their catch to either the fresh market, or for canning or curing, they must take it back to the Isle of Man or Scotland. The new Ardglass factory will do much to resolve this problem, for when it is in operation, it will be able to handle 300 crans a day.

Just before I left the *Gold Crest* I asked one of the crew why he stayed working on fishing boats when he could be earning more money for less work in other jobs.

He thought for a moment before giving me an answer that was short and to the point: "Why do we do it? It's because we are born to it and because it makes us our own masters and not somebody's slaves."

Judge's writing enhances Irish angling literature: A book review

JUNE 1960, *Belfast Telegraph*

The angler, however preoccupied during his hours on the water, is by nature garrulous about his sport and eager, once the day is over, to talk about it far into the night.

With some, the enthusiasm reaches the stage when they must record their opinions and conclusions on paper for the enjoyment and education of all anglers, present and future.

Unlike its English counterpart, however, the library of Irish angling literature has grown little since the turn of the century. Thus, it was a welcome development last year when Dr. A.A. Luce, a Senior Fellow and retired Professor of Moral Philosophy at Trinity College, Dublin, published his most readable *Fishing and Thinking* (1959, Hodder and Stoughton, UK). Now he is followed by the equally enjoyable *A Man May Fish* by Mr. Justice T.C. Kingsmill Moore (1960, Herbert Jenkins Ltd., London).

As with Dr. Luce's book, the pages of *A Man May Fish* cover territory which must be familiar to a number of Northern Ireland anglers: Lough Melvin and Lough Corrib, the River Eany in Co. Donegal and the famous Fermoyle Fishery on the moorland plateau to the north of Galway Bay.

In his preface, the author says: "What fishing has meant, and means, to me may be summarized in a plea and a protest. A protest against the itch to make records, the urge to extract every possible fish in any way that is not illegal, the desire to go one better than the next man; a plea that fishing should not be so much a pursuit as a pastime, calling for concentration to put all worries out of mind, yet not such concentration as to be in itself exhausting."

A fly fisherman of considerable experience, with one pattern, the Kingsmill, named in his honour, the author writes with complete and easy authority on both lake and river fishing, leaving it a simple matter for the reader to learn without conscious effort.

Listing the dressing for the Kingsmill he says: "It has killed more white trout for me than all other patterns of tail fly put together. It has also caught a number of salmon."

But *A Man May Fish* is no textbook, and Judge Kingsmill Moore is not long in making his way to "The Big House" on the shores of Lough Melvin, near Bundoran.

Recalling a way of life long since past, he writes: "The coachman, who had met me, was serving his fourth generation, the parlour-maid had been nurse to my host, the gardener was trained by his grandfather. But the dust was settling. 'The Big House' was dying at its roots."

He concludes the chapter: "At one stride came disaster. Father and then mother were dead; the son, always delicate, became incurably ill. 'The Big House' had fallen. Another old Irish family had come to its end. Of 'The Big House' itself only a few ruins now remain."

Gifted with a keen ear for dialect, the judge does not hesitate to enliven his writing with lively, verbatim quotations. For example, he reports his boatman, Jamesie, commenting on a rising trout, as saying: "Ye should know by this, Jimmy McDonagh, that that was a thravellin' trout and wherever he is now he is not where he rose last."

←———

Big game fishing the Irish way

AUGUST 1961, *Belfast Telegraph*

Talk of shark fishing conjures up images straight from the pages of the late Ernest Hemingway – the white paint of the boat set off by the tropical blue of the ocean; the angler, eyes shaded against the glare by a long-peaked hat, straining against the powerful lunges of a fish that has his rod bent almost double.

Such scenes are commonplace off the coast of Florida and Mexico but few realize they are also being enacted on a regular basis within a day's drive from Belfast.

It was in the seaside village of Kinsale, Co. Cork, that I first heard mention of the name or Garry Culhane. An old woman, her black, hooded cloak trailing almost to the ground, answered my enquiries.

"If it's fishing you are after," she said, "see Mr. Culhane. He knows it all." High recommendation for any man, but it quickly proved to be well-founded.

Four years ago Culhane was contracting in Vancouver, British Columbia. Today he is the driving force behind a syndicate that aims to make big game fishing a profitable tourist attraction off Ireland's south coast.

Born in Dublin nearly 50 years ago, Garry Culhane is a large, friendly man with an accent and approach that quickly confirms his transatlantic background.

He has no doubts that the venture will be a complete success but says, with persuasive frankness: "It took me more than three years to convince the Irish Government that I was on to something worthwhile."

Now, after spending the best part of 50,000 pounds he has a centre the equal of any in Europe. The visiting fisherman, whether expert or novice, can hire the most modern tackle, can live on the spot in a rented caravan and can eat his meals in a restaurant from a menu that compares favourably with the best of hotels.

And this is only a start for Culhane, who now finds his own angling time being increasingly curtailed, was soon telling me of his 10-year development plan for the centre and of the dream nearest to his heart — the capture of the first Irish sailfish.

Confident that this feat will be achieved within the next few months, he explained: "The Gulf Stream passes here about 30 miles out and we are certain that the sailfish are there along with mako and porbeagle sharks, tunny and albacore.

"More than once we have had lines broken by immensely strong, fast-moving fish and until recently we did not know what to think. But after talking to the Norwegian trawler men working in the area I am convinced they were sailfish."

Already Culhane is making plans for his first "seafari" in pursuit of these big game species, fish that, until now, have been the almost exclusive preserve of the American angler operating in the Gulf of Mexico and further south.

The necessary rods and reels have been assembled, strong wire traces have been mounted with hooks that would not be out of place in a butcher's shop and a boat has been fitted with outrigger poles and a fighting chair.

The round trip will probably involve a sea journey of 60 to 80 miles, and although the 35-foot *Moonlighter* and *Rapparee* have been built and equipped specially for the job, they will not set out in anything other than the most favourable weather conditions. Long, settled spells are common enough in both August and September and the first men to undertake the 30-hour expedition may well have the privilege of making Irish angling history.

The centre already boasts a formidable record. When the Irish Specimen Fish Committee came to make its awards last year, Kinsale-caught fish had qualified for 43 medals, not far short of half the entire total.

The committee, which issues medals and certificates for all fish exceeding a certain weight for the particular species, was presented with a list that included 12 skate of over 120 pounds and 16 blue shark of over 80 pounds.

Mr. Culhane is understandably proud of these achievements and does not hesitate to tell his clients: "Our catches are not accidental. We send you out in a shark boat and you catch sharks. If you want to fish for skate we will see to it that you catch skate."

And to prove his point he handed me a fibreglass shark rod and a massive multiplier reel – an expensive example of precision engineering, its spool filled with yard after yard of braided flax line with a breaking strain well in excess of 100 pounds.

The fishing grounds lie some eight miles off Kinsale, and soon we were threading whole mackerel bait on to our lethal looking hooks. The lines were payed out and the long wait began.

The skipper spent his time pounding up dead fish in a large bucket. Technically known as "rubby dubby," this evil-smelling mixture is contained in a fine mesh bag and then suspended over the side of the boat, to provide an almost infallible shark attractor. It worked for us, and in less than an hour, the first of the six floats was lost to view.

Its owner was soon in contact and drove the hook home. Aided by a shoulder harness attached to the reel and wearing a body belt that allowed him to support the butt of his rod at waist level without risk of injury, he was able to put tremendous pressure on the fish.

He struggled constantly for a foothold in the heaving cockpit and won back line until the float came into view with the fish already visible, twisting and turning in the translucent green depths below.

The rod's work was over, and the boat's captain grasped the heavy wire trace to finish the task by hand. The shark surfaced in a welter of splash and spray, the gaff was unsheathed and it was hauled on board without ceremony.

The final chapter in the life of this particular shark – it weighed more than 60 pounds – was written with a pick handle used club wise.

This then is shark fishing the Irish way. Before the day was over another six had been hooked and landed, each one demanding the expenditure of a quite surprising level of physical effort.

My own contribution was one of 74 pounds, a great blue brute that took the bait within a few feet of the boat before sounding to a depth where the pressure half collapsed the air-filled rubber float.

It's a form of angling that undoubtedly has much to commend it, but I would much prefer to have my feet on dry land and to fly fish for trout, where presentation and deftness of hand spell the difference between success and failure.

←——————

Bonefish in the Bahamas

JUNE 1963, *The Observer*, LONDON

The heat was beyond belief for the sun was at its zenith with not a breath of wind to disturb the still air. The skiff rode to its anchor more than a quarter of a mile away as we moved stealthily through the knee-deep, lukewarm water. Angling in Ireland was never like this.

Fishing in the Bahamas is many things to many men with the unexpected almost commonplace. This time there was to be no element of chance, no tense trolling in deep blue seas where the next strike can mean anything from a marlin to a sailfish, from a wahoo to an amberjack.

This was my introduction to a branch of saltwater angling that has gained steadily in status and appeal over the last 25 years. To the scientists, still seeking fresh knowledge, the bonefish is *Albula vulpes*; to an ever-growing army of angling specialists it is the fleeting grey ghost, the elusive white fox of the tropical warm water flats.

Don McCarthy, lifelong fisherman and full-time advisor to the Bahamas Ministry of Tourism, in Nassau, was determined that I should meet my first bonefish off Joulter's Cays, a baffling maze of low-lying islets, mangrove swamps and endless flats at the northern end of Andros Island, largest of the Bahamas chain and famous for its bonefish.

We had travelled some ten sea miles from our base at the Andros Anglers' Club, past Morgan's Bluff, with its traditions of piracy and bloodshed, and on across the mouth of a vast bay. On the horizon a tropical storm flashed and growled and there were times when it seemed that we must run aground, but there was always water of a startling clarity beneath our keel.

The reputation of the bonefish is based on its well-founded ability to defy the hook with a strength that would do credit to an Atlantic salmon or a Pacific steelhead. It's no quarry for the novice or for the fisherman who cannot go about his business with the finesse of an edgy cat burglar.

The stranger to these waters would be helpless without the company of a guide. By the end of the day my sense of direction was completely gone, but Franklin, my friendly and courteous Bahamian companion, knew his business. Without him I would never have seen a bonefish let alone have caught four or five of the hundreds we stalked barefoot across the hard-packed sand.

Just as the poorly cast dry fly will put down every trout in a pool, so a carelessly presented lure will scatter a whole shoal of bonefish, sending them on a mad, headlong dash through the shallow water. There are occasions when the trout angler can see his quarry but more often than not he fishes with a combination of touch and instinct, placing his fly where he presumes the fish to be holding and then setting the hook at the moment of response.

In bone fishing, hunter and hunted are in visual contact at all time. Polaroid glasses are essential, for the glare from the water is murderous, and it can even be blinding if not treated with the utmost respect. I noted that Franklin, who has been fishing all his life, takes no chances.

The silvery bonefish is a streamlined bottom feeder with a superb turn of speed and a taste for crab, shrimp, squid and a variety of mollusks, food that it grinds with a set of granular teeth in a small mouth. The knowledge that they can be caught on artificial flies had inspired me with visions of epic battles in the sun.

We took a good three hours to find the first school, but from the moment I began to work out line for my initial cast, they were away, leaving behind an opaque, spreading cloud in the otherwise clear water.

Franklin was not surprised and opined that the strident noise made by the check on my fly reel had done the damage. From then on we relied on lightweight spinning tackle, presenting freshly collected crab bait with great care from an extreme range. That worked.

←——

An Islander for Islanders

JANUARY 2001, *www.ariverneversleeps.com*, VANCOUVER

Ask any fly fisherman what he (or she) knows about the J.S. Foster Corporation of Saanichton, near Victoria, British Columbia, and you will likely prompt a look of blank incomprehension. Then mention Islander Precision Reels and wait for the penny to drop.

The family-owned company, its origins a basement workshop on Elwood Street in Victoria, in the home of the late Joseph Foster, has been in the precision machining business for 30 years. More recently, over the past decade, their Islander Reels operation has grown to a point where it accounts for half the annual production of the firm and its 35-strong workforce.

These are fly reels that combine stunning good looks with the prime essentials of efficiency and dependability. As you might expect, this attention to detail and appearance makes for what can only be described as a luxury product – a Porsche or an Alfa Romeo to use the auto industry analogy – with prices ranging anywhere from US$250 to $495 before taxes, depending on model and size. Not cheap by any measure, but then each reel brings to the original purchaser a lifetime warranty against defects in materials and workmanship.

The commitment to excellence goes even further than that. Take the true story of the fisherman from Campbell River, BC, who lost everything in a house fire. His Islander, useable but definitely the worse for its experience, was recovered from the ashes, and he returned it to the company for service. Instead, he received a new reel with the original retained by Islander to demonstrate the durability of the product in the most extreme circumstances.

The Islander operation has to be a classic example of an enterprise moving with the times, listening to its workers, taking a chance on a new direction and then striving to be the very best in its field. Ten years ago there were no Islander reels, no beautifully crafted, golden-hued examples of inspired engineering design to complement images of successful fresh and saltwater fishermen in magazines across North America, in Japan, New Zealand and Australia and in the United Kingdom.

And all this because company president Jack Foster, son of the founder, listened to a few of his employees when they said there would be a market for a locally made reel offering mechanical excellence, eye-catching design and total reliability under the most demanding of conditions. Skilled machinists and dedicated fishermen, one or two were already running up reels at work for their own use and, you can be sure, attracting the attention of the knowledgeable anglers they encountered on Vancouver Island's rivers and lakes.

Many of those reels, original prototypes and early Islanders, remain in regular use, treasured companions of fishermen in pursuit of Pacific and Atlantic salmon, steelhead, brown and rainbow trout, bonefish, tarpon and permit and on up to the real heavyweights on the big game order of merit. Put a fish in water, anywhere any time, and there will be an Islander model equal to the challenge. All the more so these days with the fly fishermen chasing every imaginable species, from cod to pike, from sharks to bass.

Why Islander? From the outset the name and the familiar Island-shaped logo were seen as a natural choice, for these are Vancouver Island reels, designed and produced by Vancouver Island residents. It's an apt tribute as their Pacific coast birthplace is home to some of Canada's most productive fresh and saltwater fishing. What better place to develop a product one reviewer considered worthy of consideration for display at the Museum of Modern Art?

When I spent time recently with Islander manager Greg Millar and some of the team who work on various aspects of reel manufacture, he was not prepared to divulge specific production figures. That's understandable since this is a very competitive business, one where Islander sees North America as by far its largest market and Abel Reels, of California, and Timor Reels, from Florida, as major competitors.

"Over the last three years we have also developed a good presence in Japan and we are just now making inroads in Europe. Recently we have been starting to do business with a distributor in Italy," he said.

The very nature of the company's original business as a production machine shop provided skills perfectly in tune to the manufacture of high end fishing reels. In one way or another, Greg notes, everyone has input into the way the reels function mechanically and into the aesthetics too.

"We have four or five people working in the assembly room who do nothing but reels, and everyone else is involved in some way at some point from the moment the bars of aluminum are delivered right on through design, machining and finishing.

"One of the really nice things about being the manufacturer is that you can experiment with new materials, you can turn out a couple of parts, put them in a reel and try them out. We are always pushing ahead, trying something different, listening to our customers and to the people we get to test Islanders in the field."

That includes a group of saltwater guides in Florida who were given very specific instructions to use the reels just as hard as they possibly could with no attention to maintenance, no greasing, and no rinsing off in fresh water.

"We also tend to abuse our own reels," Greg explained, "and that's because we know there are people who will inevitably fish them like that and we want to know what to expect." Incidentally, employees are encouraged to borrow company reels whenever they go out – a privilege dear to the heart of every fisherman on the payroll.

Just as the market for Islander reels has increased beyond all expectations over the last 10 years, so Greg anticipates this aspect of the business will maintain steady growth. But he says the company will never put all its eggs in one basket. "We will never be in a position where we are reliant on one product. The jobbing work we do is for a dozen or more core companies. Many are in the high technology sector here on Vancouver Island and we both manufacture and provide design input for them."

He sees Islander reel sales growing at a conservative rate and explains: "Much of this is due to the demographics – more people going fishing, more people retiring with time to fish and with the disposable income. It's also a lot to do with the new popularity of saltwater fly fishing and of all outdoors activities, from birdwatching to international travel. Fly fishing is no different and every year we see growth."

While many people still both use and treasure the Islander reels they bought in the early 1990s, others are moving on to second- and third-generation products. Says Greg: "They love them and there is no need to change. It all depends on what you are doing and what you are getting out of the reel. Rods are getting lighter and lighter and you want a reel that balances.

"You could say it's an ongoing revolution. Our reels keep changing and getting better, although the differences are often hard to spot. Last year, for example, we completely redesigned our LX (Large Arbor with cross-holes in the arbor) Series. Generally speaking, ideas happen a year or two in advance of their introduction. It's very much a matter of being in tune with the market and recognizing ways to improve. Our original FR (Fly Reel) Series is now on Revision M from the first ones but, from a distance, you probably won't see any change."

Production also continues of the Islander mooching reel, widely used by saltwater fishermen in pursuit of Pacific salmon along the coastline of British Columbia, and in the USA, but omitted from more recent brochures to avoid confusing fly-fishing dealers unfamiliar with mooching as a valid technique.

Aside from its acclaimed stable of fishing reels, the company's focus is on the manufacture of high quality, high tolerance plastic and metal parts for local and international customers. Products include hydraulic, stainless and titanium components, optics parts and marine research equipment. These can range in quantity from a single prototype to over 100,000 pieces. The firm is used to machining parts with tolerances at or below 0.0002 inches (0.005 mm).

Islander voices

JEFF WILLING, mechanical designer: "The major difference between now and when we started is having computer-based equipment. It allows you to get a little more artistic, if you like to use that word, to have a smoother transition of line. There was no engraving on the early reels although we were Islander from the minute we made the first one. The name was one of a number we bantered around. We are all islanders and it just seemed right. It sounded good. The first reels we made were centre-pin float reels for steelhead. Then came the first fly reels, eventually known as the FR2. At that time we were working pretty closely with a couple of fly-fishing schools and we exchanged ideas. Most of our design has been a group effort working with the industry and fishermen. We want to give people what they want to fish with. All the holes you see in the newer models make them look great – perhaps a bit like Swiss cheese. It lightens them up and, with the new carbon fibre rods, a few grams make all the difference. The gold colour is very distinctive (there are also identical models in black with no price distinction) and you can see them from a long way off, especially out on the ocean. If we see one in use we will often detour to ask how the fishermen are getting on and tell them we made the reel. Then we meet up later on the dock, have a beer and offer a full service."

PHIL COTTERELL, senior lathe machinist: "There was one guy who for years had wanted us to produce fishing reels. His name was Pete Gustin, a machinist, who later went on to have his own shop not far from here. He came to me and together we went with the idea to Jack Foster. Everything came from that one conversation. Pete had moved out from Ontario. He was and still is a most avid fisherman. He makes me look as if I have never fished in my life. After he came we had a slow period and we asked how could it hurt to spend a few hundred dollars on labour and materials. Right away it took off and I think it was Pete who showed the reels to Peter Morrison who worked for a distribution company in Alberta. There were so many people involved to bring us to where we are today. We have become part of the fishing scenery and that's pretty exciting."

BRANDY CORNISH, assembly room employee tuning reels before packaging: "Listen to that noise. I just love the sound when the line is peeling off."

Three bulls and a bear

DECEMBER 2004. *www.ariverneversleeps.com*,
VANCOUVER

It's still raining. That's no surprise since the day's forecast was for up to two inches, par for the course in the long valley that cuts through the mountains of British Columbia's Coast Range as the annual October deluge starts in earnest.

At the remote Pitt River Lodge Glenn Baglo is in the kitchen working up a feast of filet mignon and tiger prawns, Nick Didlick is mixing mind-numbing martinis while Mark Hume and Mike Smyth mull over the first day's adventures at the bar.

Meantime, I am scribbling notes for this piece at the dinner table with the memories of what happened a couple of hours ago still in clear focus, vivid enough to last a lifetime. Wilderness fly fishing is always going to be different and sometimes challenging, that goes without saying, but this was a never-to-be-forgotten wildlife encounter.

The Upper Pitt River had come up a good foot since first light but was still running clear and definitely fishable. Wiser men would probably have gone inside for dry clothes and warm drinks by mid-afternoon. Instead, Hume and I headed off to try a deep, broad run no more than ten minutes' walk from the lodge. Two hours passed and Hume had had enough. He was on his way with a shouted "see you soon."

The pool was long and the flow strong, the sound of moving water and the familiar rhythm of cast and step, cast and step, almost hypnotic. The deep-wading fisherman is totally absorbed, eyes only for the river and a break in the stream that will soon come within casting range, perhaps a potential holding lie.

Then a splash to my back breaks the spell: *a running fish,* I thought, *and close up behind me against the river's edge*. I turned to see instead a full-grown black bear staring straight at me from no more than 15 feet away. It had come off the gravel bar and waded out to the level of its chest. I was waist-deep in the water and, with a stretch, could have touched the tip of my fly rod against its heavy, black head.

Who knows how long it had been standing there or what was on its mind? It contemplated me with no signs of aggression, curious for sure and far, far too close for the comfort of any fisherman.

My instinctive reaction was to shout ... and shout as loudly as I could. "Go away ... f*#* off, f*#* off," I yelled, followed by a string of other equally meaningless commands. The bear stood its ground. Not moving forward ... or backwards. It didn't make a sound.

With nowhere to go for sanctuary, no one to call for help (the radio was forgotten, buried deep in a dry pocket inside my waterproof jacket) we were in the grips of a proverbial stalemate, on the horns of a true dilemma. I shouted again and then raised and shook my wading staff, as if a thin wooden stick with a wrapping of lead at its tip was going to be any deterrent.

The bear, grown heavy from feasting on the river's salmon, looked to weigh a good 400 pounds or even more. Admired across the width of the river, or better still, from the security of a vehicle, it would have been magnificent.

I did not have time to be really scared but still had time enough to wonder what would happen if the bear made a move in my direction. A few short steps, a single lunge would be enough to close the gap between us in an instant. Instead, at that moment, the bear slowly, deliberately turned toward the shore. I shouted after it and the bear paused in the shallows to look at me. After some 20 yards it stopped again, watching me for the last time, before scrambling away over a jumbled pile of logs left by previous floods.

The walk back to the lodge as darkness fell was hurried and anxious. My thoughts raced as to what other possible outcomes might have resulted. My reactions in a situation of undoubted risk had been instinctive but effective. I was left to wonder *was this just an unusually curious animal, one that had come out of the forest to check on an unknown presence in its home river? Or was it stalking me?*

Back in the comfort of the lodge, with a large shot of Bushmills whiskey to steady the nerves, I described the experience. Hosts Lee and Danny Gerak were simply astonished.

"I have never, ever heard of a black bear deliberately going into the water close to a fisherman like that, and we haven't seen a bear around here for at least three months," Danny said.

Baglo thought for a moment and offered: "Just as well you didn't drop your back cast. You'd have been out on the backing pretty fast."

And how was the Pitt River fishing that first day? For me it was a three-fish effort as the level inched ever higher, bull trout of 20,

22 and 24 inches, solid takes in heavy water with the last and largest turning and making a good 50 yards down rock-strewn rapids before coming to hand. The fly each time was a Black Egg-Sucking Leech, definitely the secret of success on a day of days for such very different reasons.

Little wonder I was entrusted with my own bear spray canister for the rest of the trip.

<--------|

Raising dam will improve Little Qualicum River

MAY 2006, *The Steelhead Review*, GREATER GEORGIA BASIN STEELHEAD RECOVERY PROGRAM, NANAIMO

The Little Qualicum has to be one of Vancouver Island's unheralded gems, an intimate, friendly river that rushes and glides over some 20 kilometres from Cameron Lake to enter the Strait of Georgia just north of Qualicum Beach.

For over a decade, the Little Qualicum's steelhead have had to endure most troubled times, like others of their kind on both sides of the Georgia Basin, while its salmon and cutthroat trout continue to show strong returns in their respective seasons.

Now, planning is underway for a $94,000 BC Conservation Foundation (BCCF) project that could add significantly to the river's overall fish-producing potential. This entails modifications to the weir at the outlet of Cameron Lake to allow an extra 67,535 cubic metres of water to be stored in late spring and then discharged to augment depleted river flows during the summer.

If it lives up to expectations, the project, made possible by grants from the Pacific Salmon Commission and the Ministry of Transportation, will enhance the river's ability to rear additional wild steelhead, chinook and coho smolts. Project completion is targeted for the fall of 2005.

The BCCF application for funding identifies summer flows as a critical factor controlling fish production, particularly for stream-rearing species like coho and chinook salmon, steelhead and cutthroat trout. "Provincial guidelines suggest optimum flow conditions for summer rearing are achieved with 20 per cent of the mean annual discharge (MAD) while the Little Qualicum flow routinely drops to 10 per cent MAD.

"The amount of water in a river dictates rearing space and directly relates to invertebrate production. A greater abundance of riffle and fast water habitat increases abundance of invertebrates (fish food organisms). Fish that are provided with a greater abundance of food during the summer will grow larger and more successfully over-winter and survive at sea."

The funding application adds: "Recent summer droughts in east coast Vancouver Island streams have accentuated the need to improve summer base flows where cost-effective projects exist. Such projects have been used on many Vancouver Island watersheds, including the Englishman River, just south of the Little Qualicum."

The modifications to the existing concrete weir (replacing existing stop logs with longer, fortified versions and installing a new sluice and fish way structure) will increase Cameron Lake storage by an elevation of 50 centimetres and improve passage conditions for resident trout recruiting to the lake. This could provide additional flow to the lower river of up to 0.46 cubic metres per second over a 60-day low flow period, translating into a significant increase in productivity downstream.

Consultations with Qualicum First Nations and lakeshore landowners are nearly complete with no objections to date. The project's key partners are Fisheries and Oceans Canada (DFO), the provincial Ministry of Water, Land and Air Protection and the recently formed Little Qualicum River Watershed Plan. DFO owns the weir and has been very supportive with significant in-kind contributions of engineering work. BCCF and federal/provincial fisheries staffs will co-ordinate all aspects of the work.

In recent years habitat restoration projects have led to the stabilization of a large clay slide on Lower Kinkade Creek, well above the lengthy federal salmon spawning channel, and to the breaching of an old irrigation dam on Whiskey Creek, below the hatchery.

Twenty thousand dollars has been invested in a program to provide additional natural cover for juvenile steelhead and coho through the installation of large woody debris structures in four strategic riverbed locations. Steel cables attached to tons of ballast rocks are used to secure the logs. This work was completed in 2004 and will soon undergo effectiveness monitoring.

For the fly fisherman, the Little Qualicum can be a river of special delight, one where catch-and-release restrictions translate into very limited pressure and, at times, sport of the highest order. If only steelhead stocks can be rebuilt, this river's future will again be filled with promise.

Stoltz Slide remedial plan announced

MAY 2006, *The Steelhead Review*, GREATER GEORGIA BASIN STEELHEAD RECOVERY PROGRAM, NANAIMO

The largest in-stream conservation project ever undertaken on Vancouver Island is scheduled to start in late summer, once all funding sources have been confirmed.

Stabilization of the 600-metre Stoltz Slide, on the Cowichan River near Duncan, will take up to three years to complete and will resolve a major environmental concern. The slide has been responsible for releasing huge amounts of glacial sediment into the lower 20 kilometres of the river since the early 1990s.

Studies have confirmed the slide has dumped between 10,000 and 28,000 cubic metres of fine sand and silt sediment into the watershed every year since 1953, representing between 35 per cent and 45 per cent of the total sediment load measured 10 kilometres downstream.

The estimated cost of restoration work in the first year will be $600,000, with the total cost of the completed project between $900,000 and $1.3 million. $250,000 has been approved by the Pacific Salmon Commission's Southern Fund and $300,000 has been earmarked for Stoltz by the Georgia Basin's Living Rivers Program. The Vancouver Island Steelhead Recovery Plan, largely funded by the Habitat Conservation Trust Fund, will direct $27,000 to Stoltz, while additional contributions are being sought from the Ministry of Transportation and other partners at the Cowichan Stewardship Roundtable.

The Cowichan has long been acknowledged as one of Vancouver Island's – and indeed British Columbia's – most important sport fish watersheds. It has significant runs of chinook, coho and chum salmon and of steelhead, while also supporting resident stocks of brown trout, rainbow trout and cutthroat trout. The brown trout, introduced in the 1930s, are well established and can grow to a considerable size, providing a special challenge to the dedicated fly fisherman.

The Cowichan's anadromous and resident fish resources have an estimated economic value of between $5.4 million and $6.2 million, but the sediment situation has had a heavy impact on the overall future of the river.

An egg-to-fry survival rate study in the winter of 2004–05 looked at redds over 40 kilometres of the upper and lower main stems. At the uppermost site, near Lake Cowichan, the mean survival rate was 86 per cent; at three sites on the heavily sedimented lower river ,the rates ranged from 0.7 per cent to 6.8 per cent, figures described by the study as "extremely poor."

The 2005 Cowichan Recovery Plan lists fall chinook as "the number one priority species" for recovery actions in the watershed. It has already been determined that, at current marine survival rates, the Cowichan chinook cannot achieve biological replacement when the egg-to-fry survival rate falls below 6 per cent. This was the case in 1991, 1994 and 1998.

If the marine survival rate is below 3.5 per cent, then survival during the early freshwater life-stage is critical in dictating future adult returns. Thus, poor habitat conditions, mediated by floods and major sediment loads "can tip the balance against achieving returns that will rebuild stocks."

The 2005 return of brood stock chinook to the Cowichan was the worst on record, and this despite reduced sport and commercial interceptions. All this gives further emphasis to the need for extraordinary measures to be taken to increase freshwater habitat productivity.

The Stoltz Slide project has the support of the Cowichan Stewardship Roundtable, chaired by Cowichan First Nations, and work is planned to start during low water flows in July and August. When complete, water quality and clarity will be greatly improved to benefit all fish species.

The planned work will involve either excavating a new channel on the inside of the bank facing the slide, or modifying the existing side channel on the south bank. This will reduce the flow of water striking the toe of the slide. A partial weir will then be built to divert some of the flow into the new channel.

These modifications will allow the continually eroding main slide formation, approximately 250 metres in length, to be stabilized more easily. The main stem channel will be widened and the excavated gravel and cobbles will be placed at the toe of the slide to create a new terrace some two to three metres in height. This terrace will be between 15 metres and 25 metres in width and will be protected by willows and large woody debris, placed so as not to inhibit public river navigation.

Remediation of the Stoltz Slide has been identified as a high priority in the Greater Georgia Basin Steelhead recovery Action Plan. The intention is do the second and third stage of the project to proceed in 2007 and 2008, assuming sufficient funding is made available.

Enhanced Ash River flows to benefit fish stocks

MAY 2006, *The Steelhead Review*, THE GREATER GEORGIA BASIN STEELHEAD RECOVERY PROGRAM, NANAIMO

The first in an annual series of planned water flow increases for the benefit of fish stocks in Vancouver Island's Ash River took place as scheduled over a 48-hour period August 30-31, 2005.

The release of water from BC Hydro's Elsie Lake reservoir raised the river's flow three-fold, from the normal minimum of 3.3 cubic metres per second to 10 cubic metres per second at a point 15 to 20 kilometres downstream. In September, a second one-day discharge of 20 cubic metres per second was completed to produce the optimum benefit for fish passage, including adult salmon and summer-run steelhead.

Hydro noted summer steelhead now have access to the Elsie Dam and its feeder streams above the Lanterman and Dickson Falls. Monitoring will determine whether the higher flows will allow coho and other salmon species to make similar upstream progress.

"The increase in river flows are similar to what would occur naturally with a storm event," says Ian Dodd, Hydro's Natural Resource Specialist. "They provide a trigger or signal for fish to migrate above river obstacles and access upper river spawning habitat. The agreement on what we call 'fish pulse flows' came out of the successful Ash River Water Use Plan (WUP) consultative committee that started work in October 2000."

Changes in hydroelectric operating procedures on the system will provide for:

‹ Increased rearing and spawning habitat for salmon and trout in the Ash River, including a nearly 14-fold increase in steelhead-rearing habitat.

‹ Reduced barriers to fish migration at Lanterman and Dickson Falls by tripling Ash River flows over 48- and 24-hour periods in August and September.

Generation of 6 per cent additional power while more water is being released into the Ash River will be made possible by revisions to the licence determining that amount of water available to Hydro for the operation of the Great Central Lake powerhouse.

The Ash River, a major tributary of the Stamp-Somass system, supports important runs of both summer and winter steelhead. It also supplies part of the Alberni Valley's power needs. Water drawn from the 672-hectare Elsie Lake Reservoir is delivered 7.4 kilometres through two tunnels and a penstock, to the 27-megawatt powerhouse on the north shore of Great Central Lake.

Membership of the WUP Consultative and Technical committees included Ministry of Environment senior fisheries biologist Craig Wightman and encompassed a broad range of water use interests, with representatives from First Nations, environmental organizations, government, industry, sport fishing and recreation groups, local residents and Hydro. The committee structure allowed for both active and observer status and 17 organizations or members of the public monitored the process as observers.

Looking ahead, the committee has recommended a number of monitoring studies to obtain more information, confirm the perceived benefits, and inform future decisions on how to operate the Ash River hydroelectric facility. The committee will review the monitoring study results annually and assess the need to recommend an early WUP review five years after receiving regulatory approval.

CASTING BACK VIII ...
to the book about Babine

⟵───┤

Strom's letters from Ejnar

Author's note: This book, Babine: A 50-Year Celebration of a World-Renowned Steelhead and Trout River *(2010, Frank Amato, Portland, OR) was a combined effort by myself and Pierce Clegg, recently retired after more than 25 years as owner and operator of the famous Norlakes Steelhead Camp on the Babine River. One of my favourite chapters, re-printed here, tells the story of the lengthy correspondence between pioneering Ejnar Madsen, who built the original camp in the early 1950s, and one of his long-time guests and friends, Clarence Stromsness, a district attorney from California. In many respects the story highlights what was a golden age in the history of steelhead fishing in British Columbia.*

Not long before Clarence Stromsness, known to all in the fishing fraternity as Strom, succumbed to cancer in 1994 he was invited to spend the first week of September at the Babine River Steelhead Camp as the Clegg family's special guest. At the time Pierce wrote: "I certainly wish this invitation was under better circumstances. I know you love the river as I do, and what better place to spend one's last days than on the Babine."

While the invitation had to be declined, it was a fitting tribute to a distinguished fisherman who had come to know and cherish the river as few others over the course of 27 years and 22 visits and many, many Babine steelhead dating back to 1967.

Strom's Pool has honoured his name for years and, as Pierce told him in his letter: "It has become one of my favourite upstream runs. I don't know that many clients from the 60s who have had runs and pools named after them, therefore I will always think of you when I cast a line into Strom's Pool."

Pierce's letter is one of a number kept by Strom's son Chris, then 25 and his father's fishing partner on that first trip, a dedicated steelheader and a seventh time Babine visitor in 2008. The majority of the letters are from Ejnar Madsen, and these extracts help to flesh out the story of the Norlakes Steelhead Camp, or River Camp, as it was originally known, almost from its earliest days.

There is also one of Strom's own letters, dated October 13, 1986, to Chris, his wife Sharon and their sons Rune and Bjorn. It describes his 18th and penultimate Norlakes trip, one during which he landed 22 of 39 steelhead hooked. "No big fish this year. I had one buck that may have gone 20 pounds. He was 39 inches long."

Strom, in his time a district attorney and, for 12 years, mayor of Tehama, CA, continues: "Because of various cancellations there were just nine in camp and really only seven as the other two were a professional guide and a photographer making a movie of the fishing. That meant considerable leeway to move around.

"Unfortunately it rained hard on Sunday and Monday so the river below the Nilkitkwa was out. Fortunately, because of the small number of fishermen, we had room upstream at Angus, Gravel Bar, Olson's, Strom's, Hansen's Corner or Halfway. Even fished Six Pound Pool a couple of days. Caught fish every day ending up 22/39." Every fisherman knows the numbers equate to landing 22 of the 39 fish he encountered over a seven-day period – superb statistics by any measure, anywhere.

"The greatest day was Thursday. I was alone at Strom's until about 11:00 a.m. During that time I hooked nine fish and landed six. Caught one more at the Gravel Bar so I had seven fish on the bank that day, mostly females. All in all, aside from the rain, it was a fabulous trip. The first day it was about 50F early in the morning and 60F during midday. That went down during the week and the last morning it was 28F."

Fishing was in Strom's blood from an early age. Kristian, his father, owned a fishing boat, trolling for chinook salmon off the mouth of the Columbia River in the summer and crabbing in the winter. He lost his life when his boat went down crossing Willapa Bar in 1931.

Chris, from Dunsmuir, CA, continues: "Dad grew up around water and boats and fish. So he just naturally helped with the boats and fuel and fish in 1967. That's why Ejnar invited him up to help and fish with no money involved for so many years. Later, he went as a regular guest for a few years before driving a camper up and staying near the weir, fishing the upper river and usually being invited down for dinner at the camp."

Years later, reflecting on his working relationship with Ejnar, Strom wrote: "I offered to help out for three or four weeks a year if they would let me fish half a day or so. Thus it developed that, for a number of years, I was a bull cook. Make beds, cut wood, make sandwiches, or do anything useful. Also fish half a day or so unless detailed to go up to the landing for gasoline. That economy moves on fuel and it is all either brought in by boat, or carried in, depending on the location. Anyway, I loved it."

Prior to his first Babine experience, in late September of 1967, Ejnar advised Strom: "We have about 12 miles of beautiful river to fish, most of which is only accessible by jet boats. We have two of these and also two cabins on the lower part of the river where we often spend the night when fishing there. There are fine stretches of fly water and good pools for spin and bait fishing. The boats are mostly used for transportation on the river and waders or hip boots are necessary for fishing.

"The fish are strong and good tackle is needed. In 1966 the largest one taken was 29 pounds and there were about a dozen over 25 pounds. Most of them are eight to 14 pounds, very few smaller ones".

Of that first visit Chris still remembers meeting Joe Brooks, the renowned American outdoors writer, and also watching his father cook steaks over an open flame that roared out of the hole in a wood stove on their one night at the River Camp. "The next year dad brought a Hibachi and showed the camp how to barbecue a steak."

The 1967 trip was a success and Strom, then living in Corning, CA, brought home a trophy steelhead. In December of that same year Ejnar wrote: "The fishing continued good and the weather was fairly mild into November. The last guests left on November 6 and Jim (his partner, Jim Price) and I spent most of that month cutting firewood and getting ready for next year.

"There were a number of fish taken over 25 pounds – one of them 28 pounds. We covered a lot of water and, after the river cleared, did most of our fishing as far as seven miles below the cabins. There are many good pools and also fly water there that can be waded but the Cabin Pool – later renamed Ejnar's Pool in his memory – is still number one.

"I wish to thank you for your generous offer of cooking at the cabins for us next October – we certainly appreciate it. For the last two years we have been working toward expanding the facilities down there so we can sleep eight or 10 and not have to go back to the lodge at all – at least not (until) the latter part of October. This would call for larger kitchen facilities and also for a full-time cook for about two months. In any event, I will write you later this winter (about) how things progress and perhaps we can work something out where you can also get some fishing in."

Thereafter a close friendship developed between the two Scandinavians, Ejnar from Denmark and Strom, whose Norwegian-born parents met in South Bend, WA, after emigrating separately in the early 1900s.

Chris again: "My grandfather's name was Kristian Johan Martin Mikklesen. As was not uncommon in those days, he took the name of Stromsness, his tiny village, when he left Norway around 1905. His boathouse remains there to this day."

In a letter dated March 21, 1968 Ejnar told Strom: "We recently got a lease on the land on the river where our cabins are. We now feel secure in building more cabins so we can sleep eight guests down there and have a cook from early in September 'til the beginning of November. We don't have one yet and I don't know whether you would want to tackle it.

"If you feel you would like to come up, we have three busy weeks, from September 21 to October 13, when we could use an extra hand and would be glad to have your help. It wouldn't likely be as a cook, but helping us on the river in a general way and perhaps running a boat for us now and again. I am sure it is something that you would feel at home at, and it would also give you an opportunity to do some fishing yourself."

The offer was obviously to Strom's liking for, on September 6, 1968 Ejnar remarked: "We look forward to seeing you again and I hope you will enjoy your weeks here. We finished a new cabin on the river for cooking and eating and have a woman cook arriving later this week. If you would help Jim and I with the daily chores and perhaps run a boat now and again, I am sure you will get a good deal of fishing in and, at the same time, help us out greatly to make the wheels turn.

"The week September 21 to 28 is very busy and will probably appear a bit confusing to you, but after that it will be smooth sailing. Please bring warm clothes and rain gear. The woman at the lodge will, of course, take care of your laundry. There are a good number of steelhead in the river and we have taken several, but are still fishing dry flies for trout as well."

The arrangement obviously worked well for all concerned with Ejnar thanking Strom warmly in a letter dated November 5, 1968. "Your assistance to us was of great help and I hope that the chores left you enough time for fishing. We have not made any definite plans for next fall but I am sure that a similar arrangement will be fine with us.

"We have only four guests this week and they will be leaving on November 8. The weather and fishing are still great. Last week there were 13 steelhead over 20 pounds landed. Olga Beck (the camp cook at that time) is still fishing from her porch and has taken several steelhead. In fact, I believe she can outcast and out-fish some of our guests.

Olga, who retired in 1971, was credited by writer Ed Zern, in an April, 1973 *Field and Stream* feature, with catching some 70 steelhead from the Cabin Pool in the four years she worked for Ejnar, with all but four of them released. What became known as Olga's Rock was her favourite fishing stance.

Ejnar continues: "The week after you left one of our guests dropped dead on the riverbank. He was 74 and the cause was judged to be a coronary or massive heart attack. We knew him quite well, as he had been coming for about 10 years, and everyone thought it was a wonderful way to pass away. Aside from that, our only excitement has been the fishing and it has been sufficient."

On March 14, 1969 Ejnar wrote: "We have enjoyed sunny and mild weather the last three weeks. I had half a moose hanging in the carport since December 10. It was completely frozen until a few days ago when I finally skinned it out and cut it up for the freezer. I was at the lodge earlier this week, shoveling snow off the roofs, and everything looked fine. There were many tracks of moose and wolves around the place and one morning I counted four wolves on the ice in the bay to the south. They are hard on game in the winter but seldom bother people."

Jim Price, Ejnar's partner at that time, describes himself as "the world's worst letter writer" in correspondence with Strom dated January 14, 1970 and goes on to say that he was able to stay at the lodge until mid-December as the weather was "so mild."

"Ejnar was with me for part of the time. Because of the mild weather we were able to put new foundations under the main lodge. Big job, we were very lucky to get it done. We also finished the wood, cleared all those willows and alders from the little creek by the lodge, put new foundations under cabin 1, and tore all the old porch off my cabin and put new foundations under that as well. The weather really gave us a jump on things for next year."

That June, Ejnar had told Strom that he had not been able to purchase plastic propellers similar to the ones he had brought up the previous fall for use with the 15 horsepower and 20 horsepower Johnson outboards. "Perhaps I could prevail on you to mail one or two to Jim and I and we will square with you later."

Strom was back again in the fall with Ejnar advising him in early September to bring "plenty of Oki Drifters" as a new regulation banning fishing with roe as bait was now in force. In August he had told Strom: "We have just finished the other cabin at the river camp and built another cabin 15 miles further down the river so we have more elbow room. Joy and the children will be at the lodge until November, the boys taking school lessons by correspondence."

A week after season's end, on November 16, 1970, Ejnar explained that he and Jim Price were still at the lodge, taking care of a few moose hunters and doing a little fishing.

"I went down to close up the lower cabin a few days ago and caught a nice steelhead right in front. The cabin was not used for the last two-three weeks as we pretty well had the river to ourselves because of Bob Wickwire (then owner of the Steelhead Lodge a few miles downstream) not having any guests.

"Fishing was good, even without the roe, and there was one 33½-pound fish taken and several in the 25-30 pound class. We only caught about 10 tagged fish – mostly small ones – and it will be interesting to see what (they) get out of the figures we faithfully collected.

"Joy (Ejnar's wife) and the children stayed at the lodge until a couple of days ago and the boys are starting school today. It all worked out well and I don't think they have missed out on anything of importance.

"Olga left on November 8 and was glad to see the end of the season. She was in good spirits all fall and I hope that she will come back again next year. I also hope that we will see you again. We will likely do some more improvements."

Strom came back to the Babine each year between 1967 and 1993, missing only five seasons. In that time Chris says his dad's catch records show he landed more than 400 steelhead, with a high of 63 (1968) and 62 (1971) and lows of two (1979, when he also suffered an aneurism), four (1981) and five (1982).

Of the 1979 heart incident, Chris recalls: "Dad would almost certainly have died in Smithers except that Joy Madsen, by sheer force of her personality, convinced the Vancouver airport to allow a mercy flight plane to land despite an air-traffic controller strike there."

Through the years Ejnar maintained his side of the correspondence with Strom by way of a succession of reports and comments, nearly all of them neatly typed by Joy. Success on the river always took pride of place along with news of the family and day-to-day events on the water.

December 27, 1971: "The fishing continued good with many fish in the river. There were some cold days at the end of October and about the 5th of November when it was uncomfortable to be on the river and the steelhead took poorly. There were a number of large ones caught, up to 26 pounds, but none larger. As usual, we had good fly fishing above the weir in October.

"From the time you left, Bob Wickwire only had three guests for a few days and then closed his camp so we had the river to ourselves and didn't fish downriver very far. Unfortunately the cold weather early in November forced us to close the river camp a few days early. It went down to zero a couple of nights and the lower end of Nilkitkwa Lake froze so we had to use the logging road and truck to get out with the last guests."

At that time Strom was considering buying Jim Price's shares in the business and Ejnar commented: "If you are serious about it, please write to me soon so we can try to work something out ... I want to emphasize that there is a lot of work involved in keeping the place running but apart from that it is a good life."

December 29, 1971: "The week after you left we had a group of four from Seattle who caught 84 steelhead. They only kept four, two 25-pounders, one 24 pounds and a small one for dinner. The two 25-pounders were caught by one person and he wanted them both mounted for his twin sons, which his wife had last year when he was up here fishing and, incidentally, was skunked. The first weeks after you left were very good with over 30 steelhead landed per day on several occasions and probably 175 fish landed per week.

"I expect to go to Vancouver early in January to see Jim and find out about his plans and desires. If you have any ideas please write or give me a phone call."

March 30, 1972: "The Forestry is making some headway with the bridge by Six Pound Pool. Whether it will be finished by this year is another question and there is not much on the other side to go across for. The big sawmill at Houston, which cut timber up there, finally went broke after losing $60 million and the pieces have been picked up by another company.

September 9, 1972: "The weather is still fairly warm and dry and we are fishing mostly for trout. Both salmon and steelhead seem to be late. The salmon run is big but there are not enough steelhead to make fishing for them very interesting. We have six jet motors running and I hope we won't have as much trouble this year as last."

November 13, 1973: "The fishing continued good and I reckon that the fellows in the week following you landed at least 150 fish and probably close to 200. One of them landed 45 and another 30. The Log Jam was one of the hot spots. In three days it came up with 28 fish and seven consecutive ones were over 20 pounds. But none of them were kept.

"The weather continued mild and we had hardly a night's frost and no snow at all before November. Since then it has been plenty cold and all the small lakes and much of Babine Lake have frozen over (in) the last few days.

"I hope to have time to make some general improvements to the

River Camp cabins next spring. I am afraid the rates for steelhead fishing will have to be raised to keep step with the costs but I don't know yet by how much."

September 27, 1974: "It is a late fall up here and fishing has been the slowest I have ever seen it up until now. We are only hooking five to 10 steelhead a day and not landing all of them either. Weather is beautiful and sunny and the river is perfect, just not many fish in it yet.

"We moved one of the front cabins back in line with the duplex and put a ceiling and oil heat in it as well as insulation. It was a good improvement and the other cabin will be moved back next year.

"Chris Barto and his younger brother Stacy are helping this fall and we have a young man cooking for a change. It is hard to find anyone to do the job these days."

November 13, 1974: "Sorry to learn from your letter that you didn't become judge – better luck next time, Strom. Fishing was slow right into October but the last half of that month was very good. The total number of steelhead landed came to slightly over 550 with only 72 killed, both figures a little below normal.

"The camp was busy and I am glad that Chris was here again as well as his younger brother. There was a record run of coho, which helped the fishing, and we made some very successful trips up to Smokehouse Island fishing for them."

August 2, 1975: "Regulations are pending which will require all non-resident steelheaders to be with a registered guide but it likely won't be the rule this year. Karl and Erik have been doing much of the guiding (for trout) this summer and are getting good at catching fish themselves."

Next from Chris's file comes a handwritten note dated November 18, 1977 in which Ejnar comments: "The last steelheader left on November 7, the last moose hunter on November 12 and I left on November 15. It was a good season and a long one. Our guests landed a total of 750 steelhead but only killed 41."

A letter dated November 11, 1980 strikes a high note with Ejnar reporting: "Steelhead fishing was the best and most consistent since the 60s and we landed over 1000 – one thousand – with fewer guests than last fall."

It begins: "First off I want to tell you that we had no heart attacks but there were about half a dozen cases of the trots which can be serious when you happen to have a top bunk. We had a very good cook, Marie, who is somewhat like Olga in that she has a very good disposition and likes to catch steelhead – not just fish."

Ejnar adds that many of his guests had been asking about Strom. "I said that you would be back next year but, please note, I don't want you to come unless you are absolutely sure you can take it."

"We opened the camp on September 6 and the fish were there in numbers and never left us, even for a day. One guest landed 26 on flies the first week and I think almost everyone caught more fish than any other year. Nobody got skunked. One odd thing was that fishing by the bridge was poor and very few people fished there. Neither were there many large fish over 20 pounds but there were certainly enough small fry, 10 to 16 pounds, to compensate for this. Fishing on most other rivers around here was good and attributed mainly to the early closure of the (commercial) salmon fishing because of small runs."

Such dramatic numbers speak clearly to the reputation of what, despite many pressing challenges, remains one of the world's greatest steelhead rivers, albeit one where present day catches can never be expected to match those of the sixties and seventies. Those were the glory days. What's gone is gone but the memories remain, wonderful reminders of what still is, by any standards, a truly exceptional fishery.

Strom and his friends continued to come to Steelhead Camp each year until 1988 when he decided to make his own arrangements, camping and fishing on the Babine, the Buckley and the Kispiox. Of this arrangement on the Babine he wrote to Chris: "Walking is very possible to the Halfway Hole (Drift), Hansen's

Corner and even to the Nilkitkwa (Gravel) Bar as well as to Strom's. I feel honoured to have a pool named for me, incidentally.

He also expressed his concerns at that time over the possibility of a new bridge being built to cross the river near Trail Drift, now better known as Upper and Lower Trail. This logging-related proposal was fought to the bitter end by Pierce and others and was eventually cancelled by the provincial government.

Strom commented in the very detailed diary he kept of his October, 1987 trip: "They have cleared the road area, about 100 yards wide, and have pushed the road bed right to the river's edge. It is ugly. Pierce thinks he can stop it, on the basis of what is best for the economy, tourism vs. timber, but we think he is fighting a lost cause.

"If the road goes in I think there will be a lot of people (drifting) down from the weir to the new bridge, assuming there is a new bridge, fishing the good spots on the way down. In that wilderness I doubt the ban on fishing from boats will be observed for long. How would the catch and release program be observed? There are a lot of places where a bright steelhead could be consumed over a campfire without being seen. Enhancement would be an almost impossible task and I can even imagine there would be those who would use roe."

In his final report, dated October 12, 1993, Strom advised Chris: "I have come to the reluctant conclusion that I have fished my last time on the Bulkley or Babine. There is a lack of interest, hard as that might be to believe, and a great lack of physical ability. I find that moving about on the slippery rocks in the river is getting to be a real effort, even with a staff."

Then he suggested a possible summer trip with his own boat and motor to fly fish the upper river. "That is fun, not physically exhausting, and holds much promise," he wrote. Sadly, Strom died the following June.

Anna Babine Stromsness – Strom's great-granddaughter, Chris and Sharon's granddaughter and daughter of Bjorn and

Elizabeth – fished on the Babine in 2004. Hopefully she will someday be the fourth generation of Strom's family to know and appreciate this special river.

CASTING BACK IX ...
to my 80th year diary

One fisherman's year

Jan.1, 2015: With an 80th Birthday coming up in July I thought it would be interesting to compile a detailed diary covering all my fishing activities over the full course of the year, both in fresh water and in the ocean. According to my count I managed to get out with rod in hand 52 times during the year, a neat average of once a week. Also included with these extracts are some relevant notes from regular and valued fishing partners Glenn DiGeorgio, Bryce Olson, Harvey Stern and Gordon Shead.

JAN. 9: Spent the day with Gordon with the Spey rods on the Stamp ... no tugs but a lovely mild day to be out and about and a good flow of clear, clear water. Heard of one fresh-run fish being taken on the fly last week but nothing else and not too many fishermen about. Of course, it's a weekday and not everyone can avoid going to work.

JAN. 22: Went with Gordon to one of the lesser west coast watersheds. Waded across the river – just – and bushwhacked for 20 minutes to a really nice pool river left. Both of us fished it down carefully twice with the double-handers and sink tips but nothing there. Gordon had four offers and landed two of them from that same spot just after the big pre-Christmas flood had subsided. Fished another spot downstream around midday with similar nil tugs outcome.

Beautiful water if perhaps just on the high side, which meant that another likely looking run/pool combination downstream had to be passed by this time. Very, very mild – around 7/8C – and felt like a day in mid-April. Almost raining some of the time and quite heavy driving back over the Hump. Forecast is for lots of rain over next 48 hours so fishing opportunities for the week ahead could be slim pickings.

FEB. 3: Cowichan River fly only section – Spent a pleasant morning on the river. Fished my way down as far as the Cabin Run with the double-hander but no sign of any steelhead there or at the Spring Pool. Still very, very mild but still winter as far as new growth is concerned. River's flow was at a nice height (62.5 cubic metres/second) and a perfect colour. Met three other rods along the way, all fishing for trout; one, a young First Nations guy, suggested few if any steelhead were that far up the river as yet. Not a good outlook for this year, I fear.

FEB. 12: Sproat Lake, Taylor River flats – At last a fishing report that includes fish. We knew there was a chance of rain and down it came – in a near-continuous downpour for most of another notably mild day. Fished from 10:00 a.m. until 3:00 p.m. and together we finished up with six good-sized cutthroats to hand and two others on and off, all playing with vigour. Gordon led the way with four as well as the two misses while my two from two were 20 inches and 18 inches. All on sinking lines, or in my case a fast sinking, integrated tip so perhaps not fishing quite as deep as Gordon, on flies with eyes or bead heads ... mainly natural in colour or chartreuse with plenty of movement from the rabbit fur dressing. We experienced a flat calm and lots of mist with the rain and both boats badly in need of bailing by the end of the session. Appropriate clothing and wide-brimmed hats meant we stayed dry and warm. Unfortunately the same could not be said for my cell phone which sadly drowned in my unfastened jacket pocket.

We had the lake to ourselves but a camper with a load of firewood arrived just before we left so perhaps that marks the start of the spring season for the "residents." The lake, as you might expect, is full and every creek we crossed along the way was pounding down with all island rivers still high but better, drier weather is in the forecast. The fact that there is no snow anywhere as this strange winter nears its end means that access to the launch site is open when it is so often blocked at this time of year. Also, recent logging activities between the lake and the road means that this particular stretch of lake is now easily seen by passing motorists and that may encourage more fishing visits by those who notice boats on the water.

FEB. 16: Sproat Lake, Taylor River flats – Pretty as a picture and a quite beautiful day on the water but not a fish (trout) to be had for this reporter. Not that others did not enjoy some action ... Gordon had one cutthroat of about 18 inches and two other good touches while, over the course of the four hours we were on the water, I saw at least eight or nine fish landed and released including a beautiful 22-inch rainbow by one of Gordon's Port Alberni friends. It was hooked well out from the sunken logs and close to the drop off. The rest of the fish that I observed being played were hooked much closer in. In total there were at least seven fly-fishing boats on the water including Ryan Henri from Gone Fishin' – as well as a couple of trollers who went elsewhere – and most of them managed at least a brace of trout. I just could not fool even one this time. Weather was remarkable for the time of year with the temperature up around 12C and only a light breeze that died away around lunchtime. On the way home, with hardly a cloud in the sky, I noted only traces of snow on Mt. Arrowsmith, surely unusual for the time of year?

FEB. 18: Sproat Lake, Taylor River flats – Another fine, mild day on the water in and around the flats where the Taylor River enters the lake. Fishing was hard slogging for a while after a 9.45 a.m. start produced just one touch for me and nothing for Gordon. He packed up to take care of other matters at home around

12:30 p.m. and I fished on with some determination all by myself until 1:45 p.m. and was duly rewarded with an 18-inch cutthroat, a beautiful fish that could easily have been labelled "fat and sassy," and two other good, solid touches but nothing more. Called in to see Ryan at the new, very spacious Gone Fishin' location in Port Alberni – just a block up from the old store in what was previously a car dealership. He had four fish show interest on Monday and landed two of them. Interestingly he prefers an intermediate tip with a bright fly – blue being one of the main colours – and a very slow retrieve while we have been fishing either a full sink line (Gordon) or a type 6 tip (me) and thus both requiring a faster retrieve to avoid touching bottom where there are snags aplenty. Will try again at least once next week. Definitely a more pleasant experience compared to the long walk down, and hard slog back up, to the Slide pool to try pink worms for the Stamp River steelhead that may or may not be present. And the Stamp is still on the high side for walk and wade from recent reports. Incidentally I saw at least six trout rise today but have no idea what brought them up. Only two other boats around when we started, a camper in a canoe whose son got a small trout on a worm and a guide in a power boat with both he and his sport using spinning gear which detracted from the usual fly-centric ambience associated with this fishery. Finally, all my fish came to a Chartreuse Leech pattern.

FEB. 20: Bryce's Report – "Well a happy report from Sproat Lake from Glenn and I. Arrived in a steady rain that diminished gradually to a lovely calm afternoon. We got into fish almost immediately both of us touching fish and then Glenn hooked and played a beautiful 22-inch cuttie. There were a few fish breaking the surface and a few hatching bugs. Glenn then hooked and lost another nice trout. I changed to the fly recommended by Peter and used by Glenn and right off the bat had a great strike on the shoreline ... a couple of head shakes and then of all things the hook broke at the bend ... but a nice fish. Shortly thereafter in almost the same spot

I hooked and played the biggest cuttie I have seen ... measured to a good 25 inches ... a superb fish. There was no other action and the surface was quiet. Hopefully this is a great start! Talk already of heading back early next week. Looking for a sunny day".

FEB. 20: My comment – Bryce, that's absolutely brilliant ... will be interested to hear all the fine details over coffee tomorrow morning ... we know there will be those in faraway places who envy your good fortune, not to mention your undoubted skill. A 25-inch cuttie is a truly wonderful fish and I am sure it played like a chinook on your trout fly rod. Funny enough Ryan and I were talking just yesterday about how hard they hit and how strongly they fight and that was all about trout in the 18- to 22-inch range. The forecast next week is really promising and bright days are often the best or so I am told. Interesting that you too saw fish on the surface as I did yesterday but there were hardly any rising at any time on my two previous visits.

FEB. 23: Sproat Lake, Taylor River Flats – Fished from around 9:30 a.m. to 2:15 p.m. in conditions that ranged from thick fog at the start of the day to bright sunshine at the finish. For all that the fish were hardly in a willing mood. Bryce had one 23-inch cut-throat and lost another good one when it went to ground (stick), Glenn registered an acrobatic 15-inch rainbow while I came home with the proverbial skunk – not even a little tug to sharpen the focus. Tried both fast sink tip and a slow sink tip and a variety of flies without making any impression on the stock. Bryce took his on a nondescript, multicoloured bead pattern, the Brazilian Bracelet, that also worked for him on his last visit. Measured against the huge, flat stump just to the right of the river mouth, the level of the lake has dropped appreciably from last week, down a good 20 inches at least. To round off my day I got back to shore to find that one of the flip-up wheels had dropped off the back of the little white boat. Here's hoping I can find a quick replacement. An Internet search followed by a visit to Harbour Chandler tomorrow should resolve the problem. Later: all good to go again for an out-lay of under $25 ... wheel and two 5½-inch stainless bolts and lock nuts for axles from Harbour Chandler, hard plastic liner and a short length of ¾-inch copper pipe from Industrial Plastics and Home Hardware, a lot better than about $140 for a complete set of two new wheels and mounts.

FEB. 24: Note from Gordon – Peter, your lack of fish may be explained by the fact that many trout have been seen at the Rest Stop Pool by the highway bridge over the Taylor. A lot of these fish seem to have gone further upstream indicating they are mov-ing into spawning mode. The number of spawners bodes well for future stocks.

FEB. 26: Another note from Gordon – I fished the mouth of the Taylor River today. Hit five or six fish but landed few. A nice 23-inch cutthroat was the best, but most were solid fish. I lost one that went airborne and it looked like a clean steelhead to me – a big, bright fish. Three boats in total, one being a troller, and it was slower fishing for the other two people. It is not over yet.

MAR. 5: Sproat Lake, Taylor River flats – Could not have asked for a better morning as far as the weather was concerned. Near calm most of the time and then a light and chilly breeze from the east that made me glad I had brought my toque and mit-tens. Fishing on the flats in the usual spots was slow to say the least of it. Gordon hooked and lost a small rainbow while my one and only offer produced a very fat, handsome and photoge-nic cutthroat that measured just on 20 inches taken on an un-weighted Muddler Minnow fished on a 15-foot, type six tip and eight-pound pound fluorocarbon leader. We fished from 9:30 a.m. through to 1:30 p.m. and did see a few fish showing, includ-ing one very big one – in the six to eight-pound range – that cleared the surface completely and could very well have been a steelhead. Gordon reckons there are still plenty of fish in and around the river mouth. They just weren't biting for us today. There's always next time.

MAR. 13: It's little wonder that Glenn sees the Little Qualicum as his home river. We were looking for cutthroat today in ideal conditions, both in terms of the continuing springlike weather and a nice river height. Glenn had his first fish on his first cast before I arrived to meet him at the hatchery and went on to land another three or four from half a dozen chances, while I had to be satisfied with one of about 12 inches from the river right in the pool below the one where Whiskey Creek comes in downstream from the hatchery. Just one other rod on the river and he arrived after us and left before we came back to the car park for lunch.

Only one of Glenn's fish, which included a single rainbow, was a solid looking "yellow belly," and it could be we were on the early side for the incoming sea-runs although we were told the chum fry are already on the move. The river was running at 13.3 cubic metres/second, which made for a difficult enough crossing just above the site of the former fish diversion gate, removed a couple of years ago along with the walkway we used to get to the far bank, river left. We fished down as far as the old railway trestle but most of Glenn's action, to a Muddler Minnow with a tungsten head, came in the Whiskey Creek pool. On the way back I crossed over well above the hatchery at the tail of a long pool that had produced for me some good few years ago. Not this time.

MAR. 18: Launched at Westwood Lake in clearing fog around 11:00 a.m. and finished shortly after 2:00 p.m., in time for a by-chance meeting with Bryce in the car park as he completed his round-the-lake dog walking routine. No fish to hand. One stocky, maybe 10 inches, was hooked and lost at the net. Three or four other gentle touches, one trolling, the others — no more than light taps — casting a Black Bead Head Micro Leech while tied off to a suitable stump on the west side about halfway down. Wind freshened to SE 12/15 after the fog lifted. A pleasant enough way to put in a few hours, but it will probably take at least another week or two to warm up to the point that the fish are more co-operative. Harvey, still sunning himself in Arizona, is the local expert and may have other ideas since he has put in many, many more hours there than I have.

Apr. 1: And off we went, on April Fool's Day as it happens, to see the sights, for this was a fishing trip without material rewards. Sproat Lake, Taylor River flats, on a bright and increasingly breezy morning. Glenn did the driving with his red pontoon boat and my little white craft safely embracing in the back of his truck. The first of the Easter weekend campers was in place where we park with two more arriving, complete with family, strollers, dogs and ATVs, while we fished (cast). The lake was up a good two or even more feet, probably close to the level we experienced first time there this year in February, and all the creeks along the way, not forgetting the Stamp, the Sproat and the Somass, were well filled and noisy too when it comes to the foaming torrent that crashes down the mountain on the far side of the lake.

There were also a few swallows around for the first time this year and Glenn noticed the occasional hatching chironomid, likely what brought the birds down to surface level. But where were the trout? We fished hard from around 9:00 a.m. to noon with Glenn covering all the right places since, with no anchor, he had to keep on the move to avoid being blown into the shore by a freshening and chilly wind that came straight down the lake while I sat casting comfortably at anchor. Rewards were minimal and three flies were lost to the bottom and its many hazards. I had one touch and another fish on just long enough to put a bend in the rod while Glenn had just one touch. And there was not a trout to be seen on the surface. That was it. Warming coffee at Timmy's and home by early afternoon with Gordon reporting four rainbows from the other end of the lake.

Apr. 9: Westwood Lake in the warm spring sunshine with Glenn.

The forecast for the next 24 hours was calling for rain so this was the day to be on the water and we saw at least eight or nine other boats during the day. But only a very few fish caught. Fished 10:00 a.m. to 3:00 p.m. for one 11-inch rainbow on a Black Bead Head Micro Leech and 15-foot sink tip. Glenn kept three, not too big, from seven or eight touches. I spent most of the time trolling slowly on the oars interspersed with some down and deep re-trieving while he drifted in his pontoon boat. Apparently the lake fished really well the previous day and there was a big hatch of chi-ronomids while we were there but I only saw two fish rise in all the time we were on the water. One fisherman, who was in dou-ble figures yesterday, suggested the falling barometer was to blame. Glenn registered the water temperature at 52F.

APR. 14: Westwood Lake again. Nothing special to report.... I had one from five offers.... the one was small (10-11 inches) while troll-ing the Black Bead Head Leech with a 15-foot sink tip on the far side ... it was quite chilly (10C) with a fitful wind mostly from the NW ... when it went calm around 2:15 p.m. a number of fish started to rise out in the middle. I think they were nymphing – lots of chi-ronomids about again – so an emerger might have worked, but I was not set up and then a heavy rain squall came sweeping down from Mt. Benson and that was that. Fished from 10:45 a.m. to 3:00 p.m. Harvey had two small ones and missed two or three others fishing with an indicator at the top end of the lake. That's it for now.

APR. 16: Westwood on a bright if breezy morning. Gave it a cou-ple of hours – 9:30 to 11:30 a.m. – and decided that was enough. Managed one trout of 11 inches on a Scud and one good tug on the same fly. Fished on a slow troll and a five-foot sink tip. Very few chironomids were showing and nothing rising. Maybe there will be more action next week if the forecast is correct and it gets warmer. It was still chilly today with wind from the SW.

APR. 19: Report from Harvey – "Glenn and I journeyed to a lake near Duncan yesterday. Arrived to find a flat calm and only one other fisher on the water. Fishing was slow but steady at the start and gradually heated up as the day went on. Water temperature rose from 51.6F to 56.9F over the course of the day and aquatic life of various sorts (but no one major group) became more active. By mid-afternoon fish were taking flies off the surface. The lake also attracted more fishers as the day went on and was the busiest in my times there – six boats at peak time. Over the course of the day I had 30+ takes, hooked 12 and landed eight. Glenn claims his best day ever on the lake with 18 or more to hand. The fish were in excellent condition, very feisty and ranged from 12 to 16 inches. Later, over coffee, Harvey told me they were both using sub-surface patterns although they felt a dry fly would also have worked.

APR. 29: For me the start of a new salmon season. Launched at 7:00 a.m. and in at 11:00 a.m. ... fished through 10:30 a.m. low tide and had only one hit (and fish) just on the turn. Started from Neck Point and on down to Rocky Point and then worked my way out to well past the Fingers. The strike was on a medium-sized Cop Car spoon at 130 feet in 950 feet of water, a just legal marble chinook by an inch or so. There was a very light ripple first thing and then the wind freshened to SE 12 when I was coming in. No Pacific cod but one flattie on a hoochie – green and white. Boats pretty well scattered with a few as far north as the Brickyard, most of them well out. Probably saw 12/15 boats in all from Fingers and on north. No seals and no algae.

APR. 30: One 20-inch chinook and one pollock on the Cop Car spoon. Fished 6:00 a.m. to 10:00 a.m. and then the wind got up.

MAY 2: To the lake near Duncan with Glenn and Harvey, a round trip of 165 kilometres. With the forest road open only at weekends and encouraged by their earlier success, we set out with high hopes. Instead the fishing was ordinary enough with very few fish showing. I managed just one rainbow of around 14 inches on a Pheasant Tail Nymph from three offers while the others did better but not that much better. There were eight or nine boats on the lake by mid-afternoon and we saw a handful of fish being landed and released but had definitely anticipated better results.

MAY 4: Just had to get out again after salmon when wind fell away during the morning. Launched at 12.30 p.m. at Charlene. Still blowing 12/14 knots from the NW and a bit lumpy at the ramp. Happily motor fired first time and I was soon in deeper, safer water. Fished until 4:00 p.m. without a touch to various spoons, hoochies and plugs. Fished north to Rocky Point and then turned and came all the way back to outside the Fingers. Wind died, as forecast, and it became quite warm, with boots and sweater discarded. Glenn was on gardening detail so missed nothing. Nanaimo reports strong for past three weeks, also Thrasher Rock, with many of the chinook either white or marbled which seems to be the pattern at this time of year. So far I have not seen any seals on four outings and almost no algae – strange. I wonder why? Some suggest regular visits by the transient orcas has made the seals a lot more wary and more inclined to stay close to their usual in-shore haunts rather than venturing offshore.

MAY 15: Definitely not my week ... out this morning in flat calm conditions and fished until 10:00 a.m. without an offer. Same story from previous two trips. Not often that happens. No salmon action at all on various spoons and hoochies fished at between 110 and 140 feet. Counted about 20 boats widely distributed from the Fingers and on north but saw no nets out and spoke to three other boats, all fishless. Either the salmon have moved on to the Silva Bay/Thrasher Rock area or I am doing something wrong? Fished from the mouth of the bay on past Neck Point to opposite the Navy spotting house and then out to beyond the Fingers and back in again. Marked a lot of something on the sounder from 100 down to 140/160 feet between the Fingers and Neck point but they could have been big schools of pollock as I had half a dozen of them as well as a small ling on the way back.

MAY 15, 17, 23 & 31: Same outcome so month of May very poor for me. Fished seven days and approximately 25 hours for only two strikes and two undersized chinook released. June was hot and very windy as was the beginning of July with a record-setting heatwave, drought and river closures here on the Island.

JUNE 21–23: Kitimat River – Here we are at the halfway point of the trip and the fishing news is not great ... I lost a good chinook on the first day, solid take, two big head shakes and gone, Doug Machuk hooked and just as quickly lost two yesterday and landed one early this morning of around 10/12 pounds. We have seen lots of fish showing and rolling in the early part of the day but few takers in bright sunshine and mid-summer heat. Darren, our guide, figures it will take rain and a bump up in the river level to make a real difference. Meantime ... spirits are high and we will keep trying. The day starts with breakfast – excellent egg sandwiches and coffee at 3:30 a.m. and we are on the road to the river by 4:00 a.m. in the hopes of finding an early morning taker. The Kitimat is definitely on the low side compared to what is usual at this time of year, but it's still big water by Island standards and we are fishing 14-foot double-handed 9- and 10-weight rods with heavy sink tips and big showy flies. Water colour is good with ample visibility and the river temperature is just over 50F which makes for pleasantly cool wading in the heat. Had a leak at the crotch for the first two days so finished on the damp side but all patched and dry again now. That's it for now. Time for a nap before supper and early to bed in preparation for days four, five and six.

JUNE 24–25: Overnight and morning rain made all the difference. The river came up about six inches and we were Johnny on the spot after a 3:00 a.m. wake-up call. This Kitimat River chinook fishery is most definitely not for the weak in heart. But what a way to mark my up-coming 80th on July 19. Last salmon of the day, of eight raised and three landed between Doug and myself, was mine and what a fish it was, in the high 20s for sure and maybe even over 30 pounds but hard to tell when they are that size. Amazingly strong and took me about 100 yards downriver despite all the pressure I could manage with a 14-foot double-handed, nine-weight rod and the truck-stopping drag provided by Loren's Hatch reel. Everything mechanical worked perfectly under huge pressure and now I know why 25-pound test is the minimum leader size used here. We finished, as usual, at lunchtime and are now back for a much-needed nap. A great finale and we still have one more day to go and the river should be at its best with fresh fish coming in on the next high tides drawn by the increased flows.

JUNE 27: Here we are home again around midnight after Harvey very helpfully collected me at the Airport, Daphne being on her way back from two weeks in Northern Ireland. The fishing trip laundry is done and the first photos have been downloaded. The last day, yesterday, Friday (June 26) started with a bang or a bust depending on how you look at it. We were fishing around 4:45 a.m. and almost immediately Doug was in touch with four successive fish, all of which came off a hook somehow having turned up thus curtailing the hold. We finished the day with either 10 or 11 touched/hooked/played but only two landed including one of around 30 pounds (38½ inches long with a girth of 25 inches). The river came up about a foot overnight with Thursday's rain and was falling back all morning. I managed to play two very large fish, both far out on to the backing and both then lost. The second one was the heavier of the two and I had it on for a good 10 minutes and on the run down the shoreline trying to regain line. Heavy-duty stuff in all regards. There is just nothing that I have ever encountered that has the pulling power of a big Kitimat chinook. The rain definitely made all the difference in the world and the fact that we had fish with sea lice still in place on both

Thursday and Friday confirmed that a fresh run was on the move while those already in residence were becoming more interested in our offerings. How soon we forget the long, hot days earlier in the week when we could not muster a single touch between us! In fact I went three days with nothing to show for all those hundreds of casts save the occasional small bull trout.

JULY 9: A long day but a good one. Up at 3:00 a.m., picked up Glenn at 4:00 a.m. and fishing for sockeye salmon out of China Creek by 5:30 a.m. Home just after 1:00 p.m. Started with a doubleheader but Glenn lost his in a tangle with me. Finished with an eight-fish limit and at least one more lost, which was a good return. Fished to the right of China Creek and well out with gear running at 60/80 feet and no pressure at all from other boats. Most boats we saw seemed to be concentrated further down the inlet around McTush. Fish not large, best no more than five pounds, and the majority about pink salmon size. But they'll eat well. Hate to report the fact but Glenn had six to my two, the first and the last. His flasher was red while mine was green. Did that make the difference? Who knows? We were both using small, pink hoochies on 18/20 inch leaders fished three to four feet off the clip with a dummy flasher below for added attraction. Lots and lots of fish showing on the sounder and plenty more to be seen jumping and finning, just like big trout. We'll give it another go one day next week.

JULY 13: We were on the water again at 5:30 a.m. after leaving Glenn's at 3:50 a.m. and were back home just after 11:00 a.m. with eight more sockeye in the box, two in the five to six-pound range. As last week we fished from China Creek up toward Lone Tree Point and had plenty of opportunities to fill our limit before we finally did just that. Some fish were lost as soon as they hit the lure while others were much closer to the boat before departing. Small red hoochies behind red/silver flashers, run 3/4 feet from the release clip, did most of the damage. Depths again ranged from

70/80 feet down to 110 feet in 350 feet of water. Most of the fish marking on the sounder were at between 80 and 100 feet. Freezers are now replenished and we will consider one more go next week. As last week the majority of the boats we saw were working from Dunsmuir Point down toward McTush and the Narrows, making for uncrowded fishing where we were. And far fewer boats around than when the fishery is targeted on chinook later in the summer.

JULY 19: The big day ... 80 years and counting ... 14 came for dinner on the 18th and then the fishermen and partners, Harvey and Nancy, Bryce and Linda, Philippe and Janet and Sandra (Glenn was away fishing at Bamfield for the weekend) arrived for afternoon "champagne" – actually pretty good bubbly – and finger food today. Lots and lots of cards and messages with many of them not surprisingly fish-themed.

JULY 21: First Eve River Report of the year ... and a healthy one it is with Bryce taking all honours as both our driver and catcher of possibly more pinks than he could count. We were on the water around 11:00 a.m., an hour before low tide, and he immediately found fish all by himself right at the mouth of the river – but not out in the ocean where I started despite a strong wind from the north that eventually prompted a move inshore. Bryce's fish came at regular intervals as inevitably did all the other dozen or more fishermen in the area and soon the "picket fence" was established on both sides of the estuary. Philippe was busy most of the time with charming grandsons Tomas (13) and Alex (11), from France, both suitably equipped with fly rods and chest waders. In his spare moments Philippe lost two or three while the boys each marked the occasion by landing and releasing their first Pacific salmon on a fly so the happy back seat conversation on the way back was endless, and unintelligible since, naturally enough, French is their mother tongue. I managed just two decent pinks, in the five/six-pound range, and we all remarked on the size of the fish, most of the ones we saw significantly bigger than the Port Alberni sockeye encountered over the past couple of weeks.

It's perhaps early in the season for the Eve fishery but the out-look has to be promising with these results while the run presumably is still in its infancy. We spent only a few hours there before moving on for a Naka Bay picnic lunch, and sighting of a small-ish roadside black bear. Of course, we missed Harvey and Glenn but their turn will surely come. PS: Pink was the color for Bryce but resident expert Jerry Stephens continues to swear by blue and green and generously, on introduction, had flies for both boys, a very nice gesture. PPS: both my fish came solidly to Harvey and Nancy's beaded pink 80th Birthday pattern. By the bye … it's a round trip of around 500 kilometres from Nanaimo and back and takes a good three hours' driving each way. I have done it by myself in a day but welcome the ride with Bryce or Harvey.

JULY 26: At this point it would be remiss not to include mention of the extraordinary weather conditions we have had and continue to experience during 2015. Earlier in this accounting I made mention of the very mild winter and virtually complete lack of any significant snowpack here on the Island and across the Lower Mainland. Well, we are certainly feeling the impacts since there has been no appreciable (just a few mm) rain over the past three months. That led to the late June closure of many Island rivers, among them the Cowichan, Little Qualicum and Stamp-Somass due to low, low water and high temperatures. Later, in August, the mighty Fraser was closed to all fishing from the mouth as far in-land as Hope in an effort to conserve the hard-pressed sockeye run also beset by high temperatures and a drought-induced low flow regime. It's early to talk of long-term impacts, but they can't be good for either the resident trout, brown, rainbow or cutthroat, or the emerging salmon fry, let alone the incoming mature salmon on their annual spawning runs. This month many smaller Lower Mainland rivers were added to the "closed to all fishing" list, and apart from heavy showers a couple of days ago, there is no sign of any improvement. As it happens, the Stamp-Somass sockeye run into the Alberni Inlet has been of record proportions with the most recent estimate in the region of 1.8 million fish, up from the original forecast of 700,000. As a result, there has and continues to be a strong commercial (total allowable catch 813,303 fish) and sport fishery with the fish unable or unwilling to enter the parched river systems.

JULY 27: Port Alberni was calm, warm and reasonably productive, at least for me. I managed four sockeye to Glenn's one with a record number lost including a big one of his that I managed to dislodge through an incompetent netting effort. In all we reckon we landed five from 16 hookups, which is far below average. There are still lots of fish showing on the sounder, not surprising since the Stamp-Somass sockeye run is now approaching two million. The quality, however, is declining and we have decided that enough is enough for this year. We fished 5:30 a.m. to around 10:30 a.m. when there was an opening timed for the seiners working from Dunsmuir Point.

JULY 30: Eve River again ... when the fish – pink salmon – were "on" for me they were really on. I don't suppose I made more than 15/20 casts in total for my five offers. At that time it was flat calm and there were fish showing on both sides of where I was wading, which was about 100 feet north of the end of the picket line. It seemed all these fish were in a taking mood where my small red fly was concerned – identified as a Kathy's Coat by Harvey. I kept the first two, two more came off and I then released the third smaller one in the mistaken assumption that more would follow. Hah.... not another touch as the northerly wind got up and the numbers of fish in sight declined to nil almost in minutes –most strange. And that was that for the day. All the cleaned/filleted fish I saw, and there were corpses aplenty on the shore waiting for the gulls and crabs, were shining bright and very obviously ocean fresh rather than starting to colour up from freshwater exposure – not that there is much fresh water coming down the river just now. Again relied on the 7136 Sage with a five-foot intermediate tip. A new Lazar running line and 30-foot Scandi head allows for long casts – when the timing is right.

JULY 30: Harvey's Eve River report – We arrived at the Eve at 8:00 (low tide 7:59) and were fishing by 8:30. Went directly to the mouth to join a picket line of 40+ anglers all stretched out across the mouth but fishing into Johnstone Strait. Quite a few fish showing and constantly being caught by those nearer the middle of the line. Peter went to the north end of the picket line and in the next half-hour hooked five/landed three/kept two. I crossed the river to the south side where there were considerably fewer fish showing and just got one. At 9:30 the tide starting flooding really well and the fish disappeared!!!!!! Not one fish was seen heading upriver from then until we left at 1:30 in spite of auspicious conditions. Most people packed up their fish and left with many limits in evidence from those there since daybreak. By early afternoon we basically had the river to ourselves. In talking to Gerry Stevens he said today was unusual in that in previous days there were not a lot of fish but at least some found their way upriver. I'm going to wait at least a week before trying it again. It seems like my journal entries from three previous "odd" year entries are correct re run timing.

AUG. 8–10: Not really fishing related but a big event nonetheless ... the whole family including brother-in-law Walter, who hit 80 in June, assembled in Tofino for a 160th Birthday Celebration.

AUG. 14: To the Eve River again with Harvey and his mountain biker pals, Tom and Al. Harvey had been to Nile Creek early on the morning of August 12 and, while seeing three schools of pinks, had nothing to report in terms of catching. After a slow start (nothing) I had a good day using the 1376 Sage and the Lazar running line, 480 grain Scandi head and five-foot intermediate tip. I made contact with a good dozen fish, mostly on a small Bead Head Green Laser pattern, releasing five or six. My report follows after a long and tiring day, made easier by the opportunity to sleep soundly in the back of the truck while Harvey looked after the driving. For those heading north tomorrow (Bryce and Co.) the advice has to be "early, early, early." We were there pretty well at low tide, just after 8:00 a.m., and the campsite was deserted. Everyone was on the beach or in place around the corner at the river's mouth. No shortage of fish but hard to catch at the start – for us at least. By 11:00 a.m. it was pretty well all over. Green worked best for me, while the others had less success on traditional pink. We saw plenty of salmon, showing in numbers and being caught on both sides of the estuary, but for whatever reason, they did not appear to be moving up into the main river, e.g. the long pool where they are often present in numbers at high tide in previous years. Get there as early as you can and find a place near the mouth of the river and then work your way back upstream as the tide fills.

Aug. 18–21: Bamfield report – Stayed at Crown Charters, which was excellent in all respects. Fished with Glenn and with Bryce, Philippe and Phil, Bryce's cousin, in their 16-foot boat, brought from Saskatchewan by Phil and upgraded and equipped for the salt after 17 years in storage! Last year we had a "one over (77 cm) and one under" rule for the Bamfield/Alberni Canal which worked well for DiG and myself. This year anything over 77 cm had to be released…. so back went a 20+ and one that was close to or possibly a bit over 30…. those two big fish apart we both rated the actual fishing as the poorest we had ever experienced out of Bamfield or Poett Nook … we caught five or perhaps six chinook in total over the four days' fishing and returned three of them and also kept two coho … all on anchovies. My contribution to all that fishing – probably close to 30 hours' trolling – was one 12-pound chinook! I think Bryce and Co. had seven good-sized chinook to their three rods. Each day we were out in the dark around 5:00 a.m., and on the last morning, came in between 9:00 and 10:00 with precisely nothing to show for our final and considerable effort. I did lose a fish just before we pulled lines, but that was it ... not good at all.

Total cost of the trip for Glenn and me worked out at $340.20 each, including $170.10 each for three nights' accommodation and $132.59 for gas ... $42.90 for the truck to and from China Creek (18 mpg) ... $44.08 for running the boat from China Creek to Bamfield and back at around 19 knots (90 mins. each way approx.) and $45.61 for boat fishing gas, which worked out at around $1.60 an hour, or just over a litre an hour at trolling speed. Very economical. We dined well each night with a different menu – pasta and shrimp (Glenn), a wonderful fish stew based on a freshly caught pink (Philippe) and lamb on the barbecue (Bryce).

AUG. 26: China Creek lived up to expectation this morning. An early (3:45 a.m.) solo start allowed for a 5:45 a.m. launch and I was first back at the cleaning table around 8:30 with two fish, one about 16 pounds, happily just a fraction under the 77 cm rule, and the other in low double figures. Both still ocean bright red chinook taken at 40 feet on anchovies on a slow troll six feet behind a green and chrome silver flasher. No other hits so I was obviously lucky to limit out. Fished from China Creek up as far as Lone Tree Point and back down again and marvelled at the very considerable numbers of sockeye finning, jumping and otherwise displaying. Talked to one other boat with two chinook landed early on and also saw a few nets out with most of the action well out from the rock face and midway between Lone Tree and China Creek. I have to admit I was dozing when the second one hit. The buzz of the Islander reel providing the perfect wake-up alarm.

AUG. 27: Two boys and a boat – mostly calm water and bright sunshine made for a perfect opportunity to take grandsons Finn and Jack fishing before the onset overnight and the next day of a forecast and much-needed major rainstorm. This storm swept the Vancouver and Lower Mainland area with very high winds and resulted in the most power outages ever experienced by BC Hydro, in the region of 700,000 in total, which took three or four days to repair. Happy to be retired and not dealing with constant media calls! We launched from Hammond Bay and ran out to the Fingers. Trolled north, while the boys napped, without any action so pulled the lines and went to look at the Hudson Rocks seals. Jack very keen to run the boat so he steered us home on the plane while sitting on my knee – just in case. Finn was happy enough to observe. Jack has a feel for the water and listened well to all instructions. Hopefully the day will come when he can do it all on his own while I sit back and enjoy the scenery.

SEPT. 1: Glenn and I had a dawn start at China Creek, leaving home again at 3:45 a.m. (crazy!) and, like pretty well every other boat we saw/watched, ended up with a nil return and some level of frustration. Glenn did hook and play a very large chinook that made one huge run and then headed back toward the boat only to come unstuck and leave him with a badly bent treble. It hit between China Creek and Lone Tree Point on an anchovy and red/chrome flasher at 30 feet. My contribution earlier on was one very stinky sockeye, also on an anchovy at 44 feet. Still many sockeye showing everywhere, an amazing number of them, in their thousands, but it could be the fresh water from the long-awaited weekend rain has already taken the resident chinook up and away. Sockeye have also been reported running the Stamp and Somass rivers in great numbers which is all to the good for the future. Lots more fish still to come from Bamfield, we were told. Perhaps we'll head back one day next week. Also noted strong flow of fresh water into Cous Creek as well as in the river that borders the highway on the Alberni side of Cathedral Grove before entering Cameron Lake.

The DFO's one over and one under 77 cm regulation came into effect again later in the day, just in time for the annual three day

Port Alberni Derby over the Labour Day September 5, 6, 7 weekend. The $15,000 first prize went to a fish weighing 40.4 pounds, caught near Bamfield on a pink hoochie. Daily $5000 winners were: Saturday 31.65 pounds, Sunday, 40.4 and Monday 25.5. Over 1000 salmon caught according to the *Alberni Valley Times* report. Most fish taken in Bamfield area with upper part of the Canal, China Creek, Lone Tree et al. reported very poor by Ryan from Gone Fishin' tackle shop. Could improve with warmer weather in the forecast for the week ahead, he thinks. We'll see.

SEPT. 20–24: To Smithers at dawn (5:50 a.m. flight) to fish for steelhead with an old friend, a long-awaited trip that was a full two years in the making. Fished the upper part of the Morice River, well above Houston, on the Sunday afternoon and then for the next three full days before heading back to Smithers late on the Wednesday afternoon for a shower and change of clothes, with the final day on the Bulkley. Our base camp was at the Bymac boat launch and campsite using a very comfortable pop-up camper. Only offer was a six-pound fish that on the first day came to my host fishing a dry line and waking fly well above Bymac. By Thursday afternoon, with a jet boat providing great access to many miles of water, we had touched/hooked/landed and released 13/14 of the 17/18 steelhead we encountered. These were divided pretty equally between a waking dry fly and my sunk fly, a Pink Pussy to start with and, when it was mislaid, a medium-sized, multicoloured Intruder. Wonderful sport with fish up to 10/12 pounds in near-perfect fall conditions, brilliant colours in the poplar, aspen and cottonwood trees and perfect river levels after rain the day before I arrived in Smithers.

The Morice is a big and most attractive river, much larger than I had anticipated, with a series of long pools and broad runs. We were never bothered in any way by pressure from other fishermen. We saw quite a few, some working from pontoon boats and rafts, others walk and wade (difficult access for the most part) or in jet boats like ours. The fish were well distributed and in fine condition. Of course they played brilliantly with most hookups really solid. One fish was lost due to mechanical failure, the pawl on my old four-inch Scottie reel, by Sharpe's of Aberdeen (see "Last day steelhead one to remember," page 205), splitting into two pieces as I played a strong fish below the Houston road bridge. The reel went into free spool and that was that. That was on the Tuesday when I landed four of five hooked, numbers that my partner repeated the next day. I had a spare reel with me, a No. 2 Islander, so it was easy to switch lines and carry on.

Living in the camper was nothing but a pleasure, with great meals and ample supplies of Tullamore Dew and red wine. As was to be expected we slept well and fished hard every day. Other than my boating mishap on the last day – see next entry – the trip was largely incident free. I did manage to wade a little deeper than was wise on one occasion, prompting a half-eaten apple to be aimed in my direction from upstream, thus drawing my attention to my situation as it floated past. All in all a perfect trip that lived up to every expectation and that we celebrated with a truly excellent Indian dinner before the late evening flight back from Smithers. Richard was waiting at Vancouver airport to drive me to Conor's for a somewhat disturbed night's sleep.

SEPT. 27: Long story but came back late Thursday (September 24) to Conor's in North Van and on to home by ferry Friday morning with a cracked and painful rib after heavy and unexpected fall in the boat on the Bulkley River – not under power, thankfully. All that on the Thursday morning, our only blank day although we kept trying until mid-afternoon. Finally went to Nanaimo Hospital Emergency Dept. this morning and got some heavy-duty painkillers, but they have not yet kicked in, so the level of discomfort/pain is pretty high. I'm afraid it's going to put a bit of a damper on my coho pursuits in October. No X-ray deemed necessary as rib injuries are simply left to mend with time, and indeed, my recovery was definitely quicker than I had originally anticipated – fishing again in two weeks – although there was still some discomfort, mostly when lying down in bed, after almost three weeks.

OCT. 8: And a positive way to start the Nanoose Bay beach season just two weeks after the mishap on the Morice. Launched at 2:30 p.m. (high tide 4:22 p.m.) and finished around 5:15 p.m. with one five-pound wild coho landed and another lost, both on one of Glenn's Nanoose Bay Specials fished on a five-foot intermediate tip and clear floating line. No fish showing on the bible camp side so rowed slowly across to the other side where there were three boats and three or four wading anglers, who soon departed, suggesting some earlier reason for their interest. Sure enough I soon saw a jumper, then another one and perhaps the same fish finning. Stopped, anchored and covered the spot – fish on and duly landed second cast. Stayed in the same place for the next couple of hours, saw a reasonable number of fish jumping and finning, both quite large and pretty small and mostly coho to my eye. The other fly fisherman, in a small white dinghy, hooked and just as soon lost a coho over to my left while the power boater had earlier taken a 15-pound chum on a spoon along with a small coho. Most of the fish showed in the hour before high tide in four/five feet of water in the middle of the bay where the creeks come in. Then it went quiet. Only noted one wading angler halfway back to the bible camp side and no fish showing there that I saw and nothing down the rail track side either when I went out. One other point of interest: the bay seems to be absolutely packed with jellyfish, in their multiple thousands probably. The largest looked about twice the size of my hand with the smallest about the size of a hen's egg. They appeared to be a pale, translucent, bluish colour. Not sure what if any impact they will have on the fishing. Not so many on the far side where we were concentrating. Now I think everything will depend on the weather and how much rain we get over the next three or four days. Heavy rains are in the forecast; too much and the creeks will come up and the fish may move on.

OCT. 10: Looked in at church side at 6:00 p.m. on way back from visiting with friends. The one boat out fishing was well up into the bay ... nothing moving ... only there for two/three minutes ... almost calm. Wednesday Bonnell Creek still bone dry and full of leaves.

OCT. 12: Bryce's report – Philippe and I spent about 3½ hours in a fruitless effort today. We put in on church side ... we could see jumpers in various location across the bay and several boats on the track side. These fish did not sit still at all ... chase one and they weren't there ... no finning fish but saw both coho and chum. Finally settled on some fish on church side who showed somewhat sporadically in same location but no takers! Finally no more fish to be seen so we left.

OCT. 13: Glenn's report – Fished on Sunday with Bryce and Phillipe. It was very windy and unpleasant. Saw a few fish and tried to target their rises but, due to conditions, could not stay over them. Monday was a bust weather wise. This morning went church side again and saw only chum. Had to go to town and stopped on camp side. Tide was rather far out. Saw one fisher in a pontoon boat in the corner by the railway. I saw no fish rising. Conditions were excellent but prospects did not prompt me to launch.

OCT. 14: Thanks to Bryce and Glenn for their recent nil reports. Here's mine for today: launched on church side at first light, around 7:00 a.m. (high tide at 7:46 a.m.) light ripple to flat calm. Glad I had a warm woolly toque. Rowed across to the far side and noticed (a) five vehicles in the bible camp parking area, (b) four gear fishermen on shore and two others wading, (c) the occasional fish jumping in the corner bay, (d) nothing showing along the railroad tracks. Really there is not much else to report. Saw two fish jump, likely chum, in the bay on the church side and that was it.

Finished at 9:00 a.m. and checked out Holly Farm and Blood Creek on the way home. Wind freshening from the northwest and nothing moving that I saw. I'll probably give it another go on Friday when the high tide is at 9:10 a.m. One last note: there were no jellyfish to be seen, quite a change from the thousands I encountered last week.

OCT. 14: Harvey's report – I have had two sessions at the beaches. Yesterday, I arrived just as Bryce was rowing from the railroad track bay back to the other side. I fished the rising tide until dark. Some fish showing but as Bryce said you drive yourself nuts trying to chase them. I got what I thought were two good shots but no takers. A young fellow in a pontoon boat hooked three and landed one on an orange & silver spoon from the school I had the good shot at. This morning I headed north before first light. Found fish just at daybreak at Henson Rd. Worked from Henson Rd. to the rock garden and back. The only place fish showed was in the Henson Rd. to power line stretch. There were fish constantly moving right close to shore, but I didn't see a fish played from any of the eight guys there although some of them were literally standing in the fish.

OCT. 14: Yet another good and detailed report from Harvey. I really do believe that we are handicapping ourselves by continuing to do all our off-the-beach fishing with fly rods. It seems to me that spoons and other lures provide a higher percentage of success. That said, it's a conscious choice and I have no intention of going over to the "dark side," or rather back to the "dark side," for I began my continuing fishing journey in Ireland using spinning gear for Atlantics and was very successful – but derived none of the pleasures since associated with fly fishing. So there.

OCT. 19: Nothing good to report from Nanoose. Spent 90 minutes there just now floating around on what was pretty well a flat calm with light rain/mist and the very occasional breath of wind.

A few fish showing before and around the time of high tide (noon) but only covered a couple and no takers. Two or three other boats with similar stories, one a gear guy who had been there since 9:00 a.m. in a little white boat very similar to mine.

OCT. 26: And it's good news from Nanoose Bay. Fished 3:15 p.m. to 5:30 p.m. (high at 5:15 p.m.) and, while only hooking and landing one, an eight-pound buck starting to colour up and so released, saw more fish showing (mostly but not all as jumpers) than anywhere or at any time previously this year. Conditions could not have been better with a light SW wind that provided a perfect onshore ripple to light wave. Went in on the church side – I was the only person fishing at the start and was then joined by one kayak spin fisherman who was still clean when I left. No fish showing in the bay where the creeks come in but plenty on the move halfway across, mostly to the right of the big blue building and well in toward the shore. Just where Glenn did so well wading last October or was in the year before? They were all sizes, including a number of pretty small fish - presumably jacks – but not great takers. Some were definitely on the dark side but there were also some that were bright silver. Tried at first with a Nanoose Bay Special on a long intermediate tip with no success and then changed to a Bead Head California Neill on a five-foot sink tip and hooked up almost immediately. Certainly enough to encourage another visit, perhaps at first light on Wednesday when there will be a 14.5 foot high at 7:24 a.m. Later: On second thoughts I am pretty sure it was a chum not a coho, bronze colour and teeth on lower jaw. Strong fighter.

OCT. 30: Rowing Nanoose – That's what I did for a couple of hours around high tide (9:24 a.m.) this morning. Just rowed and looked and rowed and looked ... and saw not one single fish from church side across to the tracks. Wind (Entrance Island stats.) came down from 22 SSE at 6:00 a.m., prompting a return to a warm bed for another hour, then to SE 7 at 9:00 a.m. before switching right around to NW 5 and 18 at 10:00 and 11:00 a.m. The wind change brought back the rain but still not a fish to be seen. One other boat out after me along with a couple of waders fishing along the bible camp shore.

OCT. 30: Harvey's comment: Peter, don't you get it? "IT'S OVER." Good exercise regime though.

OCT. 30: Later.... it was only in the late afternoon, when we were getting ready to go out for dinner, that I realized I had left my boat dry bag on the ground beside the truck at Nanoose Bay, seemingly never to be seen again. Ouch, ouch and double ouch. In addition to the bag itself I now was without my wallet, with all my ID and credit cards, along with my fishing bag, two very full fly boxes (all my beach flies, other than the half-dozen new Nanoose Bay Specials that Glenn had given me in a little container which had still to be transferred) and a decade-long collection of steelhead dries that I had planned to try at some point if the opportunity arose. Also gone was a toque, saltwater fishing licence, boat operator's card and other bits and pieces including my father's old watch that I would wind up whenever I needed to keep track of time. All missing and little hope of recovery, although every time the phone rang for the next few days I was hopeful it might just be some decent and honest fisherman doing the right thing since my name and address was on both my driver's licence and on the fishing one as well. In the days ahead I'll have to start the replacement process and to accept that much of what has gone is simply irreplaceable. Not a great way to round out the beach season. And never a phone call in the days that followed. Sad.

NOV. 24: To an unnamed west coast river with Gordon and his Port Alberni friend, George McQueen. Water clear as clear and about six inches lower than ideal. It took well over an hour to reach our destination on some really extreme gradient logging roads. Snow on the Hump coming over in the morning but then a beautiful bright day if on the chilly side with temp just below freezing. Looking down from a bridge, saw five or six steelhead in one big pool, but they were not interested despite Gordon's best efforts to cover them from river right. I had tried them from river left but nothing doing and I could not reach them.

DEC. 10: And then the rains came with a succession of severe storms sweeping in from the Pacific over the course of a full, wet week, putting an end to any hopes of further fishing in the immediate future. It could well be into the early New Year before I get out again. On the credit side the accompanying floods will give the first winter steelhead every encouragement to make for fresh water. Now it's a matter of wait and see. With Christmas looming ever closer and brother-in-law Walter due to fly in from N. Ireland on the 19th it could very well be that this will be the final diary entry for 2015. Next up Year # 81!

CASTING BACK X ...
to a pre-Olympics bomb scare

←——————|

Fly rod stops SeaBus: Bomb squad in action

No fisherman expects to find himself involved in a major police incident, more especially on February 11, 2010, the eve of the Winter Olympics, due to start the next day in Vancouver and Whistler.
  This is the untold story of that event, one summed up at the
time by the local headline writers:

> *Bomb scare closes SeaBus terminal: RCMP explosives experts arriving
> at scene (QMI News Agency)*

> *Package that shut down Lonsdale Square "harmless" (CTV Vancouver
> News)*

> *Suspicious package shuts down SeaBus: Parcel turns out to be harmless
> but cops take no chances (The Province)*

> *Suspect package a fishing rod (CBC News).*

Yes, a fishing rod, *my* fishing rod, a nine-weight Sage to be more
precise, packed for travel in a black plastic tube with orange-
coloured end caps and my name and address clearly visible.
  On our way home to Nanaimo from holidays in Hawaii, we had
been met by our son Richard off the SeaBus, at North Vancouver's Lonsdale Quay, before transferring our bags to our own vehicle and catching the 10:30 a.m. ferry from Horseshoe Bay.

Only on arrival home did I realize the rod was missing, inadvertently left behind by me at around 8:15 a.m., leaning against a fence at Lonsdale Quay, the SeaBus terminal, and close to a diesel fuel tank. It was now 1:30 p.m. and I quickly called Lost and Found at TransLink, the SeaBus operator, with all the details, which I then repeated in an email.

Richard phoned just after 4:00 p.m. to say there was radio news of an ongoing police incident in North Vancouver. We immediately made the connection and contacted North Vancouver RCMP. It was too late. The bomb squad was involved, no chances were being taken and the CBC reported "police detonated the cylindrical package before 5:00 p.m."

CBC also quoted the police as saying they had no option but to treat the situation seriously. "Our job is to keep you safe and that is why we did what we did today," said an RCMP spokesman.

What had started out as an innocent mistake on my part had quickly escalated into a major event involving local residents and shoppers, a dog squad, a police helicopter and the bomb squad while disrupting rush hour travel and SeaBus service between North Vancouver and Vancouver for some three hours.

Eventually, after weeks held in an exhibits locker, the shattered remains were returned to me by the police and I was able to complete my claim for a new rod under the Sage warranty program. I don't imagine they have been asked to replace many, if any, rods under similar circumstances.

ACKNOWLEDGMENTS

Where to start? So many people have figured in the writings that come together in these pages. An increasing number of them are no longer with us but are still fondly remembered for their friendship and their fellowship as the day drew to a close. Fishing friends make great companions for we share a love for the sport and for the outdoors, for the sound of running water, the feel of a taking fish and the beauty of our surroundings be it on river, lake or ocean swell.

Pulling all the words together was encouraged and greatly enhanced by the efforts of Rhonda Bailey, my editor and good friend. As it happens she and her late husband, Sam Bailey, have special ties to *Casting Back* for there was a time, more than 30 years ago, when they owned the little white rowing boat that figures in both my stories and pictures. It served as a dinghy for their larger powerboat, *Harmony*, and continues to go fishing with me in fresh and saltwater to this day.

Family, of course, is everything and to have, in Finn and Jack, grandsons who are also drawn to fish, much as Conor, their father, and Richard, their uncle, were in their boyhood days, means more to me than they will probably ever know. I can only hope that interest survives the oncoming teenage years and takes them into adulthood as an antidote to the more serious challenges they will inevitably face.

While *Casting Back* reflects mainly on past events it is also a reminder that these later years present even more opportunities to continue to enjoy the company and friendship of all those special people who have or continue to share my interests in fishing and the outdoors.

In no particular order thank you for your support Peter Houghton-Brown, Gordon Shead, Pierce and Anita Clegg, Harvey Stern,

Pasi Niva, Doug Machuk and Dougie Barr, Gary Flagel, Glenn Di Georgio, Bryce Olson, Ari Toivainen, Loren Irving, Moore Anketell, Craig Somerville, Fran and King Allen, Paul Macandrew, Philippe Herve du Penhoat, Darren Wright and Missy MacDonald, Dave Hall and Dave Lane, Miki Aikas, Mark Hume and Mark Beere, Gill McKean and Mandi McDougall, Brendan and Mamie Faughnan, Toni Karuvaara and Malcolm Brodie.

And finally this book would not have been possible without the editors whose permission was so willingly given to reproduce the material first used in their publications.

A FISHERMAN'S BOOKCASE

A far-ranging and personal selection of fishing books that has given me considerable pleasure down through the years and continues to do so. Fly fishing for steelhead and trout in all its many aspects is central to the collection. One antique book dates back more than 200 years, a very few focus on commercial fishing for Pacific salmon while another explores the potential impacts of greatly increased oil tanker traffic along BC's coastline.

Alevras, John. *Leaves from a Steelheader's Diary*. Portland, OR: Frank Amato Publications, Inc., 2010.

Beamish, Richard, and McFarlane, Gordon. *The Sea Among Us: The Amazing Strait of Georgia*. Madeira Park, BC, Harbour Publishing Ltd., 2014.

Bowling, Tim. *The Lost Coast*. Gibsons, BC: Nightwood Editions, 2007.

Bradner, Enos. *Northwest Angling*. Portland, OR: Binfords & Mort, 1969.

Brooks, Joe. *The Complete Book of Fly Fishing*. New York: A.S. Barnes & Company, 1958, 1968.

Bruhn, Karl, editor. *Fly Fishing British Columbia*. Surrey, BC: Heritage House Publishing Company Ltd., 1999.

Bruhn, Karl. *Best of B.C. Lake Fishing*. Vancouver: Whitecap Books, 1992, 1998.

Busch, Tony. *Trout Fishing: A Guide to New Zealand's South Island*. Auckland: David Bateman, 1994, 1997, 1999.

Caldwell, Francis E. *Pacific Troller*. Anchorage: Alaska Northwest Publishing Company, 1978.

Caras, Roger, and Martin H. Greenberg, editors. *Treasury of Great Fishing Stories*. New York: Bristol Park Books, 1998.

Catlow, Laurence. *Once a Flyfisher*. Ludlow, UK: Merlin Unwin Books, 2001.

Childerhose, R.J., and Marj Trim. *Pacific Salmon*. Vancouver: Douglas & McIntyre, 1979.

Clegg, Pierce, and Peter McMullan. *Babine: A 50-Year Celebration of a World-Renowned Steelhead and Trout River*. Portland: Frank Amato Publications, Inc., 2010.

Combs, Trey. *Steelhead Fly Fishing*. Surrey, BC: Heritage House Publishing Company Ltd., 1991, 1999.

Corbett, Ron. *The Last Guide*. Toronto: Penguin Books, 2001.

Cramond, Mike. *Game Fishing in the West*. Vancouver: Mitchell Press Limited, 1964.

Cramond, Mike. *Vancouver Island Fishing Holes*. Victoria: Pattison Ventures Ltd., 1981.

Crawford, Jim. *Salmon to a Fly: Fly Fishing for Pacific Salmon in the Open Ocean*. Portland: Frank Amato Publications, Inc., 1995.

Currie, William B. *A Gamefisher's Year*. London: Pelham Books Ltd., 1969.

Davy, Alfred G., editor. *The Gilly: A Flyfisher's Guide to British Columbia*. Kelowna, BC, Alf Davy, 1985.

Egan, Van Gorman. *Tyee: The Story of the Tyee Club of British Columbia*. Campbell River: Ptarmigan Press, 1988.

Eisenberg, Lee, and DeCourcy, Taylor, editors. *The Ultimate Fishing Book*. Boston: Houghton Mifflin Company, 1983.

Fallon, Niall, and Fort, Tom, editors. *Bright Waters: A Celebration of*

Irish Angling. Ludlow, UK: Merlin Unwin Books, 2002.

Fennelly, John F. *Steelhead Paradise*. Vancouver: Mitchell Press, Limited, 1963.

Fysh, Sir Hudson. *Round the Bend in the Stream*. Sydney: Angus and Robertson, 1968.

Gallagher, Sean M. *Wild Steelhead*, Volumes One and Two. Mill Creek, WA: Wild River Press, 2013.

Gierach, John. *No Shortage of Good Days*. New York: Simon and Schuster, 2011.

Godfrey, Will. *Seasons of the Steelhead*. Hailey, ID: Stoecklein Photography & Publishing, 2011.

Goodspeed, Charles E. A., editor. *Treasury of Fishing Stories*. New York: A.S.Barnes and Company, 1946.

Gottesfeld, Allen S., and Ken A Rabnett. *Skeena River Fish and their Habitat*. Portland, OR, and Hazelton, BC: Ecotrust and Skeena River Fisheries Commission, 2008.

Gray, L.R.N. *Torridge Fishery*. London: Nicholas Kaye, 1957.

Grundle, Jack. *British Columbia Game Fish*. Vancouver: Western Fish and Game Magazine, 1970.

Grzelewski, Derek. *The Trout Bohemia: Fly-Fishing Travels in New Zealand*. Auckland: David Bateman Ltd., 2013.

Grzelewski, Derek. *The Trout Diaries: A Year of Fly-Fishing in New Zealand*. Auckland: David Bateman Ltd., 2011.

Haig-Brown, Roderick L. *A Primer of Fly-Fishing*. New York: William Morrow and Company, 1964.

Haig-Brown, Roderick L. *A River Never Sleeps*. Toronto: Wm. Collins Sons & Co., 1946, 1974.

Haig-Brown, Roderick L. *Bright Waters, Bright Fish*. Vancouver: Douglas & McIntyre Ltd., 1980.

Haig-Brown, Roderick L. *Fisherman's Fall*. New York: Crown Publishers Inc., 1964, 1975, 1989.

Haig-Brown, Roderick L. *Fisherman's Spring*. Toronto: Wm. Collins Sons & Co., 1951, 1975, 1988.

Haig-Brown, Roderick L. *Fisherman's Summer*. Toronto: Wm. Collins Sons and Co., 1959, 1975.

Haig-Brown, Roderick L. *Fisherman's Winter*. Toronto: Wm. Collins Sons & Co., 1954, 1975, 1988.

Haig-Brown, Roderick L. *Measure of the Year*. Toronto: Wm. Collins Sons & Co., 1950, 1968.

Haig-Brown, Roderick L. *Return to the River*. Toronto: Wm. Collins Sons & Co., 1946, 1974.

Haig-Brown, Roderick L. *Silver: The Life Story of an Atlantic Salmon*. Vancouver: Douglas and McIntyre, 1931.

Haig-Brown, Roderick L. *The Western Angler*. Toronto: Wm. Collins Sons & Co., 1939, 1947, 1968.

Haig-Brown, Valerie, editor. *The Master and His Fish: From the World of Roderick Haig-Brown*. Toronto: McClelland and Stewart Ltd., 1981.

Haig-Brown, Valerie, editor. *To Know a River: A Haig-Brown Reader*. Vancouver: Douglas and McIntyre, 1996.

Haig-Brown, Valerie, editor. *Woods and River Tales: From the World of Roderick Haig-Brown*. Toronto: McClelland and Stewart, 1980.

Haig-Brown, Valerie, editor. *Writings and Reflections: From the World of Roderick Haig-Brown*. Toronto: McClelland and Stewart, 1982.

Harris, J. R. *An Angler's Entomology*. London: Collins, 1952.

Hart, J.L. *Pacific Fishes of Canada*. Ottawa: Fisheries Research Board of Canada, 1973.

Hintz, O.S. *Fisherman's Paradise*. London: Max Reinhardt Ltd., 1975.

Hintz, O.S. *Trout at Taupo*. London: Max Reinhardt Ltd., 1955, 1959, 1964.

Hogan, Dec. *A Passion for Steelhead*. Mill Creek, WA: Wild River Press, 2006.

Hole, Chris. *Heaven on a Stick: Fly-Fishing around the World*. Auckland: Harper Collins, 1993.

Hooton, R.S. *Skeena Steelhead: Unknown Past, Uncertain Future*. Portland, OR: Ecotrust and Frank Amato Publications, Inc., 2011.

Hughes-Parry, J. *A Salmon Fisherman's Notebook*. London: Eyre & Spottiswoode, 1949, 1955.

Hume, Mark. *Adam's River: The Mystery of the Adams River Sockeye*. Vancouver: New Star Books, 1994.

Hume, Mark. *River of the Angry Moon: Seasons on the Bella Coola*. Vancouver: Greystone Books, 1998.

Iglauer, Edith. *Fishing with John*. Madeira Park BC: Harbour Publishing, 1988.

Ivens, T.C. *Still Water Fly Fishing*. London: Andre Deutsch, 1952, 1961, 1963, 1970.

Jones, Robert H., editor. *Fly Fishing in British Columbia*. Calgary: Johnston Gorman Publishers, 2001.

Kent, John, and David Hallett. *Classic Fly Fishing in New Zealand Rivers*. Nelson: Craig Poton Publishing, 2003.

Kent, John. *South Island Trout Fishing Guide*. Rosedale: Penguin Group (NZ), 2009.

Kingsmill Moore, T.C. *A Man May Fish*. London: Herbert Jenkins Ltd., 1960.

Kite, Oliver. *A Fisherman's Diary*. London: Andre Deutsch, 1969.

Kite, Oliver. *Nymph Fishing in Practice*. London: Herbert Jenkins, 1963.

Koller, Larry, editor. *The Treasury of Angling*. London: Paul Hamlyn Ltd., 1966.

Kopecky, Arno. *The Oil Man and the Sea: Navigating the Northern Gateway*. Madeira Park, BC: Douglas and McIntyre, 2013.

Lewis, Adam. *Skeena Steelhead and Salmon: A Report to Stakeholders*. Smithers, BC: Steelhead Society of British Columbia, Bulkley Valley Branch, 2000.

Lingren, Art. *Famous British Columbia Fly-Fishing Waters*. Portland, OR: Frank Amato Publications, Inc., 2002.

Loewen, General Sir Charles. *Fly Fishing Flies*. Toronto: Pagurian Press Limited, 1978.

Luce, AA. *Fishing and Thinking*. London: Hodder and Stoughton, 1959.

MacDougall, Arthur R., editor. *The Trout Fisherman's Bedside Book*. London: Hodder and Stoughton, 1964.

Mansfield, Kenneth, editor. *The Fisherman's Companion*. London: Eyre and Spottiswoode, 1968.

Marshall-Hardy, E. *Angling Ways*. London: Herbert Jenkins Limited, 1934 (2), 1944, 1945, 1947, 1948, 1950.

Marston, A. Norman, editor. *Newnes Encyclopaedia of Angling*. London: Newnes, 1963.

Mayse, Arthur. *My Father, My Friend*. Madeira Park, BC: Harbour Publishing, 1993.

McKelvie, Colin Laurie. *A Game Fisher in Ireland*. Southampton, UK: Ashford, 1989.

Meggs, Geoff. *Salmon: The Decline of the B.C. Fishery*. Vancouver: Douglas and McIntyre, 1991.

Menzies, W.J.M. *Salmon Fishing*. London: Adam and Charles Black, 1935.

Merriman, Alec. *Outdoors with Alec Merriman*. Sidney, BC: Saltaire Publishing Company, 1967, 1968.

Metcalfe, E. Bennett. *A Man of Some Importance: The Life of Roderick Langmere Haig-Brown*. West Vancouver, BC: James W. Wood, 1985.

Mirfin, Zane, and Graeme Marshall, Rob Bowler, Jana Bowler. *Brown Trout Heaven: Fishing New Zealand's South Island*. Christchurch: Shoal Bay, 2000.

Nelson, Ron. *And When You Go Fishing*. Lantzville, BC: Oolichan Books, 1984.

Netboy, Anthony. *The Atlantic Salmon: A Vanishing Species?* London: Faber and Faber, 1968.

Netboy, Anthony. *The Salmon: Their Fight for Survival*. Boston: Houghton Mifflin Company, 1974.

O'Reilly, Peter. *Trout and Salmon Loughs of Ireland*. London: Unwin Hyman, 1987 and Collins Willow, 1992.

O'Reilly, Peter. *Trout and Salmon Rivers of Ireland: An Angler's Guide*. Ludlow, UK: Merlin Unwin Books, 1991 (2), 1993, 1995.

Oglesby, Arthur. *Salmon*. London: Macdonald, 1971.

Pollard, Douglas F.W. *Peetz: A Reel for all Time*. Surrey, BC: Heritage House. 1997.

Prosek, James. *Trout of the World*. New York: Stewart, Tabori & Chang, 2003.

Read, Stanley E. *Tommy Brayshaw: The Ardent Angler-Artist*. Vancouver: University of British Columbia Press, 1977.

Reid, D.C. *Fishing for Dreams: Notes from the Water's Edge*. Surrey, BC: TouchWood Editions, 2005.

Rigney, Matt. *In Pursuit of Giants*, London: Viking Penguin, 2012.

Ritz, Charles. *A Fly Fisher's Life*. London: Max Reinhardt, 1959, 1965.

Sawyer, Frank. *Nymphs and the Trout*. London: Stanley Paul, 1958.

Scharff, Robert, editor. *Esquire's Book of Fishing*. London: Frederick Muller Limited, 1964.

Sharcott, Margaret, *Troller's Holiday*. London: Peter Davies, 1957.

Sheehan, Paul. *Irish Game Fishing*. Shrewsbury, UK: Swan Hill Press, 1997.

Sheringham, Hugh, and John C. Moore, editors. *The Book of the Fly-Rod*. London, Eyre & Spottiswoode, 1936.

Skues, G.E.M. *Nymph Fishing for Chalk Stream Trout*. London: Adam and Charles Black, 1939, 1960.

Skues, G.E.M. *The Way of a Trout with a Fly*. London: Adam and Charles Black, 1921, 1928, 1935, 1949, 1955, 1961.

Spencer, Sidney. *Salmon and Sea Trout in Wild Places*. London: H. & F. Witherby Ltd., 1968.

Spencer, Sidney. *Newly from the Sea: Fishing for Salmon and Sea Trout*. London: H.F. & G. Witherby Ltd., 1969.

Spencer, Sidney. *Fishing the Wilder Shores*. London: H.F. & G. Witherby, 1991.

Stefanyk, Larry, editor, *Ultimate Trout Fishing in the Pacific Northwest*. Madeira Park, BC: Harbour Publishing, 2011.

Sutterby, Rod, and Malcolm Greenhalgh. *The Wild Trout: The Natural History of an Endangered Fish*. London: George Philip Ltd., 1989.

Thornton, Barry M. *Steelhead: The Supreme Trophy Trout*. Saanichton, BC: Hancock House, 1978.

Threlfall, Richard E. *On a Gentle Art*. London: Country Life Limited, 1951.

Titterington, Albert. *Irish Fieldsports & Angling Handbook*. Belfast: Appletree Press, 1984.

Tracy, J.P. *Low Man on a Gill-Netter*. Anchorage: Alaska Northwest Publishing Company, 1974.

Venables, Bernard. *A Fisherman's Testament*. London: Adam and Charles Black, 1949.

Venables, Bernard. *A Rise to the Fly*. London: Robert Hale, 2000.

Venables, Bernard. *Mr. Crabtree Goes Fishing*. London: Daily Mirror Newspapers Ltd., 1949.

Vines, Sydney, and Sawyer, Frank. *Frank Sawyer: Man of the Riverside*. London: George Allen & Unwin, 1984.

Waller, Lani. *A Steelheader's Way: Principles, Tactics and Techniques*. New Cumberland, PA and Mechanicsburg, PA: Headwater Books and Stackpole Books, 2009.

Waller, Lani. *River of Dreams*. Grand Island, NY: West River Publishing, 2004.

Waterman, Charles F. *The Fisherman's World*. New York: Random House, 1972.

Whitelaw, Ian. *The History of Fly-Fishing in Fifty Flies*. New York: Stewart, Tabori & Chang, 2015.

Williams, A. Bryan. *Fish and Game in British Columbia*. Vancouver: Sun Directories Limited, 1935.

Williamson, Capt. Thomas. *The Complete Angler's Vade-Mecum: Being a Perfect Code of Instruction on the Above Pleasing Science*. London: Printed for Payne and Mackinlay, in The Strand, and Martin, Middle Row, Holburn, 1808.

Williamson, Henry. *A Clear Water Stream*. London: Faber and Faber, 1958.

Williamson, Henry. *Salar the Salmon*. London: Faber and Faber, 1959.

Wood, A.H.E. (Jock Scott). *Greased Line Fishing for Salmon*. London: Seeley, Service & Co., 1935.

INDEX

PETER MCMULLAN

Peter McMullan has been passionate about fishing all his life and has written fishing stories for magazines and newspapers in Ireland, England, Scotland, Canada and Finland. Along the way his fly rods have been well tested by Atlantic and Pacific salmon, by steelhead, brown trout and rainbow trout and, from time to time, by other species as well.

Northern Irish by birth and Canadian by choice, McMullan considers himself fortunate to have been able to derive much pleasure from both his work and his leisure-time activities, especially fishing.

As a boy in Ireland he was fascinated by fish and water. He went on to become a journalist who for 16 years covered news stories along with rugby, cricket and fishing for the *Belfast Telegraph*.

McMullan emigrated to Canada with his family in 1971 and settled on Vancouver Island, where he had previously spent some time as a Victoria College student in 1953-54. His work took him away from the Island for a time, but in retirement he is back, living in Nanaimo with Daphne, his wife of 54 years. Peter and Daphne have two sons and three grandchildren.

McMullan had a 25-year career in communications in Canada, as editor of the *Nanaimo Daily Free Press*, director of public relations and information with Nanaimo's Malaspina College, now Vancouver Island University, and, from 1981, corporate communications manager for BC Hydro, in Vancouver. Between 1996 and 2000 he was in Dublin, Ireland as media and promotions manager with the world governing body of the game of rugby, the International Rugby Board, now World Rugby.

His vocation as a writer and his passion for fishing have always been connected, and his stories have found many outlets. The steelhead of the Babine River and the river's sport fishing history and traditions prompted him to conceive and co-author a book with then lodge owner and guide Pierce Clegg. *Babine: A 50-Year Celebration of a World-Famous Steelhead and Trout River* was published in 2010 by Frank Amato Publications, Inc., Portland, Oregon.

McMullan is the Canadian field editor for *Chasing Silver Fly Fishing Magazine* (www.chasingsilvermagazine.com), a high-quality English-language quarterly published in Finland. He is also a longtime contributor to the Canadian fly-fishing website www.ariverneversleeps.com.